"Matt Zeller brings a soldier's view and a keen analyst's eye [...]
understand why the training he and his unit received did not prepare them for the challenges they faced in the vital eastern region of Afghanistan. More importantly, by showing just how difficult it is to train the Afghan security forces, he illuminates the fundamental flaw in ISAF's withdrawal plan from Afghanistan: it is a fool's errand, utterly beyond the military's ability to carry out effectively. *Watches Without Time* is a crucial contribution to understanding why the war is a doomed effort—not today, but years ago."

—JOSHUA FOUST
Senior Fellow, American Security Project
author of *Afghanistan Journal:
Selections from Registan.net*

"In *Watches Without Time*, Zeller drops readers onto the battlefield by capturing the stress, grind, and uncertainty U.S. troops face in a guerilla war. It provides insight we don't often get and allows readers a much better understanding of the war our country's sons and daughters were sent to fight."

—BRANDON FRIEDMAN
author of *The War I Always Wanted*

"*Watches Without Time* is the heartfelt memoir of an American soldier's Afghan War experience. From training to deployment to combat, Zeller painstakingly lays out his experiences, his emotions, and the lessons he learned in a way that humanizes today's combatant and reveals the multifaceted complexities of prosecuting the war in Afghanistan."

—BENJAMIN TUPPER
author of *Greetings from Afghanistan,
Send More Ammo* and *Dudes of War*

"Every war produces tales of horror and heroism as told from the vantage point of the soldiers who actually fought in it, and the war in Afghanistan is no exception. What is different about this book is that Matt Zeller has given us an accurate, no-holds-barred account of what it was like to train for, fight in and recover from a war that most Americans rarely think about—a conflict that is happening out of sight, 'over there'. Matt Zeller volunteered to serve in the military for all the right reasons, and he did his duty with brains, dedication and courage. But, as he describes in this compelling volume, his experience in Afghanistan changed him, and his perspective on the military, the Afghan conflict and the world, in many ways. This is a memoir of war that is definitely worth reading."

—MITCHEL B. WALLERSTEIN
President of Baruch College

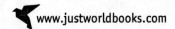

WATCHES WITHOUT TIME

For my FOB Vulcan brothers,
who taught me the true meaning
of honor, family, and friendship.

WATCHES WITHOUT TIME

AN AMERICAN SOLDIER
IN AFGHANISTAN

MATT ZELLER

WITH A FOREWORD BY

EDWARD S. WALKER

JUST WORLD
BOOKS

CHARLOTTESVILLE, VIRGINIA

Typesetting by Jane T. Sickon for Just World Publishing, LLC.
Cover design by Lewis Rector for Just World Publishing, LLC.

Second printing, 2013.

Publisher's Cataloging-in-Publication
(Provided by Quality Books, Inc.)

Zeller, Matt.
    Watches without time: an American soldier in
    Afghanistan / by Matt Zeller ; foreword by Edward S.
    ("Ned") Walker.
    p. cm.
    Includes index.
    LCCN 2012935474
    ISBN 978-1-935982-20-3

    1. Zeller, Matt—Correspondence.. 2. Afghan War,
2001—Personal narratives, American.   I. Title.

DS371.413.Z45 2012   958.104'7'092
                    QBI12-600069

Contents

A list explaining the identity of the military units and the American and Afghan personalities who are featured in the book can be found online at http://bit.ly/K9xaoB

Foreword

Matt Zeller was my student at Hamilton College, just over a decade ago. Two things stood out about him in addition to his natural intelligence and sensitivity. One was his skepticism—he had critical thinking down pat—and the other was his ability to analyze a situation and write very convincingly about it. If you read this book, which is a compilation of the e-mails he sent home to family and friends while serving as a junior officer with the U.S. Army in Afghanistan in 2008, I think you will agree with me. You may or may not agree with everything that Matt says in the book, but you will come away from this account with a much better appreciation of the challenges and responsibilities we are placing on our young men and women who have been doing the fighting in Afghanistan.

The prime strength of this book is that it provides an almost photographic account of what an American officer goes through as he or she tracks American policy—in this case, the counterinsurgency program—after it filters down from the top commanders, through the colonels and lieutenant colonels, and finally comes down to the men and women charged with implementing it on the ground. What was envisioned at the highest levels and passed down, like the child's game of whisper-down-the-lane, may have little to do with the original vision. At the end of the line, however, it brings the men and women who are tasked with implementation face-to-face with life and death situations. Matt draws a helpful distinction between "the ducks" and "the turtles," with the turtles representing those who have been engaged in combat and the ducks being those who never get beyond the wire. He does not have a lot of time for the ducks. And when you read his account, you can see why.

I respect the approach Matt chose as he wrote these dispatches to the home front. He raises questions, but they are not disloyal to the top commanders or to the soldiers who worked alongside him or reported to him.

He can be irreverent, but he is not cynical. He expresses his pride in what he and his fellow soldiers are doing. This book is not *M*A*S*H* or *Heart of Darkness*. The central concern that arises in his writing is that he believes we could be doing more, and doing it better, to gain the support of the Afghan people and to achieve an honorable exit from Afghanistan. He still believes in the mission, as fewer and fewer Americans do these days. But if the doubters and naysayers were to read this book, they would very likely come away with a new perspective and perhaps even a little hope. One of his most heartfelt observations is, "We have a more coherent strategy on how to lose this war than win it." And he wants to change that situation.

He has some suggestions for changes, such as: How can we win hearts and minds when our representatives, our military officers, are in theater for such a short time, have just begun to learn where the latrine is, and then are whisked away, never to return? That approach doesn't make sense for our military in Afghanistan (and if I can add a personal note, it does not make sense for our State Department and AID mission personnel either). I have thought about the two-force military that Matt suggests: one for the fighting and one for the wooing. In a way, it seems to make sense. But from talks with my military colleagues, I am skeptical. I am told, and tend to believe, that the skills involved are so different that you would need a completely independent service to manage and implement COIN successfully. Matt makes a good case in this book, but I leave it up to you to judge.

When Matt was in college, he was a thinking student, somebody who listened as well as talked. He was sensitive to the body language of others. Frankly, it surprised me when I found he was going into the military. He seemed more the type to be going to graduate school—and he did that, too, with great distinction. But from this book, I can see that his best graduate school was the U.S. Army and his time in Afghanistan. I have no doubt that in his service he learned far more about the world and other cultures, and about himself, in a shorter time than he could ever have learned anywhere else.

He is sensitive to symbolism. In the dispatches in this book, he worries about the messages we send when our officers attend formal dinners in full combat gear, like *Star Wars* stormtroopers. He conveys the sense that we take security too far, to the point that it is jeopardizing our mission.

He has an unfailing eye for the stupidity of mid-level officers on the make. He brings the frustration of the turtles into stark focus when it comes to the duck "Lieutenant Colonel Clueless," whom you will meet in the book. But he also has an unfailing eye for the majesty of Afghanistan, the warmth of its people, and the common, everyday life of the army soldier. He makes it all come to life. I have never been to Afghanistan, but throughout my career I have been to many army bases, and Matt tells it all. I wonder if anyone who hasn't waited for a flight to his or her duty post and had to trick the system to get there could understand what Matt was going through. What I could not believe was that the system I had experienced fifty years earlier in Vietnam seemed to have hardly changed!

He had some problems after coming home from Afghanistan, but it would be an intrusion for me to even comment on his past nightmares. He himself does the job so well.

This is a great book. It truly is a page-turner. When I came to the end, I wanted to read further to find out what happened to all these characters—the good and the bad. Maybe Matt will give us another installment. He probably has a great tale to tell about the run he made for the U.S. Congress in 2010, running on a strong veterans' rights platform.

The reintegration into American society of the hundreds of thousands of veterans from the wars of the past decade is one of the biggest challenges—and could be one of the biggest opportunities—that our country has ahead of it. Understanding the experiences these Americans have had in the battlefield will help us all in this task. In this, as in several matters of military training, organization, and policy, *Watches Without Time* can be an invaluable resource.

—Ambassador Edward S. Walker

April 2012

Preface

There's a tale of an American soldier interrogating an illiterate Taliban fighter just captured after a firefight. The American asks the Afghan Taliban why he continues to fight:

> *American: You cannot possibly hope to win. We have fighter jets, bombs, drones, artillery, armored vehicles, helicopters; we're better trained, better equipped. You cannot possibly think you can beat us, can you?*
>
> *Afghan Taliban: It is true, you Americans have all the watches, but we have all the time.*

The Taliban prisoner provides a perfect summary of our efforts in Afghanistan from 2001 to the present. A watch is an amazingly complex piece of technology that reflects a society's level of progress and development. But if a watch doesn't tell time, if there is no strategy that dictates how one should use that watch, then a watch is nothing more than an incredibly complex piece of technology that doesn't serve a purpose. For eight years and counting, we've lacked a strategy that dictates how we should use all this amazing technology; we've lacked a goal to which we can apply our strength and resources. Thus, in the current conflict, we Americans and our allies, with all our technological military might and marvel, are the watches without time.

—Chapter 34

This is the story I wrote for my friends and family so that should anything have ever happened to me, they would know what I went through. Comprising e-mails and letters I sent home, each chapter reflects the emotions of the moment in which I wrote it—a mirror to how I felt at that exact time. Simply put—this book is as naked as I can get.

The next time you hear that the United States is sending soldiers to war, chances are those soldiers will go through similar experiences, and I hope after reading this you'll have a better understanding of what it means to send our countrymen off to fight.

—Matt Zeller
March 2012

Acknowledgments

I'd like to thank: my FOB Vulcan brothers; my friends and family—for their love and support before, during, and after the deployment; my Mom and Caitlin—for their help editing rough drafts; Helena and her amazing team at Just World Books; and my Afghan brothers—who kept me alive, welcomed me as their guest, and provided me with the education of a lifetime.

PART I

Training

1

Birthday Shots and Camp Funston

Monday, January 21, 2008

The day has finally arrived. Tomorrow my unit and I head to Fort Riley, Kansas (located in Manhattan, Kansas, of all places; don't let the name fool you, we're told the town shuts down after dark), to begin two months of unit-specific training for our upcoming yearlong deployment to Afghanistan.

I officially went on Active Duty this past Sunday, arriving in the frozen, barren landscape that is Syracuse, New York. I feel as if the temperature of 13 degrees (with a windchill of 10 below) was an appropriate weather welcome for where we're about to spend the next year of our lives. We've spent the past few days packing, filling out a plethora of paperwork, and, most importantly, bonding as a team.

I'm proud to say I'm deploying with some of the finest officers and NCOs I've ever had the privilege to work with. At this point I think we're all anxious to get to Fort Riley, complete our training, and see what Afghanistan has in store. We've got a great mission: training elements of the Afghan security forces and serving as their mentors, instructors, and, hopefully, friends and allies. My personal job is as my team's Operations and Intelligence officer. I'll be responsible for training the officers and soldiers of an Afghan Army unit in all matters concerning intelligence gathering and analyzing and all matters concerning operations planning. I'm not sure where we'll be located when we get to Afghanistan, but if and when I can tell, rest assured, I'll pass along that info.

Our barracks at Fort Riley. Note the close spaces and standard level of chaos.

Tonight some of the guys and I are heading down to Syracuse University to visit a few of my old stomping grounds—two or three beloved bars on our last night of "freedom" for the next few months. We've been told we'll have two four-day passes (four days in February and four in March) before we leave for Afghanistan.

Finally, I want to thank each and every one of you whom I've visited, seen, or talked with over the past few weeks. Your words of encouragement, your friendship, your love: This is what drives me to do this. You are *my* inspiration. I couldn't do this without you. I hope each and every one of you knows just how much you all mean to me. In a word: thanks.

Thursday, January 24, 2008

The birthday messages I received from friends and family were the bright spots in an otherwise bummer day. We spent today in-processing, doing *lots* of paperwork, filling out wills and power of attorney, and everyone's favorite: shots! That's right, the army loves me *so* much that on my birthday, it gave me vaccinations for anthrax, smallpox, hepatitis A and B, typhoid, and influenza! Even more exciting, while in Afghanistan, I get to take a daily antimalaria pill. At the moment, I'm literally a walking biohazard.

We began our day at around 5:30 ("O'Dark Thirty") and just finished around 8:30 p.m. (2030 to my military brethren). I'm *very* impressed with how smoothly things are running out here. The training is thus far extremely professional and yet laid-back, especially when compared to other army training I've been through. The "no B.S." nature of this whole place is outstanding and greatly appreciated by all. The overall commander of our training is the same gentleman who wrote the book *Learning to Eat Soup with a Knife* (recommended reading!), Colonel John Nagl, and the training environment clearly reflects his leadership philosophy.

Tuesday, January 29–Saturday, February 2, 2008

This week has been a veritable roller coaster of activity. Monday was a very wonderful 73 and sunny, but on Tuesday, winter arrived. Tuesday was cold—really cold—Antarctic cold. Around 5:15 a.m., I was rattled from a deep slumber by a howling 70-mph-plus wind. Its anger at not being able to reach me was apparent with each crash against my window. The wind when combined with single-digit temperatures made for a *most* miserable day. We walk pretty much everywhere, and the headgear for our uniform is also the ultimate in winter-climate absurdity—a black beret doesn't really provide all that much protection. The worst part is that the army, in its infinite wisdom, issued us these wonderful fleece caps that are literally a pillow of warmth upon one's head; too bad we're not authorized to wear them on base while in uniform. I must extend special thanks to my Aunt Bonnie and her Daughters of the American Revolution chapter, who provided us with wonderful knit wool caps that can be worn with our uniforms; our heads were thankful for the lack of frostbite and your generosity!

Wednesday was an exercise in boredom. In the morning, the brass paraded themselves in front of us to tell us how *hooah* (it's army slang for just about anything; in this case, they used it to mean awesome) our training would be. In the afternoon, we sat in a church, of all places, and listened to three hours of a multimedia presentation on Survival, Evasion, Rescue, and Escape (SERE). This is a *very* important topic, but the best way to present it is *not* a mass briefing to hundreds of soldiers who have already spent the morning listening to speakers drone on and on. The army has two types of training: hands on and sleep mode. Hands on is interactive, participatory, and invigorating; it's also usually done in small groups. Sleep mode is also known as Receive Mode, as in someone blabs on and on in a corny video or an awfully long PowerPoint, and we do our best to pay attention and stave off sleep, all while remaining dutifully silent. This briefing was the embodiment of sleep mode. I maintained consciousness only through the numerous coffee breaks, during which I found a piano in a side room and started taking requests and jamming away. I even found a major who plays the trombone and who wants to try to start a regular jazz band while we're deployed—how very WWII!

Thursday was like Christmas. The day we get issued our gear is one of my favorite days in the army. Not only do I get loads of cool new stuff, I'm constantly active, *and* I get to joke around with my guys in line. Next to a day's worth of hard training in the field, there's nothing quite like it. And wow, did they give us a *lot* of stuff: four duffel bags' worth! After our issue, which took the majority of the day, we spent the rest of our time in frigid temperatures, packing and loading trucks into the wee hours of the night.

Friday (today) was moving day. Once again, the army in its infinite wisdom had us all get up, clean our barracks, and move the rest of our stuff out by 0600 (6:00 a.m. for you civilians) so that we could sit around and wait till 1300 (1:00 p.m.) to actually do anything. That's right: Your tax dollars paid me to watch ESPN's *SportsCenter* and CNN all morning. Once 1300 came along, we loaded up on our buses, moved to the base's armory, and were issued our weapons. Specifically, we're carrying the M4 assault rifle and the M9 pistol into combat. I take my earlier statement back; the day we get our *weapons* is my favorite day in the army. There was something strangely familiar and comforting about feeling the weight of my M9 pistol in its holder and my M4 resting silently against my chest. In the military our weapons are an extra appendage, so the day you get issued your weapons is like being reunited with a long-lost friend. In a way, you almost feel naked without them.

After picking up our weapons, we moved to FOB (Forward Operating Base) Funston. This is where we'll live and train for the next two months and where we'll eventually depart for Afghanistan sometime at the end of March. I went from my own personal room, with a shared kitchenette and bathroom, to a 40-man open bay, with 20 communal showers and 10 shared laundry machines. Personal space and privacy are pretty much at a minimum, but I also argue it's the best kind of military living, as nothing breeds camaraderie quite like open-bay barracks living. It took *forever* to unpack all our stuff and get settled.

Tomorrow will be a day of exploration, as we arrived on our FOB too late to do much else other than move our gear to the barracks, eat chow, and unpack. I'm told the gym and MWR (morale, welfare, and recreation) center down here are actually far nicer than the ones on main base.

Sunday, we plan to order an ungodly amount of pizza and wings and wash them down with delicious beer as we cheer on our beloved NY Giants to victory! I only wish I could be at home with my dad to see it live.

Monday will finally bring our first day of real training (*good-bye* paperwork and in-processing monotony; *hello* challenging physical and mental training). I cannot wait.

With that, I'm off to bed; this means putting in earplugs and placing a pillow over my face (as the lights are still on, music is blaring, and guys are sitting around telling jokes and "so-there-I-was" stories).

Sunday, February 3–Sunday, February 10, 2008

Monday: We spent the day in two of the worst classes I've ever had in the army. This is a thinking-man's war. We should not and cannot reduce our teaching of Islam and Afghan culture to base generalities. The instructor at one point began listing terrorist groups known to be in Pakistan to illustrate the potential threat if the country were to be destabilized. Included on his list were the Sikhs, who are pacifists and have nothing to do with Islamic Fundamentalism. I felt the need to argue this point; I know it's only our initial training on fundamentalist Islam and that my level of understanding probably well exceeds the norm here, but we're going to hamper ourselves if this is what we're teaching our soldiers. Soldiers are going into combat with this gross misrepresentation of the religion and culture that will take *that* much longer to undo, when we could be using the time and energy to actually make headway on our mission. Thankfully, the army provided us with a block of phenomenal instruction on

Friday from some Special Forces guys who helped correct much of Monday's misinformation.

Tuesday: We had our first "key-leader engagement" meeting on Tuesday. A key-leader engagement is a simulated meeting between U.S. Forces and some Afghan entity (the Afghan Army, police, a tribal leader, village elder, mayor, governor, etc.). The U.S. forces are played by soldiers, while the Afghans are played by actual Afghans. I was selected ("volun-told") to be the first person in the "hot seat." The hot seat represents the leader of the U.S. delegation and assumes primary responsibility for the success or failure of the meeting. The scenario was as follows: We were meeting with elements of the Afghan National Army, having just arrived in the country and replaced a team who had worked with these forces for a year. Our goals were to build the foundations of a positive relationship and ascertain the Afghan commander's immediate needs. We surpassed these goals. My men and I walked into the room, and, in my struggling Dari (a language of Afghanistan that is primarily spoken by the army), I attempted a formal greeting with all the customs that accompany an Afghan greeting. These customs include only using your right hand, kissing the cheek of the person being greeted three times, and asking a series of questions.

What I attempted to say was, "*Salaam aleikum. Chetor hastid? Jan-e-shoma jur ast? Khub hastid? Sahat-e-shoma khub ast? Be khair hastid? Jur hastid? Khane kheirat ast? Zinde bashi*," which I didn't get all out, but the effort was well received. One of my captains would later exclaim, "I only wish I had a camera to capture the look of shock and happiness on the Afghan's face when you attempted the greeting! He was clearly moved." The meeting went very, very well due to my fellow soldiers' grasp of culture and mannerisms. We drank chai, the local tea, and spoke the entire time through interpreters. The Afghans all actually speak phenomenal English, but for our training purposes speak only in Dari (thus, through the translators). After the meeting, we went to Blue Force Tracker (BFT) training.

The army uses a GPS-based computer system called Blue Force Tracker: We're blue forces, and the bad guys are represented as red forces on military maps. Basically, it's a program that shows us where we are while in our Hummers and where known and suspected enemy forces and obstacles are on a digital map. For those of us who've grown up with computers, it was easy to grasp how to use the program within the first hour of eight we'd spend using it on Tuesday. Class was supposed to go until 2300 (11:00 p.m.) but was ended early because of a massive snowstorm. On the bus ride back to our barracks, one of my former soldiers called me from his training at Fort Bragg to update me on how things were on his end: not good, in fact, downright awful. Before I was assigned to this embedded training team mission, I was the intelligence officer for a battalion in my unit. The majority of our brigade is training for this mission at Fort Bragg, while only those of us on the embedded training teams are training here at Fort Riley. The guys at Fort Bragg are in tents outdoors, apparently just got hot water for their showers installed last week, and have spent their time in embarrassingly substandard training: How does simply walking an 800-meter path count as counter-IED training? What totally shocked me was that my soldier claimed they had spent two entire weeks counting weapons, over and over again. One of the unusual duties of the intelligence officer in an infantry unit is to act as the unit's security officer, which includes accounting for all weapons. Usually you do one total physical inspection (literally touching every single weapon in the unit, which can be thousands), reading off each weapon's unique serial number and comparing it with the master authorization list. If the serial numbers all match the list, you're good to go. If not, you've got a *big* problem on your hands, especially if you're missing something. This process normally takes a day or two. My soldier told me they've done more counts than he can remember. Instead of training, the intelligence soldiers of this unit have spent their weeks at Fort Bragg counting and recounting weapons, which every time are all present and accounted for. It frustrates me beyond belief to not be there with them to do something about this. I told my guys that they're gonna have to step up and be responsible for their own training. I went to bed Tuesday night with a storm raging both outside and in my heart.

Wednesday: *Hello Winter!* Wow . . . it was cold, I mean really cold today. So cold a snowman would look around and say, "Forget this! It's too cold out here, I'm heading indoors!"

I decided to let my guys sleep in as we had the morning off and could do our physical training at the gym later in the morning. After PT, I went to Ash Wednesday services and then on to another 10 hours of Blue Force Tracker training. By hour six, I think we were all ready to bang our heads on the table in an attempt to knock ourselves out and end the suffering. Computer training somehow is just not that exciting when you've got meetings with Afghans and weapons to fire.

Thursday: We had our first formal instruction in Dari today. I should point out that where we're going in Afghanistan, the predominant language is Pashto, but go figure; the army's infinite wisdom strikes again! Our teacher was rather arrogant and cynical. I think he's simply seen too many bad classes of soldiers come through here and now assumes we all are just doing these classes because we have to "check that box." I like to think that my class is different. I was a little taken aback by his condescending manner and the fact that he really didn't cover all that much. Having a working knowledge of Arabic, I'm grasping Dari very quickly. Dari is based on Persian, and Persian and Arabic share similar rules and script. Unfortunately, only three or four other people in our class understand as well; the others are all beginners. Thankfully, we've requested and received a better instructor for the remainder of our training. The other highlight for Thursday was that we went on our first tactical road march. A tactical road march is basically a long walk with all our gear and weapons, including all our body armor, helmet, magazine clips, and first-aid pouch. It usually weighs around 30 pounds, depending on the size of its wearer (bigger vests and armor plates for bigger people). Mine weighs about 40 pounds without ammo. We covered about three or four miles in an hour. While I was proud of my guys, we can obviously move faster, and so I resolved to significantly increase the intensity and duration of our physical training, something that earned me their ire on Friday.

Friday: I got my men up around 530 and proceeded to fall in with Captain Fraser's team for PT. Captain Fraser is a PT stud, and I figured we'll get better PT with him than on our own, but I had no idea how right I was until it was too late. He kicked our butts. You'd think that the simple task of walking up and down stairs with body armor on wouldn't be all that hard, and you'd be wrong. In all we ended up doing weight lifting with our body armor, rifle drills, walking up and down stairs for 10 minutes with all our armor on (a task that smoked me), and then went on a nice two- or three-mile run. You can see how this would cause resentment in my guys. But, once I explained my thinking to the first sergeant (our head sergeant), he agreed with my reasoning (we need to be in the best physical shape possible, and the road march showed me how far we have to go). While my guys got some phenomenal instruction on Afghan culture and do's and don'ts for our upcoming mission from captivating Special Forces soldiers, I spent the day at the armory adding M203 grenade launchers to about four of our weapons. The paperwork is why it took so long—bureaucratic ineptitude at its finest! The highlight today was our Afghan dinner. The Afghan role-players cooked a *massive* feast of traditional Afghan food, which is *incredible*. I love it. I cannot wait to eat the real thing over there. If it was this good with army food supplies, imagine what it must be like when "Mom" makes it with local ingredients! We had rice (a mixture of brown and white) with carrots and raisins (an amazing addition), a beef stew with beans, and a type of salad called *salada* (cucumbers, onions, cilantro, lemon juice, and tomatoes, basically a lot like tabbouleh). After the dinner we went to Dari lab, where we spent an hour sitting on computers listening to phrases in Dari. I think that is the *worst* way to learn a language. You can listen all you want, but unless you start speaking regularly with a native speaker, at least for me, you'll never really get it, and especially not by learning for a few sporadic hours. I spent Friday night in the barracks reading and setting up one of my captain's laptops. I've sort of become my team's de facto IT guy because of my ease with computers. I should probably start charging for my services!

Saturday: We fired our M9 pistols and (for those of us with them on our assault rifles) our M203 grenade launchers (it attaches to the bottom of the rifle barrel, rather than a hand grip). I qualified as a first-time go on each weapon system by passing each qualification fire on the first try. Apparently I'm quite the shot on the grenade launcher: I shot 16 out of 18 targets, at one point putting a grenade round right through the tiny two-foot-by-two-foot opening of a bunker. Though it adds about three pounds to the weapon, I'm actually happy to have the extra attachment for my weapon; if I ever get into a firefight, it'll be nice to have all that extra firepower. Shooting took most of the day. We had our second Dari class (this time with the new instructor we requested, who just rocks), and we learned a ton. Now that I know the basic sentence structure (in Dari it goes pronoun, noun, then verb) as well as the conjugated endings for verbs, I've got the basic foundation of the language. I just need to start memorizing nouns and verbs. I'm still looking for a Pashto teacher, and I think I found one. My buddy Jeff (a fellow lieutenant on my team) and I decided we needed to get off base last night, so we headed out to Aggieville, the local hangout for students who go to Kansas State University. In typical college-town fashion, it's basically a string of bars and restaurants. Jeff and I spent our night barhopping, exploring the area, and marveling at the sight of women! Yes, after nearly three weeks of only being around men, we've begun to seriously crave female companionship. After spending a great deal of time draining one Irish pub of its supply of Maker's Mark bourbon, Jeff and I walked across the street into a Texas-themed bar and couldn't believe what we saw: our Afghan role-players sitting around a table smoking cigarettes and drinking! Jeff and I ended up having one of the guys join us in our exploration of the area, and, to our delight, he kept up with us in fine form. We ended our night at Pita Pit and Burger King and shared a very memorable cab ride back to the base with the Afghans, teaching each other the finer points of cursing in our respective languages. I can't wait to walk into the next key leader engagement meeting and use my new Dari profanities (while the role-players speak Dari, the U.S. soldiers who evaluate us do not, so for all they know we're just conversing as normal). Last night we built up a good rapport, and I think they'd really get a kick out of it.

Sunday: Today I slept in till about 2:00 p.m. (I went to bed around 4:00 a.m. last night and haven't gotten more than three or four hours of sleep each night this past week), although I was briefly awoken at 9:00 by the team in the bunks next to ours. They're sort of on their own loud schedule; seriously, who really feels the need to blast Ozzy Osborne at 7:00 a.m.? Yep, barracks living is loud, smelly, and significantly lacking in personal space. It'll be nice to get out of here next weekend. A few of my teammates and I are headed for "luxurious" Kansas City. We've booked ourselves into the Intercontinental Hotel (it used to be the Ritz), the city's only five-star establishment, for two nights. I plan on seeing the sights, hitting up a casino for novelty's sake, and finding a few jazz clubs in which to ensconce myself. It'll be great to sleep in a bed that isn't bunked and in a room that doesn't contain 39 other snoring (loud, really loud, chain-saw loud) men. I wear earplugs, and that does a pretty good job of keeping out the noise. Later, Jeff and I are heading over to the Afghans' quarters for chai. Tomorrow we begin two days of firing and qualifying on our M4 assault rifles. We've got more Dari training midweek, and we receive our armored HMMMVs (Hummers) on Thursday. Friday begins our long weekend in celebration of Presidents' Day.

Interesting tidbit on Camp Funston: Apparently this was the site of the first outbreak of influenza in 1918 in the U.S. Army! And, for those interested, my smallpox is nearly healed, though Wednesday brings the second of six anthrax inoculations.

2

Tools of the Trade

Monday, February 11–Monday, February 18, 2008

What a week! Winter continued to wallop the prairie with a vigor and intensity more fitting for the Arctic than for America's breadbasket. If there's anything to be thankful for, it's that shared suffering often builds bonds between men and soldiers like no other, and this week, we suffered.

Monday: We awoke to find our beloved Camp Funston a veritable Arctic wasteland; the once-barren grounds were buried by nearly a foot of snow and encrusted in a thick layer of ice. The temperatures had plummeted into the single digits as the sun and all its warmth decided to take the majority of this week off. Making the best of the situation, we bundled up in our gear and marched off to draw our weapons for the week. We basically live attached to our primary weapons from Monday morning to Saturday night; they only leave our sides when we shower (yes, we even sleep with them). We turn our weapons in at the end of training on each Saturday, which allows us to have Sunday off without having to leave behind a weapons guard. Anytime you want to go somewhere without your weapon, you have to leave a guard behind to watch it. Turning our weapons in to our arms room on Saturday removes this responsibility. It's also great training, because when we're in Afghanistan, these weapons will never leave our sides. Everything is slower with your gear on. Movements that once seemed so natural often have to be planned out. For example, I'm happy each time I'm able to get in and out of a vehicle while

---

My tools of the trade: an M4 assault rifle with an M203 grenade-launcher attachment, an M9 pistol, and the pistol holster I wore around my thigh.

wearing all my body armor, my M4 slung over my shoulder, and my M9 strapped onto my leg without getting too tangled up or banging myself around.

After weapons draw, we headed over to several classes on how to best fire the M4 (we call it PMI, or primary marksmanship instruction). We spent the remainder of the day "boresighting" the M68 scopes atop our M4 assault rifles. These scopes have what's commonly known as a "red-dot sight." Prior to the M68, a rifleman would aim using a front and rear sight post, carefully aligning the front sight post with the rear sight post, ensuring the front sight post sat center mass on a potential target. Thanks to the M68 and one AA battery, all one needs to do is place the tiny red dot one sees through the scope center mass on the target, squeeze off a round, and move on to the next target. The beauty of the M68 is not just the ease of aiming but also the fact that any soldier can pick up another soldier's weapon and use it as if it were his or her own. Prior to the M68, each weapon was adjusted to the individual soldier. Once the adjustments were made, only that soldier could fire that weapon and ensure accuracy; another soldier using the weapon would likely be firing too high, too low, or too much to one side. The M68 removes the needs for adjustments to the weapon itself, because only the scope is moved. Once the scope's red dot is in line with the front sight post, the weapon is aligned, and anyone can use it.

Tuesday: Earlier in this letter, I talked about how shared misery often forges strong bonds between soldiers; Tuesday brought such moments. We awoke around O'Dark Thirty to begin the laborious process of putting on our body armor, making the minor adjustments to an armor plate here, a Kevlar insert there, etc. Sixty-five pounds of gear later, we stepped out into our Arctic playground. The extreme cold dictates *so* much of how you will prepare for the day; you've got to pack extra clothing, dress in appropriate layers, maybe even carry an extra pack with all the extra gear you'll need to keep warm. This Tuesday, for the first time ever in my six-year military career, I wore the majority of my cold-weather gear: for the first time ever, I wore the long poly-pro underwear bottoms. This is a monumental admission. Most soldiers refer to our cold-weather gear as "snivel gear," as in, "Quit your sniveling and drive on with the mission! It's not that cold!" Tuesday *was* that cold.

It was also weapons qualification day on our M4, meaning we had to qualify in both daytime and nighttime. We boarded the lone school bus to the range at 0700, packing in 48 of us in all our gear, 2 to a seat, a literal sardine can of men, musk, weapons, and gear. I ended up in the first daytime firing order. As we moved from the warming shed to the firing line, I began reflecting on just how different my daily life is from most other members of my generation. It was barely light out. It was cold. The wind is probably the *worst* part about the cold. It is one thing if it's single digits and nary a breeze, but it's a whole new level of discomfort when one adds the wind into the mix. The wind pierces; it finds every conceivable crack and opening in your gear to cut right at your skin, down to your bones, each gust an attempt to freeze you in place, a physical reminder that you volunteered for this mission and that you're cold and tired. Frustration doesn't even come close to describing your hatred for the wind in those moments. You'd give anything for it to just *stop* blowing. It becomes personal. You start comparing the intensity and amount of wind blowing in your foxhole to the wind attacking your buddies nearby. You're convinced it's going after you, personally. It's a creature and it's alive, evil, malicious, and incredibly annoying. And then, just when you're about to let it win, you start laughing; or at least I did. There I am, sitting in my foxhole, the wind doing its worst, I can barely feel my fingertips and toes, I'm shivering, it's affecting the accuracy of my fire, all I want to do is go inside and get warm, and then it hits me: I'm getting paid to do this! Someone is paying me a great deal of money to shoot a weapon today. Better still, I'm not sitting at a desk. I'm outdoors. The hours are long, the work is endless, and in a few months danger could literally be lurking around every corner—and yet, this is awesome. I cannot believe someone would actually pay me to have this much fun. At this moment of stark enlightenment, one of the guys happened to catch me laughing and shouted, "What the fuck is so damn funny, Sir?" in manner and inflection that is truly unique to an infantryman. I turned, smiled, and shouted, "This is great! Can you believe we're getting paid for this right now?" At that moment, he smiled too and nodded in agreement. Yeah it sucked, but it was the suck that we'd come to love, because it bonded us.

After qualifying, I spent the remainder of the day outdoors volunteering as a range safety; this got my guys indoors and warm. Around 1500, we finished qualifying everyone in daytime hours, and I went into the warming shed to lie down and take a brief afternoon siesta. There are two universal constants among soldiers: (1) The suck bonds us, and (2) we can sleep anywhere. I managed to get three better hours of sleep on the dank, hard, chilled concrete floor of the shed than I have in all the nights I've spent in my bunk.

Around 1900 (7:00 p.m.), we started the nighttime qualification. I'd never really used night-vision goggles ("NODs," or night optical devices), let alone fired with them, so I had looked forward to this moment all day. I ended up on the second firing order, which was perfect, because by the time I fired, it was nice and dark. Firing with NODs involves using a laser attached to your weapon.

The concept and process couldn't be simpler: Turn on the laser, point the beam (which is infrared and thus only visible while wearing the NODs) on your target, pull the trigger, move on to the next target. Now, add 29 other people doing the exact same thing (30 beams total), and what you get is a laser light show the likes of which you've never seen. NODs turn the world green. The beams from the weapons are a near white in a sea of varying shades of green. It's like something out of a lime-colored *Star Wars*. The best part, for me, was seeing the nighttime sky. Without the NODs, only a few of the brightest stars were visible, but with the NODs, multitudes were visible. I've never seen so many stars; I've never felt so small and yet so blessed to be alive. The sheer vastness of the Milky Way is daunting. It's a memory I'll hold close and dear for the rest of my life.

We finished firing around 2230 and were fast asleep in our bunks within 20 minutes of getting home. Satisfying grunts and snores rumbled from the men around me, a sign the barracks were happy.

Wednesday: Nothing truly exciting to report for Wednesday. The day after the weapons range is much like the day after Christmas or one's birthday: always a letdown. We had classes on the operation and maintenance of the M1151 up-armored Hummer and the military-issue portable power generator we expect to use in Afghanistan. Vital classes and great learning, especially for me, as electrical engineering and vehicle maintenance are not my strong suits (yet).

Thursday: I'll never forget this Valentine's Day. I spent the morning catching up on paperwork and preparing a few classes I'll be giving in the coming weeks on how to do intelligence work. I'm the lone intelligence guy on our team, and we each have our area of expertise; the army claims mine is intel. Around 1130, Sergeant First Class Postman (our mail guy and my staff NCO, the guy I'll be most likely to work with in Afghanistan) walked in with the day's mail delivery. I was busy attempting to eradicate a virus from our first sergeant's computer, so I barely noticed the three packages (one of which was enormous) he carried into the barracks. I finally looked up and saw these packages piled on my footlocker. I sleep on a top bunk, and Sergeant First Class Postman sleeps on the bunk below. I thought that he had simply placed all the packages the group had received on my footlocker and had yet to hand them out, so I was extremely surprised when he told me that they were all for me. I was dumbfounded. I'm not used to getting this much personal mail—normally it's junk and bills.

Once again, my Aunt Bonnie and her DAR chapter saved the day. Thursday started out warm and sunny. We assumed it'd remain warm. We assumed wrong. It was a warm day until we had to step outside and draw (get issued) our up-armored vehicles. This process, like any other equipment issue, takes time. For us, this meant four hours spent outdoors with our old nemesis, winter, and his evil companions, wind and snow. Most of us (me included) had only worn our basic uniform. The equipment issue turned into a fiasco, a prolonged moment of extreme confusion. I don't really blame any one person, we were all at fault. It was cold, and we were angry at ourselves for not predicting the temperature drop and preparing appropriately. We also were hours away from our long weekend in celebration of Presidents' Day. I got the package of wonderful, warm, knitted wool helmet warmers as we were walking out of the barracks, and I handed them out as we left. Without them, I'm convinced we'd have had cases of hypothermia and frostbite.

My friend Bailey had asked how many soldiers (16) were on my team and in our bay (40). She wouldn't explain why she wanted to know, but I found out on Thursday. Inside the *enormous* package were 56 individual valentines. Forty were wrapped in red tissue paper and contained a handful of chocolates. A personalized valentine, signed by Bailey, came with each package. Her simple message ("Thank you so much. Happy Valentine's Day, Bailey Jennifer") touched my fellow soldiers deeply. My team of 16 each received a gold tissue paper–wrapped mini-package of candy and heart-shaped boxes of Russell Stover chocolates with their cards. When we got back to the barracks after the fiasco of our vehicle issue, the chocolates erased our anger, and our stress melted away with each bite.

Around 2030 (8:30 p.m.), three captains and I set off for Kansas City and our long weekend. We spent the night at a hotel by the airport (as one of the captains needed to catch a flight). I've never been more thankful for a real bed. My sleep was long, sound, and peaceful.[1]

---

1 To read more about our trip to Kansas City, go to http://bit.ly/J2Ko6r.

3

Salaam Aleikum, We All Want Our NODs Back, and How I Became an Embedded Combat Adviser

Tuesday, February 19–Sunday, March 9, 2008

The main problem with this whole deployment is how we're actually being deployed. Most reserve and National Guard units get activated and are then sent to a mobilization site (e.g., Fort Bragg or Fort Riley) for around six months, where they transition from being weekend warriors to active-duty soldiers. They then deploy for around 12 to 15 months and return home for a 1- to 3-month demobilization. The process, while not perfect, works and, at times, even works well. The original process took around a year and a half to two years total. That can be a long time and a very tough thing for people who joined to only be in the reserves, and it's even harder on families. The concern is that these lengthy deployments will hurt recruiting and retention in a way that will break the reserves. Thus, they've decided to try something new. The first reserve unit deployed under Defense Secretary Gates's tenure would go on a one-year cycle. That meant (in theory) one year away from families and home total (including the training at mobilization, the actual deployment, and the demobilization). The unit selected for the experiment was mine. Progress report: It has failed thus far.

A group of the Afghan National Army soldiers and my team at Fort Riley after a training operation.

As I mentioned earlier, all other deploying reserve and guard units got six months at their mobilization stations, while we got three three-week training periods throughout the course of last year and are now getting two months at Fort Riley or Fort Bragg. The benefit of six straight months is that you adapt and transition from civilian to soldier, with nothing else on your mind. Train, deploy, and bring everyone back alive: That's the entirety of your focus.

Our two months here are hardly enough time to flip the switch for most. The Active Duty (they oversee everything, including deployments of the reserves) mandated that our unit show up having already completed training normally done during the six-month period. My unit's solution was, simply put, stupid. Rather than just call us up and send us to Fort Drum for nine straight weeks of training before we came down here, they called us up in increments (three weeks in June, three in October, and then three one-week hiccups scattered throughout November, December, and January). It didn't work. Can you reasonably expect anyone to remember what they learned in June 2007 when they arrive in Afghanistan in April 2008? Moreover, as I said before, the beauty of six months straight is that the mission and training become one's focus. With the training spread out, by the time you're getting into a rhythm and starting to gel as a team, the period is over, and it's time to go back to your family and civilian job. Honestly, I hope we're the first and *last* unit ever to undergo this process. It's nothing more than a disservice to our soldiers and their extremely patient families (all of whom ought to be commended for putting up with this chaos). The *only* foreseeable benefit is, if the army holds its word, we'll only be gone for a total of one year (I should be back in the country and demobilized sometime around January or February 2009).

In other news, our team chiefs *finally* returned from their recon of our areas of operation in Afghanistan. I have so many questions. I cannot wait to pick their brains.

This week we're doing driver's training on our up-armored Hummers and three days of Combat Life Savers (CLS) training: basically EMT training for soldiers going into combat.

Tuesday, February 19–Saturday, February 23, 2008

We've been in Kansas more than a month, and we're already at our midway point in training! This week brought a decrease in the intensity and pace of our training as well as a welcome respite to winter's fury. I know it may seem that I speak of Kansas in hyperbole, but, I swear, it really is an extremely cold, barren wasteland, or at least Fort Riley is. Thank God this week the sun returned from its vacation, allowing temperatures to venture into the high 30s and low 40s. The snow and ice have been replaced with deep puddles of varying shades of chocolate and filled with thick, rich mud. But, and this may come as a surprise, I'm actually thankful for all of this, for I've discovered two things about my army-issued boots as a result of these temperature changes:

1. On ice, they're worthless—all considerations regarding traction seem to have been left out of the design process.
2. They can accumulate an unholy amount of mud in a very short time.

I'm glad I learned these things here rather than in Afghanistan.

Tuesday: We spent the day in the motor pool (the depot where we store all our vehicles, do maintenance, etc.) becoming extremely familiar with the ins and outs of our M1151 up-armored Hummers. It was extremely valuable training. We learned how to change the tires, which involves at least two jacks (one *has* to be hydraulic), and how to tow the vehicles when one breaks down. Our mechanical maintenance training was conducted by this wry, good-natured sergeant whose eyes did not blink once in four hours. It's amazing how some people can be so positive and generous after facing such adversity. This man clearly has seen some awful things in his life, unspeakable horrors. And yet, the only sign that he's haunted is the fixture of his eyes. You first notice it when he looks at you: A thousand-yard stare is permanently etched into his rugged face. There's an emptiness that seems ready to consume him at any time. Then he smiles, and the turnaround is uncanny. The guy is the definition of team player. He doesn't have to care; he's retiring in two months. He could simply do the bare minimum, go home at the end of the day, and lose himself in a daze of cheap booze and self-despair, but he doesn't. He's active. He's alive. He stays beyond late. He offers up all his free time to help out complete strangers, fellow soldiers whom he's likely never to encounter again. He's not getting paid extra for this; there is no overtime in the military. He's not eligible for promotion. No, he climbs down on a dirty garage floor, slides under the vehicle, and spends the next hour pointing out key parts and suggestions for how to fix them should they break, because he's the ultimate team player, the quiet hero, never seeking recognition, content with the knowledge that he consistently does the right thing. General Meigs, a professor of mine at Maxwell (where I went to grad school) once told me, "Do what's right, sleep at night." I got that adage before, but I *get* it now.

The most dramatic part of the day was when we did the rollover training. The M1151 Hummer is eight tons when fully loaded. At times, when exposed to angles over 22 degrees, it has a tendency to roll over; thus, we must all be trained on how to react if this happens. Training involves being strapped into a mock crew compartment that's attached to a machine that can spin the compartment 360 degrees in either direction. We went through three iterations of being flipped completely upside down. The first is to prove to us that our safety belts will actually hold us in place wearing our body armor. The second is to show us what to do with our weapons if the vehicle should roll over (if possible, place the muzzle end toward the nearest door and brace it with the hand closest to that door on the ceiling). The third scenario was the same as the second, only this time two people were given "injuries" (rendering them immobile and thus requiring those of us who were uninjured to extract them from the vehicle, while under simulated fire). I actually got quite spooked during the third iteration. The vehicle rolled over. I braced my weapon up onto the ceiling. I reached down with my free hand and unfastened my safety belts. I dropped down on my helmet. I began to right myself. Then I got hit—hard. The person seated behind me dropped down in such a way that he came crashing down on my helmet, his whole body flying into the upturned gunner's turret. What freaked me out was that he missed hitting my neck with the full force and weight of his body by about three inches and one second.

At the time, I was quite shaken and extremely angry at the person who had nearly paralyzed me. It was a foolish anger. It's not his fault for how he fell; it's gravity's and chance. Looking back on the event now, it was actually great training, for should this ever actually happen in combat, I guarantee I'll be equally spooked. It was also a good confidence booster, because, despite my emotions, I was able to drive on and perform my duties (escaping from the vehicle, establishing security, extracting the injured, etc.).

Thursday–Saturday: We spent these three days going through Combat Life Savers training. We all considered this *extremely* important and useful; it's just a shame our parent training unit did not. All other units going through Fort Riley get everyone deploying certified as CLS providers, but we aren't getting certified. We were told there wasn't enough time in the training schedule to get us certified and provide us with all the training we'd need. It's these answers that infuriate me. We shouldn't be training to time at the sacrifice of standards.

The only positive about this training was that we got at least a little of it (better than nothing) in the two scenarios we did on Saturday. The first had us "patrolling" a village with the Afghan Army and police (civilian role-players). During the patrol, the village comes under fire and the Afghan security forces take casualties, and we have to provide them with initial aid and evacuate them. Movement to and from the training site required a three-mile march in all our gear. I really enjoy tactical road marches, a.k.a. dismounted movement. I find the vehicles too claustrophobic.

The second scenario involved a mortar attack on a dining facility (D-Fac). This scenario is based on an actual attack that happened in Iraq a few years ago, only that attack involved a suicide bomber, rather than mortars. The scenario was as follows:

We're on our way to chow when the D-Fac is hit by a mortar. We've just become the initial-aid providers. We have to run into the building and get as many people out as possible before it "collapses." For the scenario, they filled a building with smoke, turned off all the lights and covered the windows, and threw chairs and other furniture all over the floors to act as debris. As we came across casualties, we had to perform rapid field assessments of the injuries, provide tourniquets if needed, and move them out of the building to the aid station (where they received additional care). We all found the training very useful, for it stressed the importance of developing a quick plan (where will each team go in the building, where will we bring patients, who will triage patients, etc.) before just running in and trying to help people.

Our team leader, Captain (soon to be Major) Malok, returned from his three-week recon of Afghanistan. We have a pretty good idea of where we'll be going and what we'll be doing. Unfortunately, I'm not at liberty to pass this info on at the moment, and "Nothing is guaranteed until you're actually there." Suffice to say, if we do end up where we believe we will, it's going to be a very active, but likely rewarding, year. Captain Malok gave us a great briefing on his adventures and what to expect. One thing I can say is that once we get there, it'll probably take about 7 to 10 days for mail to reach us, so baked goods probably won't survive the journey. I ask that if you feel inclined to send me a care package, you send soap, shampoo, shaving cream, baby wipes, lotion, etc., in lieu of baked goods.

I actually haven't had a chance to look at the training schedule for this week, but if my memory serves me, we're doing a bunch of training on crew-served weapons (the M2 .50 caliber machine gun, M240B machine gun, etc.). There's also RUMINT (Rumor Based Intelligence) that around 10 Afghan Army personnel will be joining us for this week (as part of an exchange program we have, where we bring their best guys over here to train with us).

Monday, March 3–Sunday, March 9, 2008

Another week has passed, bringing us one week closer to our inevitable departure and the start of our yearlong adventure. I'm going to try a new tactic and try to not anger the weather gods by refraining from my usual mockery of Kansas weather. I hope that my restraint will bring us favorable weather for what promises to be one of the more intense and hectic weeks we'll undergo while here at Fort Riley. As for this past week, we picked up on Monday right where we left off on Saturday: fast, stressful, and intense. By week's end, however, we'd slowed down to a much-needed relaxed pace, which allowed us to recover a bit and recharge our drained personal batteries. As our departure date rapidly approaches, the reality of what faces us sits heavily upon our shoulders like a silent constant companion: never outwardly acknowledged, its existence too taboo to say aloud. Yet, there's also a palpable excitement pulsing through the barracks. We're nearly ready. We want to go out, do our jobs, do them well, serve with honor, make our nation proud. The dichotomy of deployment: On the one hand, you hate to leave your loved ones behind for this year, but on the other, *wow*, what an adventure! What an amazing opportunity to do some incredible good!

Monday: We began the morning with several briefings on interrogation and tactical questioning techniques. Given the sensitive nature of these briefings, the Afghans were not invited to join us. For those interested, yes, we covered all the things we are prohibited from doing; we were told explicitly that we cannot use stress positions, water boarding, or all the other questionable and controversial methods we've all read about in the news. We were supposed to have a live-fire (real ammunition) exercise in the afternoon, but the range was covered in ice, rendering it unusable. Instead, we executed our backup plan: stack training.

"The stack" is used when clearing rooms during urban combat operations. Typically, it involves four people. I really like stack training. We drove to our training site with the Afghans in tow. In hindsight, we should have realized these grizzled veterans would be pros. Truthfully, the Afghans taught us more than we taught them. They've been doing urban combat operations for three years straight. And, as I've said before, these guys are the ones who've survived; they're either incredibly lucky or very good at their jobs.

Looking back on the training, it was very funny how quickly they showed us up. As we were going to set up the training, the Afghans realized exactly what it was we wanted to do and set themselves up in four-man teams. They lined up in stacks and began clearing rooms at will. I sat back and just started to laugh: Their expertise was frighteningly obvious. The rest of my team sat there dumb-founded. We pressed on with the training, which ended up being more for us than for the Afghans. I was actually quite satisfied with how well my team (Major Malok, First Lieutenant Gibson, Sergeant First Class Postman, and I) performed together. By the end of the training, I felt we had a really good rhythm down, our communication was clear and efficient, and we even seemed to be anticipating each other's movements.

Tuesday: Battle Drill 6 is apparently a big deal in the course of our training. We've heard about it for weeks: "Just wait till you get to Battle Drill 6." "Battle Drill 6 is a defining event." "We'll see how you all do on Battle Drill 6." I can honestly say it doesn't live up to the hype.

On the way to all our training, we drive down an IED (improvised explosive device) lane. The lane is actually a dirt road with numerous stations that employ the gamut of IEDs. Each station focuses on a particular kind of IED. Some are detonated via remote control (radio signal from a garage-door opener, cell-phone signal), others are detonated via a timer, while others are detonated via a tripwire or pressure plate. Because we drive up this lane *every day*, we've become very good at spotting most of the IEDs, with one glaring exception: pressure-plated IEDs. We've missed the pressure-plated IEDs every time.

We move in convoys. Prior to SP'ing (Start Point), we all get out of our vehicles (still inside the walls of the FOB) and go through a convoy brief. The convoy commander reviews the planned route, the predicted threats derived by the intelligence section, our plans on how we'll react to any danger/attacks, what radio frequencies to use, the order of the vehicles, etc. During Tuesday's convoy brief, Major Malok (our convoy commander for the day) said that his priority for this movement would be to ensure we spotted the pressure-plated IEDs, highlighting the fact that we've missed them every time thus far. The challenge sent my motivation skyrocketing: I was determined to find that SOB this time through.

We turned on to the tank trail (dirt road) and began to aggressively scan our surroundings. We passed the artillery shell wired to the cell phone on our right: remote-controlled IED, check. We crept along past the explosives wired to an observation post on our left: command-detonated IED, check. And then I saw it: a small tube with a wire attached to it that ran off onto the side of the road. "IED! Pressure plated! To the right of lead vehicle" I yelled over the radio. Instinct and adrenaline kicked in. Our driver floored it. The convoy commander began coordinating the movements of the convoy over the radio. Because it was a training exercise and I was the only one who had seen it, we decided to dismount from our vehicles and walk back to examine what the device looked like (the goal is for everyone to notice them). As we walked back down the road, I kept replaying the events over and over again in my head. I hadn't been 100 percent sure it really was an IED: There was a 20 percent chance it had just been a stick with shadows that looked like a wire leading off into the brush. I said a silent prayer that I'd actually find the thing. We searched. Nothing. We searched again. Still nothing. Butterflies flapped with increasing ferocity in my belly. Embarrassment set in. I turned a bright shade of magenta. I could see it now, all the ribbing and joking I was going to endure. The calls of "Lieutenant Zeller, look out!" that would ring out for months on end every time I took a walk. And then I saw it. Well camouflaged, a tan tube blending into the dirt of the road, a thin wire attached at its base, running off into the brush on the side of the road: a pressure-plated IED. "Found it!" I exclaimed with more relief than pride. Everyone smiled. We finished our review and mounted back up on the trucks. We found two more pressure-plated IEDs along the way. We noted how well they blended in to the road and how difficult it's going to be to spot them. With a little bit of luck, prayer, and an ever-vigilant eye, I'm hoping we'll prove ourselves experts.

Battle Drill 6 is a series of urban combat simulations (two during the day, and one at night). In line with the status quo of our training thus far, the night simulation was canceled for some unexplained reason, leaving only the two daytime iterations. The first simulation involves reacting to an ambush while conducting a patrol through a village. Our team decided to do our drill without the aid of our gun trucks, something that would *never* happen in real life. Nothing too exciting to report here, other than I got to fire blanks out of my M4. I hate blanks. Without some sort of laser-tag system, there's no way to tell whether you hit the target you were shooting at. During the simulation, our team was engaged while patrolling the village. I took cover behind a building and saw a sniper engaging my team. I "shot" the sniper, but, because we're using blanks, he had no idea that he was actually dead and continued to just fire away, killing a great deal of our patrol in this simulation. Yelling *"bang bang"* would have been just as effective. All shooting blanks accomplishes is simulating the noise of battle and reinforcing the importance of cleaning your weapon.

The second daytime simulation involved tactical questioning and interrogation techniques: finally, my time to shine. In this scenario, we roll into a village that has already been cleared and secured by the Afghan Army. They've detained seven people (six men and one woman) and found bomb-making material in one of the village buildings. We know ahead of time that a bomb maker by the name of Ahmed Amir Khan lives in the village. It's our job to determine if Ahmed is among the detained and whether the rest are friendly or enemy. We divided our mixed U.S./Afghan patrol into four teams: a site-exploitation team (they collect evidence), a detainee-ops team (they do the initial pat-downs of the detained), a security-liaison team (they do security with the Afghan Army), and a tactical questioning/interrogation team. Because I'm our intel guy and the most highly trained in questioning and interrogation, I was placed in charge of the tactical questioning/interrogation team. I decided to really incorporate our Afghan allies and brought along Safi as my translator/co-questioner. One by one, the detainees were led into our room, and we put our skills to work. I'm not a big fan of aggressive and mean approaches; I find befriending the detained is the most effective at eliciting information. I instructed the guys watching the detainees outside to keep them separated, not allow them to talk, keep them blindfolded, and be polite, but strict and stern. Once they got to me, I was kind, speaking in warm, sincere, gentle tones. Before I even got down to questioning them or checking their biological stats (iris, fingerprints, which are used to determine whether the detainee is in our database of known enemies), I'd offer them something to eat and drink, a cigarette, inquire about their health, and reassure them that everything was going to be okay, so long as they cooperated. I'd introduce myself and ask them for their names. I treated each encounter like meeting someone in church or at a party: I was polite, friendly, inquisitive, kind, outgoing. All of this was done on purpose. I wanted the contrast between the treatment they'd received before me and with me to be as great as possible. I do this to disorient the detainee as much as possible. People want to talk after emotionally traumatic events, it's human nature. By denying them that outlet (i.e., having the outdoor guards keep them silent, blindfolded, separated), I increased the desire to discuss, to talk that much more. Typically, by the time they got to me, they were so thankful just to see a smiling, kind face who seemed like he would take care of them that they were very forthcoming with information.

It didn't take too long to find our bad guy as well as determine that two other men were in cahoots with him. The evaluators for the simulation said we ran it perfectly and that my questioning was "spot on, excellent, some of the best we've seen." It was nice to finally show my team some of my skills, to raise my value beyond "intel guy." Intel is such a secretive world that often the guys don't get to see my value added. This simulation finally allowed them to see just what I can bring to the team.

We got back to our FOB and said our final good-byes to the Afghans, who join a new group of Americans every week. I spent about two hours drinking tea with them in their barracks, sharing stories and learning as much as I could about their culture and customs. For example, I have to make sure that every time I visit them, I stop by and say hello and good-bye to their commanding officer and invite him to join me on my visit. I learned that I must remove my shoes once indoors and that bringing a gift on each visit is a sign of my great respect and friendship. They brought out this instrument that was part piano, part accordion and played it for me. We attempted to tell jokes but agreed the punch lines ultimately got lost in translation. When we said our good-byes, each firmly squeezed me three times by hugging me and placing their hands in a fist upon my back. It really hasn't been the same without them. They brought an energy and joy to everything that we've sorely missed.

Wednesday: Call-For-Fire (CFF) and Call-For-Attack-Aviation (CAA) are critically important skills. CFF involves calling in artillery, while CAA involves calling in attack helicopters. We spent our entire day back up on the main post going through a series of classes that taught us how to call in these assets should we ever need them. The training involved massive TV screens and a rather cool video game that simulates incoming artillery and attack helicopter weapons. Performing these skills involves a combination of geometry, typography, and correct radio operation. We all found it very easy to learn and had it pretty much down within two or three practice sessions. We returned to our FOB around 4:00 p.m., fully expecting to grab dinner and move on to a series of briefings we had in the evening, but what we got instead was an exercise in stupidity.

The military has certain items that are considered so sensitive that, should one ever go missing, entire bases can be locked down like prisons, with no movement in or out until it's found. Night-vision goggles are such items. As we drove back to our FOB, a radio call informed us that we were on lockdown, that all training for the evening was suspended, and that we were to report immediately to the assembly area behind our barracks for a battalion formation. Battalion formations are rare. They're huge (numbering in the hundreds of soldiers), require lots of space, and are normally only used in ceremonies. We knew something big must be afoot if it required a battalion formation. We lined up and waited, the rows of soldiers abuzz with theories as to why we were on lockdown.

"Battalion, *attention*!" brought a quick and deafening silence to our ranks. The battalion sergeant major climbed atop a parked Hummer and called us to gather around him. Within seconds a mass gaggle of soldiers encircled the sergeant major upon his armored chariot. "Men, we've got a pair of NODs missing. So we're in a lockdown! You know what that means! Training from this point on is canceled! Dinner is canceled! Meetings are canceled! Until we get these NODs back, everything is canceled! Now, I'm gonna give you all 15 minutes to go back into your barracks and search through your crap! If you find my NODs, go into the latrine, and place them upon the sink counter! Fifteen minutes of amnesty! No questions asked of the guilty party! But, if after those 15 minutes my NODs aren't found, well, you've all been here before, you know what happens next! We're gonna all stand out here in the cold! Team by team you'll be called into your bay! We're then gonna tear apart your gear and shit! Yes, I know it's tight and cramped in there! Well, if my NODs aren't found in 15 minutes, it's gonna get a lot worse! Do my men want to search through your stuff and watch you tear apart your bunks and lockers? *No!* But are we gonna do this all night and day until I find my NODs? *Yes! Men! I want my f'ing NODs back!* Your 15 minutes starts now! So help me God, if I find a pair of NODs in one of your crap after this 15 minutes, well, to that person [sadistic smile], you're mine!"

Three hundred men went running into the barracks within 30 seconds. A chorus of grumbles rang out. Everyone hates barracks tossing (as this process is known). We especially hate it when we know we cannot possibly be the guilty party; we had turned all our NODs in that morning to the company arms room. Furthermore, we all knew that the NODs wouldn't be found. Not in the allotted 15 minutes, and certainly not during the inevitable barracks shakedown. We joked about all the things we would have loved to yell back to the sergeant major:

"We all *want* things in life, Sergeant Major, doesn't it suck when we can't have them?"

Or

"We'll make you a deal . . . you stick to your training plan [they're *constantly*, at times hourly, changing it . . . much to our supreme annoyance and frustration], we'll give you your NODs back!"

Or

"Yeah . . . and we wanted CLS certification . . . but just because we *wanted* it doesn't mean it's gonna happen!"

It's times like these when I truly appreciate the profound sarcasm that seems to be a requisite for all soldiers.

Through a bit of snooping around for info, I determined that one pair of NODs was missing from Alpha Company. We're Bravo Company. Thanks to Alpha's incompetence, we were sharing in the punishment.

Fifteen minutes passed. No NODs were found. The barracks tossing began. For the next five hours, we went in by team and ripped apart our homes. We tore everything out of our lockers. We dumped everything out of our rucksacks, backpacks, and footlockers. We turned all our pockets inside out. We watched as soldiers assigned from another battalion went through our belongings, carefully searching for the elusive pair of NODs.

Five hours later, the barracks were a chaotic mess, gear strewn in all places, and not a single pair of NODs had been found. We rescheduled our briefings. We trained late into the night.

The NODs were never found; they're still missing. Turns out, they've been missing for three weeks. From what I've been able to piece together, Alpha Company's armorer was recently brought up on charges for going AWOL. Now that he's been fired as their armorer, Alpha Company has to do a full items inventory of everything in their arms room. In other words, Alpha Company's commander and his new armorer have to go into the arms room with the fired armorer, pull out every single item in that room, and compare each item's serial number to the master serial-number inventory list. Problems arise when the numbers do not match or, worse, items are missing. Alpha completed its sensitive-items inventory and found it was missing a pair of NODs. The Alpha Company commander asked the fired armorer if he knew where they were. The fired armorer claimed that he had issued 17 NODs to a team of 16 people and that when they went to turn the NODs in, they only turned in 16. The Alpha Company commander went to this team to get its side of the story. That team claims the armorer tried to issue 17 NODs, but that it refused the extra pair and made the armorer sign a statement proving he had only issued 16, despite his claims otherwise. Hence the barracks tossing!

The funny thing about all this is that the missing NODs are commercially available, cost around $3,000, and have been around for almost 20 years. It's not like they're some super-secret equipment we don't even want falling into the hands of our allies. What will most likely happen now is that that armorer will be responsible for the $3,000 they cost, and he'll get in even more trouble for lying, not to mention the bad karma from sending an entire battalion on a wild goose chase.

Thursday: We had another in our never-ending series of Dari classes in the morning. I've gotten all that I can from these classes, and I'm not going to move forward unless it's via my own instruction. The remainder of the day was a nice respite from the frantic pace of the previous week and a half. I spent the afternoon on the main part of post getting some much needed paperwork taken care of (medical stuff, pay issues, etc....).

In the evening, we celebrated Staff Sergeant Craig Morrissey's birthday. We celebrated the entire day in full army fashion. We sang "Happy Birthday," to his extreme embarrassment, at the morning formation *and* at lunch in the chow hall. We even gave him a cupcake with a match in it as a makeshift birthday cake.

Morrissey is close to my age and a veteran of Iraq. Three weeks into his tour in Iraq, he was shot in the abdomen and almost died. The fact that he's so positive and funny is a testament to his character and excellence. I'm beyond proud to know him and call him my friend. He's definitely one of my favorite team members. We all chipped in and bought a ton of pizza, beer, whiskey, and Jager (Morrissey's favorite drink) to celebrate. I volunteered to take his rental car and pick up the pizza. It took about an hour, but it was well worth it. By the time I returned, the party was in full swing, and a joyful chorus rang out at the sight of food. Morrissey rushed up with a glass of Jager in hand, proclaiming, "Thanks, Lieutenant! Let's do a shot!" We drank heavily and ate heartily. Through a very inebriated conversation over many Peanut Butter Girl Scout cookies, I learned how I ended up on this embedded training team.

Major Hunt, my old boss and perpetual mentor, approached Lieutenant Colonel Summers (our overall commander) back in May when he first found out he'd be on an ETT for this mission. Lieutenant Colonel Summers was looking to staff his teams with the best and brightest our brigade could offer. He had asked Major Hunt for his recommendations, and apparently my name was on that list. Thus began the months-long secret effort to steal me away from my previous assignment with the 427th Battalion as the battalion intelligence officer, a position and unit I've previously described as one of the worst assignments in my career. Major Hunt's plan was brilliant, cunning, and diabolical. Once the 427th realized I was the only competent intelligence officer they had, they would be loath to give me up. Thus, Major Hunt had to convince them that it was *their* idea to get rid of me. He was confident I'd play my part by being a constant pain in the ass once I realized the extent of incompetence that flowed through the unit's leadership. He knew I wouldn't just sit back and do nothing, but that I'd keep trying to fix things and do what's right. Eventually, they'd get so sick of my refusing to go along with the shortcuts and half-assed jobs that they'd be happy to let me go. Apparently I played my part perfectly. He submitted my name, Lieutenant Colonel Summers requested me. Request denied. By midsummer, I had become so fed up with my previous unit that I'd requested reassignment. Request denied. Major Hunt approached the unit's executive officer (XO) to "check up on me." The XO went to town with how he didn't get me, why I couldn't just go along with the team and accept the levels of performance to which they were accustomed. Major Hunt circled in for the kill: "Well, if he's such a problem, why not get rid of him? We need people on the ETTs, you want him out of your hair. If you guys volunteered him up, you'd look like great team players, and you'd get to get rid of him on your terms, not his, because he's not gonna let up, that's Zeller, he won't stand for anything less than people's personal best." That conversation took place at the end of October. Two weeks later, I was reassigned to my current team. I'll never be able to thank Major Hunt enough.

Friday: Seriously, what is it with this place and the Arctic winter? When we woke up it was 18 degrees outside, but −16 with the wind chill! It was *so* cold and windy that when you walked, it felt as if the wind was constantly punching you in the gut, knocking all the air out of your lungs. We spent the day in personnel recovery class where we had yet another PowerPoint presentation interspersed with clips from the movie *The Guardian* starring Kevin Costner. What does a movie about coast guard rescue jumpers have to do with rescuing captured U.S. soldiers in combat operations in Afghanistan?

Most of the class was classified, so I can't discuss the details other than to say I learned five minutes of useful information and spent the majority of the class reading a book, *Six Minutes to Freedom*, which I highly recommend. We had another Dari class in the afternoon, after which we turned in our weapons and prepared for our first real two-day weekend in nearly a month. I ended up going to Buffalo Wild Wings with our team leader, Major Malok. Eventually, we were joined by First Lieutenants Pulley, Gibson, and Foldes. I think we got in around 3:00 a.m. after a much-needed night out.

Sunday: I awoke around noon, just in time to find out I'm going to be Tuesday's convoy commander. I've now got a few hours of planning ahead of me where I'll have to determine our routes, the order of our vehicles, the radio frequencies we'll use, contingency plans, file a trip ticket (the document outlining all of this) with our higher headquarters, etc.

Today the weather is actually gorgeous outside; sunny, blue skies, mid-50s. For about an hour, we took advantage of the nice day and talked through how we'll respond to ambushes, IEDs, disabled vehicles, obstacles blocking the road, etc.

Next week, we will spend Monday and Tuesday doing live fire exercises with my favorite weapon, the M2, a.k.a. "Ma Duce." Wednesday through Friday we'll be doing a series of mounted combat patrols and exercises, all in preparation for our capstone exercise next week. Then it's Easter vacation (off for four days), two days of cleaning up and turning in our training gear, and our graduation from training on March 26. We also found out our flight window, the approximate dates on which we'll actually fly to Afghanistan. Our window is April 6–10.

4

Ducks and Turtles

Monday, March 10–Sunday, March 16, 2008

This week has been an emotional roller coaster of epic proportions, a study in the highest of highs and the lowest of lows.

Monday: By far our slowest day of the week, Monday found the men of Team Mohawk familiarizing one another with the workings of the M2 .50-caliber machine gun. We learned how to assemble and disassemble the weapon, which parts to clean, and practiced firing it using a computer simulation (which I think is worthless). We spent the remainder of the day doing the same type of training with AK-47s, RPKs (Russian Machine Guns), and old Soviet sniper rifles—all weapons one may encounter in Afghanistan. We ended the day with tow drills, practicing how to tow a disabled vehicle.

Tuesday: I was the convoy commander for the day, a position that required a *lot* of preparatory work. Two days earlier I had to compile a "trip ticket," a detailed plan outlining what routes we would travel on, the exact time we'd leave, all the radio frequencies we'd use, who was in each vehicle, our final destination and activities along the way, and contingency routes we'd take should one be closed. I woke up at around O'Dark Thirty to ensure I was the first person out to our vehicles. Our normal routine in the mornings we travel off the FOB is as follows:

My Fort Riley training team at our last group dinner before flying to Afghanistan the next day. Clockwise from the left: Sizemore, Boggins, Pulley, Darden, Eichler, Postman, Fraser, Malok, Escobedo, and me.

We get up, shower, eat breakfast, put on our body armor, gather up our crew-served weapons (the M2 and M240-B machine guns), and walk the quarter mile to the motor pool where we store our vehicles. First Lieutenant Gibson and Sergeant First Class Postman usually mount the M2 on top of our vehicle while I go about getting the vehicle ready to move. First, I have to unlock all the doors. There are no power locks or key locks on an up-armored Hummer, we use master locks (like one would use on a gym locker) to lock our front doors. The rear doors are "combat locked"—locked from the inside. Once the front doors are opened, I have to reach around to the rear doors and unlock each by pulling up on a handle attached to each door. Once the doors are unlocked, I turn on the engine. There is no remote start, there isn't even a key! In their stead is a switch that one must first place into standby and wait for the *wait light* to turn off, a signal that the engine is ready to be started. With the engine on, I then lift the hood up and check to make sure all the fluids are at their proper levels and that nothing is broken. Next, either Major Malok or I turn on our "Blue Force Tracker." Finally, I turn on all the radios and the internal communication headsets, while someone else (usually First Lieutenant Gibson) sets up the turret. With the vehicle ready to move, I order our other team vehicles to move out to the convoy staging area at their leisure.

Trying to get your vehicles lined up in the correct order in the convoy staging area is an exercise in futility. At times there can be up to seven other convoys attempting to do the very same thing, all without any kind of cross-team coordination. I wasted about five minutes and fed my growing ulcer a healthy meal of worry as I attempted to conduct an orchestra of eight-ton military vehicles in an intricate ballet of "move left, turn right, back up, no, go forward, no not that way, this way, no right, no not your right, my right!"

With the vehicles in their proper alignment I got the first FRAGO (fragmentary order; an on-the-spot change) of the day: My convoy would be falling in with another team. See, we're not allowed to travel outside our FOB without an OC (officer-in-charge). Normally, each team gets an OC, allowing us to travel as individual convoys. Just my luck, the day I'm in command, there aren't enough for each convoy to have their own OC. We were told we'd be joining another infantry team on their movements. No problem. A quick adjustment to our radios (we had to use the other team's frequency), and we were all set to move.

To actually leave the FOB, one must first give the people traveling in the convoy a briefing: where we're going, how we're getting there, what frequencies we're using, what to do if we get ambushed/find an IED, which vehicles will call up medical reports (i.e., medevac), our speed of travel, the distance that should be maintained between each vehicle (i.e., intervals), what call signs we're using, and the order of the vehicles. After the briefing, I called up to "higher" (our OC) to report we were ready to move.

To our OC:

"Bull Dog One-One, this is Mohawk Two, over."

"Mohawk Two, this is Bull Dog One-One, over."

"Bull Dog One-One, Red One Report to follow. Status Green [we have accounted for all our people and sensitive items, weapons, night-vision goggles, etc.]. One-Six PAX, U.S., Four Victors. How copy over?"

"Mohawk Two, roger that, good copy, One-Six PAX, Four Victors, move when ready, over."

"Roger that, Bull Dog One-One, Mohawk Two moving now, out."

Bull Dog One-One (aka Bull Dog 11) is our OC, and I'm Mohawk Two. Army trivia: The intelligence officer is *always* the "Two."

With permission to move, I radioed the other team (the Wolverines) and relayed the same info. Then I radioed my team:

"All Mohawk elements, this is Mohawk Two. Prepare to move. Follow my move. Move. Move now."

As we left the FOB, I stole my first calm breath of the morning; it would be the last one I'd take all day.

We turned onto IED alley, the dirt road we take *every* convoy, and I began calling out the familiar IEDs. This was turning out to be an easier convoy than I had imagined. The radios worked. Our intervals looked great. And now we were in a mass convoy with another team and not likely to be ambushed by the OPFOR (opposition forces, the bad guys of our training). The OPFOR usually only ambushes single-team convoys, because some teams are better prepared than others. The better-prepared teams get tougher ambushes so that they can learn from them and adjust accordingly. Some convoys only get gunfire, others get complex ambushes with IEDs, gunfire, artillery, or obstacles.

I laughed when I heard the crackle of the day's first gunfire. "You're kidding me, right?" Nope. IEDs, multiple machine guns, a squad's worth of OPFOR. At first we reacted just as we'd practiced. Each vehicle simultaneously returned fire while increasing its speed to get out of the kill zone. That's when the IED hit my vehicle with a flash of white and a dense plume of smoke. Is that baby powder I smell?

Had it been a real IED and not just baby powder, everyone in my vehicle would have died. Just my luck, the first time I command a convoy and we get the most complex ambush we've seen. Even better, my vehicle is a mobility kill (everyone inside is alive, but the vehicle cannot drive and must be towed). To make matters worse, we've stopped in a gate, and a metal chain-link fence sits at either side of my vehicle. There isn't a chance that one of the other vehicles will be able to tow us unless we move out of the gate. The OC realizes this and gives my vehicle permission to move to a place where we can simulate being towed.

"Bull Dog One-One, this is Mohawk Two, over."

"Bull Dog One-One, this is Mohawk Two, over."

"Bull Dog One-One, this is Mohawk Two, over!"

"Lieutenant Zeller, fight your battle, call higher later!" screams Major Malok. "Mohawk Elements, this is Mohawk Two, my vehicle is a mobility kill. Mohawk

Three-Zero, move your vehicle to my front to provide security. Mohawk One-Two, move your vehicle up to mine and tow us the hell out of here. Mohawk . . . [I stopped, trying to remember his call sign] Lieutenant Pulley, continue to provide rear security for the convoy."

He replied, "Roger that, Mohawk Two, good copy, remember to use call signs while on the radio."

I'm proud to say my vehicles responded in rapid military precision. Within seconds my vehicle was "towed" out of the battle, and we moved on to conduct our AAR (after action review). We reviewed our actions, and I took the ding on forgetting call signs and trying to call higher first. Other than that, we all agreed we did actually quite well. We followed our plans. We utilized our training. Was it perfect? No. Did it work? Yes.

Around 8:30 that morning, we fired the M2; only two people on the team actually got to qualify, the rest of us (including me) only got to do a "fam fire" (familiarization firing—just shooting targets, no score kept, no time standard to meet). Our team would be shooting last; we had about an hour or so till it was our turn. Major Malok took the time to brief us on what the rest of the week's training entailed. As he briefed Thursday's missions and assigned roles, I took mental note of the fact that he was assigning the same four people to leadership roles over and over again. While he, Captain Mcintire, Captain Ford (who would later be relieved for cowardice in war and yet still find a way to get awarded a Bronze Star while riding a desk), and Captain Fraser were off evaluating the Afghans' ability to conduct a checkpoint, the rest of us would be pulling security. While they met with the village mayor, the rest of us would be pulling security.

After the briefing, I pulled Major Malok to the side and pointed out the fact that only four people were really getting training that day; the rest of us on security would be so far from the training that we really wouldn't get much out of it.

Me: Perhaps you could change up the roles a bit. I mean, these guys are already the most senior and experienced people on the team. If anything, they're the last people who really need this training.

Maj. Malok: Lieutenant, the reason why they're in these roles is that in country they're going to be my company mentors. Regardless of their seniority and experience, they need this training more than anyone else.

Me: Sir, you're assuming that we're all going to end up together and in these roles. There's a very good chance we'll be split up and performing other jobs than our current positions. [In other words, just because I'm not a company mentor now doesn't mean I won't be one in country.]

Maj. Malok: Roger, got it. But that's just the way it is.

Me: Okay, Sir, well, do you think we could possibly use some of our free time to do additional training? Get some of our guys into leadership positions in key leader meets?

Maj. Malok: Right now my priority is additional medical training. I'd rather you all know how to stop an arterial bleed than know how to properly conduct yourself in a leader meet. I mean, at the end of the day, those things really only require you to use your common sense. So, the answer is, no. Not until we get better at medical.

Me: Sir, I disagree. The leader meets are equally. . . .

Maj. Malok: Stop. End of conversation.

I was beyond angry, I was fuming. Didn't the major realize that, yes, obviously additional medical training is supremely important, but so are the leader meets? In country they could be the difference between being shot at or rolling through a village unharmed. Doesn't he get that the basic principle of counterinsurgency is to deny the enemy a sympathetic or apathetic population? It's *all* about the people.

Wednesday: Our day began with an Escalation of Force class taught by our training battalion's commander, Lieutenant Colonel Siegel. Escalation of Force can be summed up in five words: Shout, Show, Shoot, Shoot, and Shoot.

Shout: "Stop or I'll shoot!"

Show: Point your weapon at the person you intend to stop.

Shoot: Fire a warning shot.

Shoot: Fire a disabling shot (e.g., into a vehicle's engine block).

Shoot: Shoot to kill.

Chaplain Yates, our unit's chaplain back in New York, spoke to us this week. He looks as if he's in his late 40s or early 50s, speaks with a powerful voice, and carries an energy that is equal parts warrior and healer. He can go from soldier to spiritual leader in a heartbeat. His discussions are often very frank and rock; he doesn't dance around the point but moves straight in for the kill.

I'll remember his talk for the rest of my life. It was a definitive moment, a turning point.

We sat in a semi-circle around the chaplain in the TV room. He took a deep breath, looked each of us in the eye, and began:

"Men, I'm here tonight because I wanted to take some time to talk to you about the things you mentally need to do to prepare yourself, as best you can, for what you're about to experience. Let me be honest, brutally honest. You're not going to be the same men you are now when you come home. You're going to change and in ways you cannot predict. You need to be ready for that. Are these changes going to be all bad or good? No. They'll be a mixed bag. You're going to have some tough times. You will see combat. You are all warriors. Warriors accept that death may come. Warriors do not let the fear of death prevent them from completing their mission. You need to get that down right now, before you go over. There is a chance you will die. Deal with it. Move on. You cannot let the regular worries of life impact you; that half-second hesitation could be fatal. You're all warriors. You will see combat. That changes a man. When you get back, you may not feel like talking about these things, but you need to. You see, you're going to find out that there are two types of people in the world. There are ducks and there are turtles. Combat veterans are turtles. When they get home from combat they often like to take refuge in their shell and not deal with what they've just been through.

"Then there is everybody else, all the people who will never experience combat: the ducks. Ducks like to talk, and talk, and talk. They're loud, they're ever present, and they're constantly talking about things that only a turtle can really know. The problem is, ducks don't speak "turtle" and turtles don't speak "duck." That's why it's *so* very important that we get you together so that you can talk to each other, fellow turtles.

"I want to close our talk with a word of final advice. Find yourself some sort of faith, be it religious or something else, but find it. Carry it with you. Maybe it's a rock from home. Maybe it's a cross around your neck, or a letter or picture from a loved one. Whatever it is, find it. Hold it, keep it close. Return to it daily and as often as needed. Be sure you do this. Faith is what will keep you sane, what will make all those hard moments endurable. Faith is what will help you internalize the most difficult events you will likely encounter. Men without faith, whatever it may be, fare far worse than those with faith. I've seen it. I've been to war many times now. You're all warriors. Right now some of you are ducks and some are turtles, but *all* of you will come back as turtles."

And then we prayed together. Chaplain Yates asked God to protect us, to give us the strength we'll need, and to help all of us find the faith we'll carry.

As he spoke, I couldn't help but think about my own mortality. I worry about death, but not for all the reasons you might think. Sure, I'd be disappointed not to get to live out the life for which I've always hoped (a beautiful wife, kids, family, successful career, presidency, grandkids, owning my jazz club, climbing Mt. Everest . . .), but with death I don't get the chance to be disappointed, so getting bummed about that is kind of pointless. What I'm scared of, what worries me and what I couldn't stop thinking about, is how my passing would impact my family and my friends. What I've realized is this: They are my faith. They will be the faith that will help me through this.

I went bed that night thinking about "The Letter." Does writing it jinx you? What I've realized is that you don't write it for you; you write it for those you leave behind. I once came across an online blog from a deployed soldier. He had recently been killed in Iraq, and he had left instructions to a friend to post a final entry he'd written ahead of time in case the unthinkable occurred. What struck me was how many places he seemed to be ending the letter only to go on. How do you end something like this letter, other than with the obvious "I love you and always will"? It's a bit like clinging to life: You don't want to stop writing, but you know you eventually have to find an end; everything has an end. It's something I keep coming back to; I realize there will be a moment in the near future in which I sit down to compose the hardest thing I'll ever write and that eventually I'll have to find a way to close it. Just as that letter would be for you (God forbid), this is for me. I needed to write this. It's helping me prepare myself, transition to the warrior. I cannot even think of how to end this segment. Thanks for listening; I love you all. (That works.)

5

See Ya Later

Wednesday, March 26, 2008

One of the more difficult days of my life, I spent the morning anxiously awaiting the arrival of my mom and stepdad, who graciously drove all the way from Colorado to see my graduation ceremony. In a moment of sheer army irony, the standing around in formation waiting for the ceremony to start lasted longer than the actual ceremony.

The army will *never* cease to amaze me with its timing. As I walked into the ceremony, Major Malok pulled me aside and said, "We're not on an Afghan Army training mission anymore, we'll be training the Afghan National Police instead." We had just spent the last 2.5 months training to be army advisers, and now we're on a police mission! Aside from a few soldiers who are police officers in civilian life, the rest of us have had *no* police training, let alone training to be police mentors.

After the ceremony, Mom, my stepdad, and I went out to a nice lunch. I gave them a tour of the desolate wasteland that is Fort Riley and then a tour of the barns that are our barracks. Then it came time to say our "see ya laters"—no good-byes on this trip! I tried my best to stay strong and composed, but I'm sure they both could see me holding back my tears. I cannot imagine what it must be like to be a parent and to see your child off to war; in fact, that's why I'm doing this—I want my future kids to *never* have to go through this.

The entire Fort Riley training class of embedded combat advisers waiting in the Camp Funston gymnasium for our flight to Afghanistan.

Thursday, March 27–Tuesday, April 1, 2008

I spent these days in the U.S. and British Virgin Islands, falling in love with the Caribbean and island life.

Tuesday, April 1–Saturday, April 5, 2008

I spent these days in my hometown, Rochester, New York, with my dad, brother, extended family, and friends from high school and college. Saturday morning I had to say my "see ya laters" to my brother Andy and my dad. This time I lost it. Andy held on tighter than he ever has when he hugged me. Dad literally lifted me up over his head (like he used to when I was a small child) when he hugged me. I've seen my father cry three times in life, and this was one of them. I'm resolved to come home alive and well; I couldn't bear to put you all through such torment if the unthinkable happened.

I spent the afternoon driving down to Washington, D.C., where I had a *very* eventful weekend with my dear friends. I needed those two days to get my head straight and calm my nerves (I had been having silent panic attacks while at home in Rochester); the reality of what I was about to do was getting to me in ways for which I wasn't prepared. I now have clarity in a way I never before imagined, breathtaking clarity.

I returned to Fort Riley, and, truth be told, I've missed these guys way more than I ever thought I would. We spent Tuesday packing and yesterday in advanced medical training that was actually quite awesome. We went out for a final steak dinner last night and got rip-roaring exuberant. I took the time to savor every bite and drip of my onion rings, three salads, four beers, Maker's Mark bourbon and Coke, glass of cabernet, and of course my 20-ounce porterhouse cooked medium rare. Delicious doesn't do this meal justice. I topped off the night with a good cigar and went to bed.

Friday, April 11, 2008

It's now 11:00 a.m. on Friday, and I'm taking today as a lazy day, because this will be my last day to relax. We leave for Afghanistan tomorrow night.

PART II

The War

6

We're Not in Kansas Anymore

Saturday, April 12, 2008

Our last day at Fort Riley was bittersweet. In a fitting end to our incarceration there, the weather was a lovely cold rain capped off by the ever-loving wicked wind. Our gear already packed, we spent the majority of our last day sitting in the barracks watching DVDs or surfing the Internet on our laptops. Around 1830 hours, we headed over to the "reception area" to begin our lockdown. Reception is an interesting process, to say the least.

You are weighed with all your carry-on luggage and weapons—have to make sure the aircraft won't be overweight. Finally, your ID is scanned into a database, and you are released to an area with volunteers from the USO who prepared a lovely assortment of treats. Two large screens display an NBA game, but tensions are too high to pay much attention. You could literally cut the nervousness with a knife—reality was finally sinking in.

We sat in this area for about an hour, just waiting. Interestingly, the outside of the building is surrounded by barbed wire fences to keep us in; not like we could get very far even if we tried. I spent my hour calling friends and family to say my "see ya laters" from U.S. soil. Around 9:00 p.m. we boarded our first flight, which took us to Bangor, Maine, and then on to Leipzig, Germany. Interestingly, we were allowed to carry our weapons aboard and as many liquids or gels as our hearts desired! We landed in Bangor around 2:00 a.m. and left the plane for an hour while

A village outside Camp Phoenix, with more of the mountains that ring Kabul in the background.

it was refueled. Upon entering the terminal, we were greeted by a two-star general and several USO volunteers and veterans, a real honor to say the least.

I slept the entire flight to Leipzig, Germany—a rarity, as I seldom am able to fall asleep aboard aircraft. Our arrival in Germany must have been a sight: two streams of soldiers pouring out the front and aft ends of the aircraft, stretching and soaking up a bright afternoon sun. From Leipzig, we flew to Manas Air Force Base in Kyrgyzstan on one of the most terrifying flights of my entire life. The turbulence was so strong it actually threw a flight attendant off his legs at one point. I found it thrilling to look out the window at an absolutely pitch-black ground and sky, interrupted by the occasional solitary light of some nomad's fire upon the Asian steppe.

We landed in Kyrgyzstan as the dawn crept into the sky; a grey haze enveloped and masked the impressive scenery to our east, while a calm breeze blew moisture across the tarmac. We piled onto crammed coach buses for a very short drive to the entrance of the air base, which buttresses the Kyrgyzstan airport. We only ended up spending a day at Manas. Despite this being the nation's capital, I was told that most people lived in mud huts and shantytowns–a real pity considering the friendliness of the locals who worked on the base and the breathtaking beauty of the Tian Sian Mountains that sat on the city's eastern edge. The Tian Sian are said to be the Alps of central Asia. When we first arrived, they were hidden in the faint light of dawn. They are massive; these things just appear to soar into the heavens. Around 1:00 p.m. the next day, we put on our body armor and helmets and boarded the coach buses for the very cramped drive back to the airport and our C-17 transport flight to Kabul International Airport (henceforth referred to as KIA). To say the flight was cramped and unbearably uncomfortable would be an understatement. The lucky ones got the outside seats along the inner walls of the fuselage; the rest of us got the standard airline coach seats that sat on sliding platforms. Every time the pilot braked or sped up on the runway, one was sent slamming forward into the seat in front or back. As the flight chief announced we needed to fasten our seatbelts and explained that our emergency oxygen masks were under our seats, a deafening laughter erupted: We couldn't reach our own thighs, let alone our seatbelts or underneath our seats. Should we crash, we were confident we'd be wedged in with enough force to replace the safety offered by a seatbelt; the oxygen was another matter. About 10 minutes into the flight, I noticed one of the air crew had adjourned to the cockpit area, leaving a seat along the inner walls free. I promptly grabbed it and stretched my legs in a moment that can only be described as pure ecstasy. At one point, I noticed an army major enter the cockpit area with camera in hand. I decided to follow suit, as I've always wanted to see what it's like up front. Amazingly, we were flying through a whiteout of clouds; with the exception of the noise from the engines and the instruments indicating we were around 30,000 feet, there'd be no way to tell we were actually flying. It appeared as if we sat in a void of unending white.

I've never been on a roller-coaster ride that even came close to capturing the sheer thrill and terror of our landing. It felt at one point as if we were in a nose dive, and we hit the runway with more force than I ever thought a plane could survive. We rapidly deplaned and at a near run made our way to a sheltered hanger; no one wanted to give some errant sniper a chance at a lucky shot, especially on Day One. On our way I found myself floating with a sense of joylike excitement at the stark beauty of the mountainous landscape that surrounds Kabul. This place is truly gorgeous from a geographic standpoint. Our armored personnel convoy took us only a few miles, but from the scenery we might as well have landed on Mars. Donkeys pulling carts, burka-draped women, white-bearded men hobbling along, people defecating in the streets with no thought to privacy or hygiene, homes without doors, filthy kids running alongside the convoy begging for water, candy, or a dollar—every stereotype portrayed in our brief jaunt "outside the wire." Every now and then my heart rate would skyrocket as a civilian vehicle attempted to get too close to the convoy; the pervasive threat of the potential suicide bomber always lurks nearby, too close for comfort and close enough to prevent complacency.

Our entrance into Camp Phoenix was like entering another world. Just like Manas Air Force Base, Camp Phoenix is a little pocket of America dropped square in the middle of a desolate foreign landscape. Outside is absolute poverty; inside is the wealth of a nation on full display. The gym has plasma TVs. The dining hall offers lobster and steak. Outside they're starving, while inside we're feasting like we're on a cruise. The housing has cable TV and high-speed Internet. Everyone is entitled to as many hot showers as one can fit in a day. There's definitely a lack of the standard "roughing-it" experience that is necessary for any true war-deployment experience here at Camp Phoenix.

Our welcoming committee was made up entirely of my former soldiers, who made no attempt to contain their happiness to see me. These are soldiers from the unit I left to join this ETT (embedded training team) mission. Specialist Aaron Addison and I met up right after our welcoming committee explained the standard rules (no drinking, no sex, wear the proper uniform, incoming artillery bunkers are located here, etc.). He gave me a quick layout of the base, and then my team and I went to work collecting all our gear that had been shipped via cargo. A cold rain soon fell from the sky as we trudged through mud and puddles with our 100-pound rucksacks and duffel bags; a bit of Kansas seemed to have followed us all the way to Kabul.

We spent the following day in a repeat of all the briefings we received while at Fort Riley. The IED-threat brief scared the living daylights out of me and most of us who haven't been deployed before. The guy who gave it used examples from friends he had personally lost. The reality of the danger here punches you hard in the face when you see the charred remains of an up-armored Hummer that was split in two and then fragmented beyond recognition.

I spent a great deal of the evening with one of my former soldiers, Specialist Mike Meraz. He told me that in his military career, he had always been looking for that one officer who'd help him grow and achieve things and who he could always turn to. He said I was that officer and then profusely thanked me for always being there for him. There is no greater joy than taking care of soldiers. These guys never cease to amaze me and make me proud. After my talk and dinner with Meraz, I met up with Specialist Addison and headed over to karaoke night. I ended up singing in a chorus made up of my old soldiers, all of whom insisted I join them in their horrendous rendition of "American Soldier."

I awoke to one of the most beautiful mornings I've ever seen. The sunrise painted the snowcapped mountains hues of pink, purple, and yellow, and not a cloud hung in the sky. It was a sunrise and a morning view fit for Monet.

In the evening, I volunteered to pull a few hours of guard duty with Specialist Meraz on one of the guard towers. As we ascended the tower to relieve Specialist Rhodes, we could hear a crowd of children beckoning Rhodes to give them candy and money. Rhodes was all smiles as he regaled us with tales of his shift: the kid who ran around naked, the fights that broke out among the children vying for his attention, the rocks they hurled via their slingshots, and the teenagers who offered him hashish [marijuana] and whiskey. Within minutes, we had replaced Rhodes as the targets of their attention: "Mister, Mister. Give me a dollar. Give me water for baby. Give me candy!" At first I just smiled, but then I decided to have my fun as well. "Salaam Aleikum!" I shouted. Stunned silence. The kids didn't know what to make of the strange body-armor clad American suddenly speaking Dari. The oldest finally responded with "Aleikum Salaam!" "Chetor Hastid?" I asked. A more pronounced stunned silence. I'm guessing they'd never encountered an American who could speak even my limited amount of Dari. "Khoob hasti," the oldest responded.

We then exchanged names in a mixture of Dari and English. I must admit their English is far superior to my Dari. Eventually an older kid would come along and replace the previous boy as group spokesman. The kids must think they're clever, because all of their names are either "Bob" or the name of some wrestler from America. Just as the conversation begins to die out, the oldest offers to sell you hashish or whiskey. I told them that such things were "haram" to sell or consume. And then the rocks started.

Some little punk would begin firing a barrage of fist-size rocks at us, and we'd retreat into the armored guard shack. This would prompt the oldest to admonish the rock throwers who had suddenly ruined his "business deal." He'd chase off the rock throwers, beckon us to emerge from the tower, and the cycle would begin anew. Every now and then an adult male would come by and I'd say hello, ask them how they were, and then wish them well, all in Dari—just my simple attempt to win some hearts and minds. At one point I even called my mom on my Afghan cell phone and had the crowd of children scream, "Hi, Mom!" She promptly laughed and then told me to get back to doing my job!

The reason we don't hand out water or food is sad but simple: A few weeks ago, navy sailors on one of the towers tossed down some water and food to a few little girls. The girls were then severely beaten by a bunch of older boys. Our rules of engagement do not allow us to physically interfere with that type of behavior while on the towers. By the time a team could be formed to go outside the wire and protect the girls, the boys had dispersed. The girls received medical treatment, but the gifts from the towers stopped. We now only hand out food and water via humanitarian assistance missions, proof that all it takes are a few bad apples to ruin it for everyone.

As the sun set, the call to prayer sang out across the land. All across the village and its fields, people ran to their rooftops to pray. One simply cannot help being taken aback by the beauty of these people and this land. Meraz and I both agreed that this place is truly amazing, one corner of the world where globalization has yet to completely transform a culture.

7

Down South, Where the War Is

Thursday, April 17–Monday, April 21, 2008, Ghazni

Our team, sadly, has been broken up by the powers that be. I'm now at my job destination in Afghanistan, FOB Vulcan in Ghazni. Ghazni is both the name of the city we're in *and* the province. I'm really anxious to get started with our mission. First Sergeant Boggins is the only other member of my team here with me. I'm very thankful I'm with him, as he's an amazing NCO. I'm absolutely confident I'll learn a ton from him over the coming months. I know he'll make me a better officer and a better man.

I'm fine, healthy, extremely satisfied, quite excited, and in great spirits. For those of you looking to send care packages, the Afghans (especially the kids) could use all the pens, old clothing, and shoes you can spare. Children's toys, soccer balls, and volleyballs (they are crazy for it here) are also quite welcome.

Pens are key. Afghanistan provides all its children with free primary education. They do not, however, provide them with writing implements. If a child's family does not own a writing implement, their parents will not send them to school; to do so would be a major disgrace for the family. The children end up farming and herding animals rather than receiving an education. The primary recruits to the Taliban are the uneducated in search of an income or children who were sent to madrasa. Madrasas are religious schools for boys in which the primary instruction is basically memorization of the Koran. They are usually funded by the Wahabi School of Islam that dominates Saudi Arabia and are best known for the brand

Our compound on FOB Vulcan, with the "suburbs" of Ghazni city in the background.

of Islam adhered to by Al-Qaeda and the Taliban. Parents often send children to madrasas because they cannot afford to keep them in their household; sometimes parents simply cannot feed all their offspring, and madrasas take care of this basic need. Madrasas also provide their students with writing implements. Pens are vital to winning this war; they keep kids in government-run schools, which in turn increases the number of educated people in this country, improves the economy, and, most importantly, decreases the Taliban's recruiting pool. Please send pens. We can only win this war by preventing today's children from becoming tomorrow's terrorists. Many of you have asked how you can help me during this deployment. My answer is: Help me help give these kids a better life. Send pens. Send clothing. Send shoes.

Friday, April 18, 2008

I've been assigned as an operations mentor to the Afghan National Police at a base down in Ghazni known as FOB Vulcan. As an intelligence officer with absolutely *zero* training as an operations officer, I feel I am 100 percent unqualified to serve in this role. My whole 16-man team from Fort Riley is pretty much being broken up into two- or four-man elements. We knew this was likely to happen, but reality has finally arrived with an upside blow to our heads, hearts, and spirits. To be honest, when my position was announced, the first thing I thought was, "I'm not going to make it out of this mission alive." Of my Fort Riley team, only the first sergeant is assigned with me. I have mixed feelings about being with him. On one hand, he's hard working, seldom displays emotion, and is tough as nails. On the other hand, he's rock, up front, tough as nails, straight forward, and a bit gruff. Of all the people I've met in my life, I've never had a harder time reading someone.

I spent the rest of the day packing to leave for my new home—allegedly we're convoying down tomorrow. Once packed, I helped First Lieutenant Escobedo move his gear over to the convoy that will take him to his new home. While we were loading his gear onto the cargo truck, I got my first look at what an IED can do to an armored SUV. The front end was completely blown off one vehicle, the other was barely the form of a truck. Crumpled masses of steel and aluminum, the vehicles sat as testaments to man's destructive nature. Thankfully I couldn't see any bloodstains on the shattered, but still intact, glass panes and surprisingly undamaged seats. I can only hope this is an indication that everyone made it out of this attack alive.

Saturday, April 19, 2008

For hours, First Sergeant Boggins and I could not get a firm answer on whether we were leaving today. When I returned from my afternoon Internet session, I was surprised to discover that all my gear was missing from my bunk. Either I had been robbed, or Boggins had done me a favor and moved my stuff onto our outbound convoy cargo truck. I rushed out the tent and bumped right into him. Grinning ear to ear, he exclaimed, "Got us a ride, Sir! We leave at 1500!" One hour and we'd be gone. We were finally moving "outside the wire." As we walked away from my family of the past three months, Major Mcintire waved and yelled "Good luck boys! Have fun storming the castle," a quote from *The Princess Bride* that's become our de facto motto. As we approached our new teammates (they had convoyed up that morning), they struck me as quite laid-back, a ragtag group of tired-looking souls close to the end of their tour. Their mind-set was clearly on their mission's end and "getting the hell out of Dodge." It was safe to say we'd be taking all the safety precautions with these guys; no one wants to get hurt or killed with only a few days left in the badlands. I chatted a few up and got the latest assessments of our AO (area of operations) and the overall status of the mission. They said the ride down to Ghazni would take roughly three hours and was relatively safe. Our FOB was so close to the city that it had never been attacked, because the Taliban and Al-Qaeda are afraid of civilian casualties; they don't want to anger the local population. I asked one of the outgoing lieutenants if he had seen any action. He just laughed and said, "Yeah, man, you'll definitely earn your CAB [combat action badge]. That's guaranteed."

As we rolled out of the wire, I took a deep breath, said a silent prayer, and started to scan out the window across from me. To my left sat the captain. Across from me was First Sergeant Boggins, and next to him sat First Sergeant Rock. The vehicle is so compact inside that to seat four men, each guy must sit with one leg in the crotch region of the man to his front. Arranged in our zigzag pattern, Rock promised me that if my knee made contact with his groin, he was going to take out his knife and "beat you to a bloody pulp, Sir." I think he was kidding. I *think*.

Our ride out of Kabul was exhilarating. We drove past ruins, Soviet-era bases, the soccer stadium where the Taliban held public executions, numerous bazaars, beggars, some of the dirtiest apartment complexes I've ever seen, old-world dwellings of mud brick and soot, and all of it teeming with children, merchants, burka-clad women, men with turbans, soldiers, police, and the ever-present daredevil motorcyclists and bicyclists. As we left the filth of urban Kabul behind, the land turned into plains with farms, wild grassland under siege by numerous flocks of sheep, and finally into an ever-encroaching desert, all surrounded by breathtaking white-capped mountains rising toward the heavens. By the time we arrived in Ghazni, it was dark, and I could barely see anything other than the multiple restaurants that buttress Route One (the main highway between Kabul and Ghazni).

Route One is actually part of "Ring Road," a paved, two-lane road that forms a circle around the rugged mountain terrain of Afghanistan's center. Should one continue south, one would eventually come to Kandahar, the birthplace of the Taliban and the most violent part of the country.

Our FOB is currently a "blackout" FOB (no lights of *any* kind after dark). At first, this makes sense: We're in a war zone, and we don't want to give the enemy a shining target at which to aim their artillery. But we're on the edge of a city and in the middle of an Afghan National Army Base (which *isn't* a blackout FOB). So, right now, we're the big *black* spot at night in the middle of a well-lit city at night. This will *all* change in the coming days as my unit takes over from the guys from South Carolina who are RIP'ing (relief in place) out. Apparently, this base used to hold a nightly bonfire. A team of combat stress personnel visited and saw everyone sitting around the fire "smoking and joking" and declared it the "best combat stress relief they had ever seen." First Sergeant Rock has resolved to light a massive bonfire the night we officially take command.

We ended up being housed temporarily in the MWR (morale, welfare, and recreation) b-hut while they figured out our permanent housing assignments. For the next few nights, I slept on the most luxurious bed I've ever had in the army: two plush leather couches pushed together. I even got the fortune of bunking in the room with the giant wall-projected TV.

Sunday, April 20, 2008

We spent today getting our RIP/TOA (transfer of authority) briefings. This amounted to a very general intelligence assessment of our AO and a description of each teammate's job duties. We spent the afternoon helping clean weapons; these guys have become *very* lazy and complacent. I'd later come to find out that they seldom, if ever, do PCI (pre-combat inspections; you do them on all your gear before heading outside the wire) or PMCS (maintenance on vehicles and gear). We've also been briefed that the ANA (Afghan National Army) and ANP (Afghan National Police) mentors (all U.S. Army personnel) do not have a great relationship on our FOB. Thankfully, most everyone here is leaving, and the ones staying behind seem like quality people, and the majority of incoming ANA and ANP mentors all went through Fort Riley together.

My new team consists of Captain Morriarty, myself, First Sergeant Boggins, and Sergeant First Class Alderson. Captain Morriarty is the team chief, Boggins is his NCOIC (noncommissioned officer in-charge) and the logistics mentor, I'm the operations mentor and the default intelligence officer for the whole FOB, and Alderson is the personnel mentor and the all-around information technology guru.

We're such a small FOB (fewer than 60 people total) that we've all got to pitch in when needed. We also have some security forces on our team, but they have yet to arrive—save for Sergeant Blasker. Sergeant Blasker and I get along great just because we're the closest in age and therefore have more in common. Sergeant First Class Alderson and I are both intelligence soldiers by training and trade, so we approach tasks from a very similar mind-set. First Sergeant Boggins and I have grown closer in just these past few days than we were at Fort Riley. I think being the only two members of Team Mohawk has bonded us. And then there's Captain Morriarty, my ideal officer: special forces, ranger, witty, sarcastic, great natured, self-deprecating, confident, and extremely intelligent.

Monday, April 21, 2008

In the afternoon we had a few classes on how to call for a medevac (medical evacuation by helicopter) and how to call for close combat attack (munitions fired from attack helicopters). Thankfully for us, we're opcon'd (operationally assigned) to the 101st Airborne Division. The guys for whom we're taking over were opcon'd to the 82nd Airborne. The 101st is an air assault unit—meaning they operate *all the time* with helicopters—whereas the 82nd Airborne is an airborne unit (jumping out of planes) and only has marginal helicopter assets. The main difference as far as we're concerned is that the 101st helicopter pilots are unspeakably more proficient than those of the 82nd. Tomorrow, we would head out on our first mission. Surprisingly, I slept soundly, with only the occasional butterfly visiting my stomach.

8

Leaving the Wire

Tuesday April 22, 2008

To say I was nervous as we crossed out of the relative safety of our FOB and into the oncoming traffic of Route One is a severe understatement. I was terrified. As we drove through the streets out to our first stop, an unfinished hydroelectric dam from the Soviet Occupation, I was taken aback by Ghazni's extreme filth. Mud-brick buildings, smog everywhere, human excrement running open in troughs along the street—my first daylight view of Ghazni was my introduction to what I refer to as "the fifth world." This place is simply too poor to qualify as third world.

Our arrival at the dam aroused the sleeping and seemingly unprofessional police who occupy a checkpoint on either side. My first view of the Afghan National Police was not very encouraging. Of the 10 men, only one had a weapon, two wore some sort of uniform, and the rest seemed too tired, hungry, or cold to rouse themselves from their relaxed reclined positions leaning against a condemned building's wall. At least their outpost had a few glass panes in the windows; most of the buildings did not have exterior walls and were pockmarked with rocket and bullet holes.

Our visit to the dam also marked my first real "dismount" in country, getting out of an armored vehicle and entering a potentially dangerous place on foot. It also marked the first time I went "red" (magazine in and a round chambered in the weapon). I talked to a few of our interpreters and attempted to say hello to the

The ruins of a Russian truck and building in Andar district, Ghazni province, that bear the scars of Afghanistan's 30 years of war.

assembled Afghan police as we waited for a lieutenant colonel and navy lieutenant to arrive and join our convoy; these VIPs would be traveling with us for the next two days doing district assessments to see what each district center (local government compound) needed in terms of engineering, force protection, personnel, etc.

We left the dam after about an hour and convoyed over to the Andar district center. Andar is one of the three districts my team covers. We spent the first hour waiting for the district police chief to finish his meeting (also known as a jurga) with the local elders. During that time we dismounted, took off most of our body armor (something that made me uncomfortable, but we need to show the Afghans that we trust them), and took in the sights. I found a lone boy no older than 10 sitting by the center's well looking very forlorn and timid. Smiling, I walked up to him and handed him one of the many granola bars I keep with me at all times. Hesitantly he took it and managed a weak smile in return. I walked away hoping he'd eat it and not throw it away (fear of the unknown). My camera in hand, I kept glancing back hoping to catch him eating it. Finally, after several minutes of looking around to make sure no one was going to steal it from him, he ripped open the wrapper and devoured it in three bites.

The jurga finished, and the police chief came out to welcome us into his office and my first key leader engagement. We shook hands, said, "Salaam Aleikum," and asked each other how we were doing. With his hand, he bid us to follow him into his office. As we entered, the assembled elders stared at us from their positions of seated scorn upon the ground.

The police chief's office was sparse yet tidy. The only wall decoration was an Afghan National Police recruiting poster that hung at the foot of the room. Our interpreter sat to the chief's immediate right, followed by Captain Morriarty, myself, and First Sergeant Boggins. Across from us and to the chief's left sat Sergeant Blasker, Major Garrison, his terp (interpreter), and Sergeant First Class Alderson. In typical Afghan custom, the chief began the meeting by ordering his manservant and chai boy (the child to whom I had given the granola bar) to bring us some chai and Iranian cookies. One by one we introduced ourselves to the police chief, who took diligent notes of our names and rank. I attempted to introduce myself in my best Dari, but I must have screwed up because our terp, Fareed, had to translate. With the introductions complete, Captain Morriarty got right down to business, recapping his last meeting with the police chief and inquiring about his current needs, the readiness and state of his men, and his relations with the local and higher levels of government.

Five minutes into the meeting, the manservant returned carrying a piping hot pot of tea. The chai boy followed close behind with a silver tray of glass teacups filled about one-fifth full with sugar. The chai was delicious—hot, sweet, and minty.

The meeting lasted around an hour and finished with a round of questions from those of us assembled in the room. A key thing I learned was that having two terps in the room simply does not work. Eventually they sort of duel for control or even dual interpret for different audiences (i.e., Fareed for us and Major Garrison's for him). The remainder of our day, including our drive back to the FOB, passed without notable incident.

Wednesday April 23, 2008

Wednesday's travels brought us to Deh Yak district and its district center. For the first and only time thus far, our terp wore body armor; I'd later come to realize they do this when they expect contact with the enemy or if we're entering a generally more dangerous area.

The differences between Deh Yak and Andar could not be more striking. Deh Yak is in the middle of FDD (focused district development); Andar will start FDD in a few weeks. FDD is a long process in which we retrain the local police to a standard of professionalism and proficiency seldom ever seen in Afghanistan. We also rebuild government centers, schools, hospitals, sometimes building these structures for the very first time, and improve the quality of life and security for the locals. During the process, the local police units are taken out of their area for retraining elsewhere in the country. They are replaced by the ANCOP (Afghan National Civil Order Police) while away at training. As we arrived in Deh Yak district center, one could tell instantly the high degree of professionalism that exists in the ANCOP. Every police officer wore a common uniform, all carried weapons, each man looked vigilant in his job, everyone moved with a purpose. We spent several hours at the district center while the lieutenant colonel and the navy lieutenant did their site assessment.

During our drive back to the FOB, I couldn't help but notice all the children we passed. One can usually gauge a village's friendliness by how their children react to U.S. convoys. If the kids come running up smiling, waving, and flashing thumbs-up, the place is generally on our side to indifferent. If the kids stand and sort of stare or run away, the village is likely indifferent to or against us. It breaks my heart to see so many emaciated-looking toddlers without shoes sprinting alongside our convoy because their lives literally depend on our handouts. I wonder what happens in their lives that transforms them from the smiling, thumbs-up waving, sprinting, carefree, innocent children to the standing, indifferent teenagers who later become scowling adults and finally sad, tired elders?

I cannot wait to do my first HA (humanitarian assistance) drop, where we roll in and hand out tons of food, clothing, clean water (one-fifth of kids die from water-borne diseases in this country), supplies, and medical care.

Friday April 25, 2008

For some unknown reason, we traveled to FOB Warrior today. The drive was uneventful other than to say that as one travels south from our FOB, the land becomes desert and the locals hostile (smiles and waves thoroughly replaced with glares and scowls). We drove down in a massive convoy made up of our vehicles, ANA Hummers, and ANP pickup trucks. We got to the FOB and watched one of the most dangerous and hysterically chaotic refueling experiences of my life: The ANP literally smoked as they refueled. Other highlights of our stupid meaningless visit to FOB Warrior were eating at the best chow hall I've seen outside Camp Phoenix and watching the Blackwater Air Force (yes they even have their own cargo planes) drop resupplies of food, water, and ammo to the troops on the FOB. They drop these in four giant pallets pushed out the back of a low and fast-flying propeller plane as it skims over the ground. The pallets fall via parachute and land in a cleared field, and watching it was thrilling. As we walked back to our vehicles, not really sure why we had driven all this way to eat a meal and watch some cargo fall out of the sky, we got word that the Deh Yak district center was surrounded by the Taliban and in need of assistance. Before you could yell, "*Go*," the ANA and ANP were mounted up and hauling ass out of the FOB, the cavalry off to save the day.

We finally got moving and actually floored it back up the road toward our FOB. Deh Yak is a good 45 minutes northeast from our FOB, and we were a good two hours south of that. We got back to our FOB in record time but didn't continue to Deh Yak. We just sat there and did maintenance on our vehicles and weapons (which is at least a step up from what the guys who are leaving have done). Eventually a water resupply truck arrived, and I helped unload 16 pallets with cases of bottled water (around 100 cases per pallet) by hand. Lacking a forklift, we unloaded each case by hand using a human chain. Two hours later, the rest of my team came back and updated everyone on what had happened in Deh Yak: nothing. They had driven all the way out there to find the situation normal, no Taliban to be found. Secretly I was glad nothing had happened. I would have never been able to forgive myself had I missed out on my team's first contact with the enemy.

Saturday April 26, 2008

For lunch today, I had my first real taste of the local cuisine: an Afghan version of a burger. To make an Afghan burger, take beef sausage, french fries, hardboiled egg, lettuce, cabbage, onions, basil leaves, and cilantro, and wrap it all up in warm, fresh na'an (the local bread, to which I am thoroughly addicted). It's dinnertime now in the plains of Ghazni, the sun is setting, and for the first time since our arrival, the smog has cleared to such an extent that we should have a spectacular night for stargazing.

9

MRAP Down

Sunday, April 27, 2008

Today began with a sense of exuberant optimism. Our plan was to drive through downtown Ghazni and head out to the Khogiani and Jaghato districts, where we would conduct site assessments of the district centers and Afghan National Police detachments. Along the way, we'd stop at random villages to hand out food, clothing, shoes, hygiene kits, and pens. Joyous, excited, I couldn't wait to leave the security of our FOB. Finally, we were on our first humanitarian assistance mission of my tour.

The drive through downtown Ghazni was uneventful. The city is crowded and dusty, but cleaner than most other Afghan cities I've seen thus far. The streets were alive with people buying goods, visiting with friends, and taking in the celebrations of Freedom Day (Afghanistan's freedom from Russian occupation).

As we headed out of town, we entered the Hazara section of the city and turned onto the lone dirt road that leads out to the districts. Dirt roads are significantly more dangerous than paved roads, as the Taliban and Al-Qaeda can more easily plant IEDs. The Hazara are Shia Muslims and the descendants of Genghis Khan's army and as a result are also the most persecuted ethnic group in Afghanistan (the rest of Afghanistan is Sunni). The Taliban brutally hunted them down, indiscriminately killing thousands during their rule. The Hazaras also love us; we brought security and an end to their persecution, a fact easily noted by all the people running out to wave hello (children, teenagers, adults, even the elderly).

Children swarm us and beg for food aid in Khogiani district, Ghazni province.

We left the city and drove out into open farmland surrounded by impressive rocky mountains on both sides of the road. Eventually we stopped at a village; dismounted from our vehicles, leaving the gunners and drivers in their positions; locked rounds in our weapons (status: RED); and made our way to the trailer of humanitarian-assistance goods. Word of our arrival spread like wildfire, and within minutes we were surrounded by at least 30 villagers (mostly kids) eagerly awaiting our aid. We ripped off the trailer tarp to reveal all that we had brought; the villagers' faces lit up to a degree I have never before witnessed, beyond the joy of a child's first Christmas.

I reached into a box and started handing out Muslim meals, shoes, hygiene kits, blankets, fabric, and clothing. All around me hands clamored for the goods. Fights between children broke out as I desperately tried to keep order in our distribution. I tried to hand things to the youngest and the girls first, but greedy boys would come and rip things out of my hands. Mass joyful wonderful chaos ensued. *"Ney! Ney Shoma!* [pointing to a little girl] *Bale, Bale Shoma!"* (Which in Dari means, *"No!* Not you! Yes, yes you!") My euphoria level soared. Smiling abundantly, the people simply could not adequately express their thanks. After about 10 minutes, the order came down to move on to the next village. I hated to leave; I kept thinking just one more minute, just a few more meals or clothing, these could be the difference between life and death for these kids. But, alas, we had to go; we had more aid to give, more villages to see.

As I walked back to my UAH, I spotted an old man carrying a young child. *"Sayed!"* I yelled out. (Sayed is an honorific and means "sir.") He turned. I ran up, unclipped my spare canteen pouch that I use to keep snacks, and handed him the last of my granola and PowerBars. I'll forever treasure his smile and kind, grateful eyes. I wished him well in Dari, and we mounted up and drove on. As we drove away, I remarked aloud, "I could literally do this every day for the rest of my life."

Twenty minutes later, we came to our next village, dismounted, and went through the same process as before. This time a crowd of nearly 50 people mobbed us. Even grown women, unveiled, came out to meet us and accept our aid. Once again, I tried to focus on the youngest, thinnest, and women. Once more fights ensued, but the general mood remained optimistic. Ten minutes after we started, it was time to leave. The order came down to wrap it up and move out, and yet I couldn't stop. These kids were just so wonderful, so alive, so fragile. I was compelled to help; my movements were all instinctual. I hated leaving. I felt so guilty. We Americans simply don't know this level of poverty, of need. We're sheltered from these horrors. I find this a good thing, because when we do confront it, we are compelled to do all we can. Driving away is just the most awful feeling, as if you haven't done enough, that you've let all those desperate families down. You feel, as you take your leave, that you are abandoning them to a painful, horrible existence and, ultimately, death.

Begrudgingly, we moved on.

Thirty minutes later, we arrived at the Jaghato district center. I panicked as our vehicle lost radio communication with our other two vehicles for five minutes. Eventually, we rectified the problem, dismounted, and went to meet with the local ANP detachment. Our meeting with the police lasted 30 minutes. We discussed their equipment shortfalls, personnel needs, and overall status of the district. They said they hadn't seen any enemy forces in weeks and that they were in overall good spirits. We told them we had some aid to distribute. They offered to help us and to call the local village elder who would decide how to distribute the aid. We walked back to our trucks, opened up the aid trailer, and started loading the supplies into the back of the ANP trucks. Children mobbed us. Bags of shoes were literally ripped out of my hands; a free-for-all erupted among the assembled children. About 75 percent made it onto the ANP trucks; the rest we handed out to the kids mobbing us.

As we prepared to leave, a boy no older than 12 walked up to me and attempted to talk to me in a smattering of Dari and English. Eventually he said something in Arabic, and, bingo, we were in business. I asked him about the security in the area. He told me that there was an Al-Qaeda cell in Khogiani and that they were going to ambush us on our way back. When I got back to my vehicle, I relayed this information back up to Captain Morriarty. We turned our vehicles around and headed back down the dirt road toward the Khogiani district center and ultimately Ghazni City.

The drive back is usually the most dangerous, as the bad guys have had time to plant IEDs and set up an ambush. Normally we try to leave via a different road from which we entered, but in Khogiani and Jaghato, it's one road in, one road out. Lord knows how many informants the enemy has in the area, but it was guaranteed they had to know we were in the area and on our way back.

Forty-five minutes after leaving the Jaghato ANP, we arrived at the Khogiani district center. We pulled our vehicles inside the hesco-walled compound and dismounted. Captain Morriarty reminded everyone to be vigilant and to do their "tiger walk." A tiger walk is a zigzag movement that keeps one constantly changing direction, making it vastly harder for a sniper to hit you. Captain Morriarty; our terp, Fareed; Sergeant Blasker; Captain Kingsley; and I walked with the local police commander to a building, where he showed us an IED he and his men had recently found. It was in the same position where Captain Kingsley had been hit five weeks prior. Captain Kingsley remarked it was a pressure plate, the exact same type of IED that had hit him. When a vehicle's wheel contacts the plate, an electric charge is sent to a detonator encased in a pressure-cooker filled with high explosive powder. The police had found this one on a foot patrol of the road, a rarity in these parts, as the ANP are usually loathe to patrol even in vehicles due to their deep fear of the Taliban and Al-Qaeda. I was instantly impressed by the fact that these guys were voluntarily patrolling the road without *any* U.S. guidance or prompting.

From the IED, we made our way into a mud-brick building and shared chai and cakelike biscuits with the local commander as he updated us on his status and the overall enemy threat in the area. He remarked that he thought there was a sizable element of Taliban and Al-Qaeda roaming around, tormenting the villagers, stealing their food, instructing them not to cooperate with the government, and periodically attacking his police. Nevertheless, he was determined to take them on and win. I wish all the ANP were like this guy. At the meeting's conclusion, Captain Kingsley shared a long good-bye with the ANP. We mounted up and rolled out.

Looking back, I was half-expecting an attack. The kids in Jaghato told us we'd be attacked, but other soldiers in my group dismissed that intel as the norm; "the kids always tell us we're going to get attacked, and nothing ever happens." The police commander had also relayed his concerns that the enemy was down the road. As a result of these reports, my senses were on high alert. I kept scanning the road around me for suspicious devices and a lack of activity. Villages active in the morning but suddenly vacant and dead in the afternoon can indicate an imminent attack.

For the most part, things looked good. Kids ran up to our vehicle, farmers farmed, life appeared normal. Every now and then we'd stop at a suspicious site, and the MRAP (Mine Resistant Ambush Protected Vehicle) in the lead of our three-vehicle-convoy would scan the road with its thermal camera in search of the heat signature given off by buried metal that might indicate an IED). The MRAP would report the road was clear, and we'd move on.

Eventually, we came to the site where Captain Kingsley had hit the IED. We stopped to scan the road with the thermal camera. Specialist Monsanto noted that the village around us was completely devoid of activity. I looked up; he was right. This village had been totally alive a few hours ago, and now there wasn't a soul in sight. Not a good sign. I noticed that our counter-IED device was going crazy. A lot of IEDs are radio detonated; we have electronic devices that can jam many of these transmissions. Just because it's actively jamming doesn't mean someone is trying to blow us up; many times it's normal cell-phone or radio use from the surrounding locals. This time, however, the light wasn't just flashing orange, it was a solid orange. I mentioned these signs to Sergeant First Class Alderson, who agreed that it was all very unnerving.

The team in the MRAP reported that the IED hole was clear, and we moved on, breathing a collective sigh of relief; in 10 minutes, we'd be in the relative safety of Ghazni city.

We turned a left corner around a hill topped by a decrepit tree and headed down into a dried-out creek bed (a wadi).

Boom!

We froze in disbelief. My first thought was, "Who in the hell is throwing artillery simulators?" That's when it hit me: We'd just been attacked.

"IED!" I yelled.

Adrenaline kicked in. Sergeant First Class Alderson floored it. First Sergeant Boggins grabbed Second Lieutenant Shen from the gunner's seat in the turret and pulled him down into the vehicle. We turned right out of the wadi, and machine-gun fire erupted all around us, from both sides of the road. RPG rounds streaked by the front and rear of our vehicles as mortar rounds dropped in and exploded all around us. I looked out my left window and could not believe it—they were really shooting at us!

"Keep going! Keep going!" Captain Morriarty shouted over the radio.

We drove on.

A mortar round suddenly impacted 10 meters outside my window. *Holy shit!*

The MRAP in front of us and the UAH returned fire with their turret-mounted machine guns. Explosions rang out all around us, rocking our vehicles with each concussion blast. Rounds zoomed by us. I looked out my window and saw the muzzle flash of a machine gun coming from a small hole in the floor of a compound wall. We pushed on and came to a bridge. *Holy shit!* They're gonna blow it! I held my breath. We drove across. The bridge didn't come down. I looked back. The third vehicle made it over the bridge. The firing subsided. We had cleared the ambush.

As we drove back, we gradually came down from our adrenaline high. Everyone was in a state of shocked excitement. Did that just really happen? We looked at the MRAP in front of us and noticed that one of its antennas was listing to its side, having been struck by a round. The ballistic glass of the MRAP's gunner's turret was, by design, shattered in place from enemy fire. Yep. That really just happened. We sped through the city back to our FOB. As we rolled in, I felt like the conquering heroes returning from battle. Someone remarked that we had all just earned our CIBs and CABs (Combat Infantryman's Badges and Combat Action Badges). But as I reflected on what had happened, I didn't feel like I had earned anything. Sure, we took fire, but I didn't really do anything. I don't really deserve any kind of accommodation or citation for being a passenger.

Moreover, and this is the weirdest part, I can't recall ever being afraid. To be honest, it was thrilling. I remember coming back from FOB Warrior the day before and wondering if there really was a war going on here. I had heard reports of enemy contact, but up until today, it didn't feel real.

We took pictures as a group in front of the MRAP and its minor damage. Smiles abound. We wrote up our sworn statements and went to our bunks to reflect on the day. As I drifted off to sleep, I couldn't help but smile: I was finally a real combat veteran.

. . . had I known what the future held, I never would have smiled.

Monday April 28, 2008

Sunday was the Afghans' Freedom Day. Unbeknown to me, Monday was Martyrs Day. The thought that frequently crosses my mind: how weird it is that when someone wakes up on the day they are to die, they have no idea it's their last day. When I woke up on Monday morning, I had no idea that it would absolutely be the scariest day of my life.

Monday's mission took us to the Waghez district to help another team assess the ANP, the old district center, and the new district center that had been recently built.

Like Khogiani and Jaghato, Waghez is only reachable via dirt roads. Unlike Khogiani and Jaghato, Waghez has more than one road in and one road out. Our plan was to come in via a road to the north and exit via another to the south.

Our drive to the district center went without incident. We'd stop periodically, use the thermal cameras on our MRAPs to check out a suspicious hole or turn, find nothing, and continue on. Due to the relative threat of attack in Waghez and yesterday's attack, we decided to roll with two MRAPs leading and one UAH at the rear. We figured if an MRAP hit an IED, there was a much greater chance the crew would survive than if the UAH hit one.

We stayed at the old district center for two hours while Captain Ricker's team did its site assessment. Periodically I'd talk with the assembled police and try to acquire any intel about the enemy operating in the area. The police claimed there was a small group of Taliban roaming the area on motorcycles; I took note.

Around noon, we left the old district center and drove to the new district center. The ANP are reluctant to move into the old district center, because it is in a remote location far outside the main village and surrounded by commanding mountains from which they could be easily attacked. As we drove out, Captain Morriarty cautioned our gunner, First Sergeant Boggins, to be vigilant as we passed rooftops.

"You never know who might be waiting up there to drop a grenade on us."

We made it to the new district center and cautiously approached. In recent visits, teams and the ANP had found IEDs planted at the center's entrance. Thankfully, the coast was clear, and we rolled in. As we dismounted, Captain Morriarty again reminded us to be vigilant and perform our tiger walks. As I scanned the area through my weapon's scope, I could not help but feel small in such a large area. The terrain is commanding and impressive, with jagged mountains dominating the west and east sides of the compound. We spent about 30 minutes on site and headed for home via the different road.

The army operates on 1:50,000 scale maps. Throughout all my training, that's *all* we ever used. However, after seven years of war in Afghanistan, the Department of Defense has yet to issue us *any* 1:50,000 scale maps. Instead, we have 1:100,000 maps, useless for trying to determine roads, routes, and specific terrain. Had we had 1:50,000 maps, we might have been able to plan an adequate route out of the district. But we didn't and as a result found ourselves lost in a village on a road that ultimately ended in a dead end. We had to turn around and go back and try another route—not good. Turning around 30,000-pound vehicles that are 12 feet tall and 20 feet long by 6 feet wide on tiny-ass Afghan dirt roads no wider than 6 feet is an exercise in futility. How we managed it is beyond me; suffice to say we did and moved on. As we rolled out of the village, our extremely tall vehicles ripped down power wires. I felt awful. This was the absolute worst way to win hearts and minds. I made a mental note to one day return to the village with a massive HA drop and try to repair any damage we caused these people's homes.

We made our way out of the village and drove down a road that became a creek with running water. We didn't have a clue as to exactly where this road led, but at least we were traveling in the right direction out of the district and toward the main, paved, highway that leads back to Ghazni. At some point, we turned out of the creek bed and onto another dirt road that our *wonderful* 1:100,000 maps indicated led to the main highway. Within five minutes, however, we found ourselves lost, again. This time, we stopped and had Fareed jump out and ask a local Afghan farmer for directions. He pointed us down a road to our left and claimed the highway was about 10 minutes down that road.

We drove along the road between two hills to our right and left and headed toward the outskirts of a village. To our left were a farm field and a wood line about 150 meters off the road and down a hill. To our right was a hill that gradually rose in a rolling fashion about 50 feet, its apex roughly 100 meters off the road. To our front was a fork in the road with a mosque off on the right fork and the entrance to and through the village toward the left. Next to the mosque was a small compound surrounded by an eight-foot-high mud wall. To our front and left going down the hill toward the village was a larger compound surrounded by a similar wall. This village is burned in my memory.

The road was hard, compact, shimmering with white as rocks reflected the hot early afternoon sun. Dust from our vehicles kicked up all around us. No sign of any threat below.

It was 3:10 p.m.

As the first MRAP negotiated a gentle gradual turn to the left, a massive explosion erupted. The MRAP catapulted forward 20 feet, its front passenger's side tire flew 30 feet; the engine was totally shredded.

Holy shit! Not again!

We were out in the middle of nowhere, lost, at least 30 minutes from the cavalry. Adrenaline kicked in.

I immediately sent our medic, Specialist "Doc" Caswell, to the front of our vehicle to read our current grid location off the dagger; we needed to send a precise location to call for help. I grabbed our TACSAT radio and transmitted Doc's readings as to our location and situation, and requested QRF, a wrecker and air support. Because we had been experiencing communication problems all day, I was transmitting "in the blind" (they could hear me, but I could not hear them).

Within seconds of the blast, Captain Morriarty began calling the first MRAP.

"MRAP One—what is your status?"

An interminable 30 seconds passed.

Captain Ricker answered, "All personnel okay."

Captain Morriarty jumped out of our vehicle and ran to MRAP One to evacuate the crew and equipment; Doc Caswell vaulted out to check on their medical welfare.

Moments later, Second Lieutenant Jesse Shen (a dismount from the injured MRAP) entered the back of our vehicle, and I handed him the TACSAT.

"Radio Ghazni TOC and the 101st Airborne! Give our SITREP [situation report], and request for QRF, a wrecker, and air support!"

I exited the rear of our MRAP and swung around to its right passenger's (truck commander) seat and transmitted our location, SITREP, and request for QRF, a wrecker, and air support to FOB Vulcan's TOC and FOB Ghazni's TOC via the BFT (it also has the ability to send text messages to individual trucks or TOCs).

About 10 minutes after the blast, the crew of the first MRAP finished moving its gear and personnel into our MRAP while Lieutenant Eastwood repositioned his M1151 between two village buildings at the top of the hill and set up a .50-caliber machine gun to provide overwatch and security.

Doc Caswell returned with Fareed.

"Looks like a serious concussion. I'm putting him in the back of our MRAP to rest."

The radio crackled: Help was on the way.

I started to breathe again. The worst was over. We were going to be all right.

Captain Morriarty and I strolled down to MRAP One to take several photos of the blast crater and damaged vehicle. When we returned to our MRAP, he began assigning security positions and sectors of fire to both MRAPs' dismounted soldiers.

I took up position on a ridgeline along the road 10 meters in front of our MRAP. From there, I noticed a man in a building 50 meters in front of me, observing our position. When I raised my weapon to study him through my ACOG, he ducked down out of sight along the compound's wall. Later I'd see this man walking with what looked like a radio antenna.

Fifteen minutes later, a man wearing a red helmet riding a red motorcycle approached from north to south along the road toward our position. I called for assistance. Doc Caswell and another soldier quickly joined me.

"*Estad-Show!*" ("*Stop!*"), we yelled.

He kept coming. We raised our weapons and again yelled, "*Estad-Show!*"

The man got off his bike, cautiously took off his helmet, and raised his hands in the air. He looked terrified.

I motioned him to place his helmet down on the road and called Fareed.

"Fareed, I know you're hurt, but I need you to tell him to go away."

Fareed relayed the message. The man rapidly put his helmet back on, turned around, and sped away. I heard a loud, distant roar above me, looked up, and saw fighter aircraft and an aerial drone circling overhead.

The cavalry.

We're going to be okay.

Five minutes later, a small flock of sheep and two little Afghan girls exited the same building where I had seen the man watching us. The girls, never taking their eyes off us, walked around the compound's wall and reentered the building. Looking back, I should have realized how odd this was. Here we were, in a deeply religious Muslim country where women *never* go anywhere without a male relative, and yet two prepubescent girls casually strolled with their sheep, alone, around their compound, surrounded by a bunch of armed American infidels.

I believe the guy in the compound called in our position to the enemy but was afraid to peek over after I pointed my weapon at him, and so the cunning coward sent his two little girls outside to recon our position. Jackass.

I returned to my MRAP to check on Fareed and Doc Caswell. After a few minutes, I left to talk with Captain Morriarty and nervously smoke a cigarette. Doc Caswell followed me. Needing to urinate, Fareed also dismounted.

As I paced about, I looked up to see the same red-helmeted motorcyclist who had approached our position before. He seemed to be observing us from the hilltop approximately 200 to 250 meters away to our south. I raised my weapon to see him better through my ACOG scope; by the time I found him, he had turned around to speed away. In hindsight, I think he, too, was a spotter for the enemy, and I feel foolish for having let him go.

"Why in the hell aren't we blowing up the damaged vehicle?" I asked Captain Morriarty.

"We've been ordered by the 101st Airborne to secure the vehicle and wait for the recovery crew to arrive."

My nerves skyrocketed at the prospect of having to sit out here in the open indefinitely all in order to defend a destroyed vehicle that was by now a really expensive ($1.7 million per MRAP) piece of scrap metal.

At 4:10 p.m., the 101st QRF reported they had left their base at FOB Ghazni, one full hour after our request and the IED strike. So much for *quick* reaction force. Captain Morriarty, Second Lieutenant Shen, Fareed, Sergeant First Class Meyer, and I clustered around the south side of our MRAP. Captain Morriarty suggested we separate ourselves and continue to monitor our positions. As we began to return to our security positions, a massive explosion erupted behind us, sending us all flying with a massive force into the ground.

Our MRAP had just been hit by an RPG.

All hell broke loose.

Machine-gun fire erupted all around us, coming from the west and north of our position (along a ridgeline and a wood line that buttressed the village, respectively). The enemy was close, too close. Bullets skipped and skirted all around, kicking up dust; we scrambled to get behind the safety of one of the MRAP's massive tires.

Adrenaline and instinct kicked in. I fired at the western ridgeline. When I turned to check our rear, I saw Captain Morriarty hobbling back toward a compound wall. He appeared to be injured. Panic and fear kicked in. Captain Morriarty gives me comfort. I feel safe with him. The thought that he may have been hurt was unbearable.

I ran to evaluate his condition. *Thank God* he was okay.

Together, we sprinted back to our MRAP to our crew and the other dismounts: no injuries.

But I also noticed our gunner wasn't firing his weapon from our MRAP's turret.

"Sir, First Sergeant Boggins isn't firing!"

Captain Morriarty and I ran to the driver's side of our MRAP—the same side the enemy was firing on—and screamed, "Boggins, fire your weapon!"

"I don't have a clear target, gentlemen," he casually replied, as if we were back on a training range in the United States and he were trying to conserve ammo.

Standing in front of our MRAP (where we were severely exposed to enemy fire), Captain Morriarty and I pointed to the enemy's position and ordered Boggins to fire. He immediately began firing into the tree line (we'd later determine this is where they shot the initial RPG that hit our MRAP), even though the enemy now targeted his position with small-arms fire.

I turned and looked up the hill to see how the other UAH was faring just as an RPG went flying over the top of their vehicle and exploded behind them.

Despite the violence and horror, there sat Sergeant First Class Postman, appearing calm as ever, aggressively unloading thousands of lead .50-caliber rounds at the ridgeline to our west.

An RPG round bombarded the compound wall behind me, shattering what was left of my nerves. I felt like crying. Countless rounds kicked up underneath our MRAP. Confused, dazed, utterly terrified, I ran with Captain Morriarty back toward the compound wall. As I ran, I blurted out, "Captain Morriarty, I'm really fucking scared!" He looked at me and in the calmest, most fatherly voice he could muster said, "Yeah I know, buddy, I'm scared too. Just keep fighting, and we'll get out of this."

That one sentence turned the tide. Instinct kicked back in. I went on autopilot and began to scan the ridgeline for enemies. I thought I saw a head pop up. I fired a barrage of shots. They hit right in front of where I thought I saw the head. Captain Morriarty yelled.

"Zeller! What the fuck are you doing?"

"I saw a guy pop up, sir!"

Immediately his tone of voice changed back to the calm, nurturing tone he normally uses. "Well, in that case, good job, keep firing!"

Captain Morriarty began firing with me.

Time slowed down. Panic returned. I wanted to go home. I wanted my parents. I wanted my friends. I wanted to be *anywhere* but here. Why couldn't I leave?

Why were we out here risking our lives on a hunk of metal? What had we done to deserve this?

Up until now, I had no quarrel with these people. I had done them no personal wrong. Angry, horrifically terrified, all I wanted was to curl up in a little ball inside the safety of that vehicle and pray to survive. I was so afraid, I couldn't even cry. Yet I stayed in my position and continued to return fire. Even now, I feel like a coward, like less of a man for being so acutely and visibly afraid. I was just thankful my soldiers weren't around to see me break, to see me lose my military bearing to such a degree.

I stole a look to see how my guys inside the MRAP were faring. First Sergeant Boggins was firing away as our driver, Sergeant First Class Alderson, sat patiently in his position (drivers are not supposed to leave the vehicle unless they absolutely have to). Throughout the entire horror, with all the gunfire and explosions erupting around him, Alderson managed to remain calm enough to take prodigious notes of the events and their corresponding times, an invaluable aid.

The firefight escalated in a violent crescendo. I continued to fire.

Boom!

A mortar exploded 15 meters in front of us, throwing Captain Morriarty and me from our feet and back into the compound wall. What the hell happened? Where am I? What's going on? Oh, right, this damn firefight. It's not just an awful dream.

We staggered up, Captain Morriarty immediately in front of me as we took up position along the wall. I scanned my sector of fire and thought I saw that head pop up again. I returned fire. Looking back, I had no qualms or hesitation about killing whoever was doing this to me. At that point, it was us or them, and to be Rock: Fuck them. The head dropped back down. I yelled to Captain Morriarty that I had three high explosive (HE) rounds for my M203 grenade launcher.

"*Zeller!* Load a round into your 203, and give me your weapon!"

I did as ordered. He fired it at the ridgeline.

"*Again!*"

Mortars continued to rain down and explode all around us. That's when I heard someone yell, "The .50 cal on the 1151 is up! I can't reach anyone on the radio! I can't see anyone on the .50!"

In one of the bravest actions I've ever seen, Captain Morriarty looked around the corner of the wall behind which we had taken cover to see if he could make visual contact with First Lieutenant Eastwood's M1151. A barrage of bullets impacted the wall all around us. Still, he did not duck back (while under continuous fire) until he saw Sergeant First Class Postman emerge from inside the M1151 (where he had taken cover) and continue to return fire.

Captain Morriarty ducked back to rejoin me along the wall. Someone yelled that they were taking fire from a grove of trees 150 meters to our west, just off the road and below the ridgeline. I fired my final HE 203 round at this grove of trees, impacting just behind it. I hope the shrapnel killed whoever was firing at us.

An eternity passed.

Bullets continued to crack and pop all around me, kicking up a constant cloud of noxious Afghan dust. Panic returned.

Why in the hell won't they stop and just leave us alone? Where in the hell is our support?

"Friendlies approaching from the rear!"

I turned and saw them—not the 101st QRF, but guys from our own FOB. Against orders, they took matters unto themselves to rescue us. No question about it: These guys saved our lives. Our personal heroes barreled up the road into oncoming fire. Captain Morriarty pointed toward the ridgeline to our west and ordered them to return fire. Explosions erupted in military precision along the ridgeline. Each blast resonated with precision, a finely adjusted metronome keeping time. Enemy fire slowed significantly. Like the modern metal-vehicle mounted cavalry they are, the QRF element drove toward the western ridgeline and assaulted the enemy's position while under fire. Within minutes, firing ceased.

We had survived. By some miracle of God, we had *all* survived. Not a single injury other than some concussions from the initial IED and very rattled nerves of all involved.

The fight was over. Captain Morriarty ordered Jesse, an interpreter, a soldier from the FOB Vulcan QRF element, and me to take up security positions along the ridgeline on the road. As I moved toward my position, Captain Morriarty, Captain Ricker, and Captain Goodman began setting up the QRF vehicles in a security perimeter.

All the while, I kept thinking, why can't we leave? Where in the hell was the 101st? Why didn't we just blow the damn IED'd MRAP in place and *stop* this senseless risk of soldiers' lives?

Captain Morriarty came over to see how we were doing.

"Captain, I'm a coward and a pussy. I was scared."

He just stared at me. "Zeller, you're not a coward. I'm scared too. It's okay to be scared. We're gonna make it out of here. But you did great. You didn't curl up into a ball and hide or run. You did your job. You returned fire. That's all anyone can ever ask. You did good."

As he walked away, I felt a bit better, but I was still terrified. I knelt down and prayed the 23rd Psalm aloud . . .

"The Lord is my shepherd, I shall not want . . .
He maketh me to lay down in green pastures
He leadeth me beside still waters . . .
Yea, though I walk through the valley of the shadow of death . . .

I shall fear no evil for thou art with me
Thy rod and thy staff comfort me. . . ."

It's all I could remember . . . those few disjointed phrases.

I turned and saw Doc Caswell.

In a very sheepish voice, I asked, "Doc, would you mind praying with me?"

In an equally shocked voice, he answered, "Sure, Lieutenant."

Together we prayed for our safety, our leadership, our lives, our strength, and, ultimately, God's love. For a brief moment, despite all the horror and chaos around me, I found a fleeting serenity.

Reality struck back with a violent blow: We weren't out of the woods yet.

Captain Goodman joined me at my security position. "How ya' doin', Lieutenant?"

I couldn't respond. My eyes said it all: an engraved thousand-yard stare that would remain for the next 24 hours. Shell shock.

Every now and then I'd see a motorcyclist approach. Villagers would peek out to see what was happening. I'd call this out but heard no response. Just when my nerves were beginning to calm, loathsome panic would return. I'd have to turn around and yell back to the various captains what I or my soldiers had seen.

"Zeller, turn the fuck back around and scan your sector!"

They didn't mean to be angry. They were frustrated, scared, and tired, like me. What they didn't realize was that they were also all temporarily deaf, because they'd taken out their earplugs before the fighting began. Only I had remembered to keep them in. (I simply cannot imagine life without being able to hear music at the richness to which I'm accustomed!)

Around 5:15 p.m. (*two hours after we called for help!*), I watched the 101st QRF drive from east to west in a village 1,000 meters to our northwest. They, too, were lost. We were informed that the 101st QRF was on the way and that we might be staying the night because the 101st higher command would not let us blow the IED'd MRAP in place. At that point, all I wanted to do was find this son of a bitch, beat him to a bloody pulp, and trade places with his air-conditioned, TOC-living, rear-echelon ass.

Finally, at 5:50 p.m., nearly three hours after we called for help, the 101st QRF arrived. The QRF commander immediately went to work setting up his vehicles in a security perimeter. For the next hour or so, I sat, prone, looking out, scanning my sector, ready to kill anything that moved. Unceasingly terrified, I started to panic when no one came to check on us, the lone security dismounts.

I couldn't stand it any longer. As ranking officer of the security element, I made the executive decision to put Second Lieutenant Shen in charge and went to see what the hell was going on, at least to see if I could get my guys some water, because we'd been without for nearly four hours. I joined Captain Morriarty and the 101st QRF commander as they talked about their security plan for the night and the recovery plan for the first MRAP. The 101st QRF commander said he was told by his battalion commander, "If you do not come back with that vehicle [the MRAP], don't bother coming back at all." That's right, we were under orders to die in place if needed. This jackass, this army, my government, valued a piece of metal over our lives.

For us to remain in place and secure the damn vehicle, above all else, was without question the stupidest thing I've ever witnessed in my entire life. Yet we did just that. We remained in place and waited for EOD (the IED experts who inspect every IED blast). The wrecker also had to inspect the site and recover the vehicle.

More bad news. The EOD and wrecker were stuck in the village 1,000 meters to our northwest and were trying to turn around to head back to FOB Ghazni. They would return in the morning and attempt to recover the vehicle. We also learned that we had been surrounded by 30 to 40 enemy personnel during the firefight.

A discussion between Captains Morriarty and Ricker and the 101st QRF commander ensued as to how to best tow the first MRAP into our security perimeter. One of the 101st QRF soldiers recommended using the tow winch from one of their armored support vehicles.

It was clear from the onset that this wasn't going to work. Their winch could only handle up to 30,000 pounds. The MRAP, undamaged and working (rolling), weighs upward of 36,000 pounds.

They tried, and tried, and decisively failed. The MRAP did not budge one inch.

The 101st QRF commander received permission from his higher command to leave the first MRAP under our security perimeter. I told the 101st commander that the majority of our team and FOB Vulcan QRF did not have night-vision devices, as the army had yet to issue us any.

The 101st QRF commander came up with a plan to cross-level NODs from his soldiers with our gunners and security-perimeter fire teams.

As we all walked back to the road and our MRAP, I turned to the 101st QRF commander and asked, "You're the 101st, right?" (The 101st is an Air Assault Division: lots and lots and lots of attack helicopters. We have an entire battalion of them right down the road from us.)

"Roger."

"Okay, no offense, but *where in the hell are your choppers?*"

He cracked a sorrowful smile. "Dude, I know what you're saying. I have no idea, I am so sorry. Trust me, I'd love to have them here too. I don't know what to tell you. . . ."

I moved our MRAP into position so that its front faced the wood line to our north. I then ordered Sergeant First Class Alderson to use the MRAP's thermals to scan the wood line throughout the night. If he saw anything move, First Sergeant Boggins was to send it into the next life.

Captain Morriarty established a meal rotation plan, sending one soldier at a time to either the ASV or the second MRAP to eat an MRE. We had enough NODs for one man per three-man team. Again, absolutely unacceptable.

The sun set, and the 101st artillery assets began firing periodic illumination missions. Each illumination round's boom set my panic skyrocketing and sent me back into a momentarily catatonic state. The round would explode above us with a magnificent bang and a brilliant flash, illuminating (hence the name "illume round") the entire valley with a mini sun's intensity.

The 101st QRF commander ordered the ASV to fire three rounds into a small, round hut along the tree line 150 meters to our north, a recon by fire. As the rounds impacted, all I could think was, "My God, I hope there aren't kids in there. . . ." For the next several hours, two soldiers from the 101st QRF and I would fire periodic parachute illumination rounds from our respective M203s in between the 101st artillery illumination missions.

As the breathtaking night sky cast its brilliance over our rattled heads, I looked up and tried to comprehend the magnitude of it all, in vain. It was too soon. Danger still lurked behind every shadow, any corner. Panic ensued.

I called out to Captain Morriarty. "Sir, are you religious?"

"Yes."

"Would you mind praying with me?"

"Not at all."

Together in hushed tones, we prayed, "Our Father, who art in Heaven, hallowed be thy name. Thy kingdom come, Thy will be done, on earth as it is in Heaven. Give us this day our daily bread, and forgive us our trespasses, as we forgive those who trespass against us. And lead us not into temptation, but deliver us from evil. For Thine is the Kingdom, the Power, and the Glory, forever and ever. Amen."

At 9:00 p.m., the EOD and wrecker element *finally* arrived on scene. Over the next hour, I laid on the ground, prone, attempting to scan my sector—a foolishly futile effort without NODs. Eventually, I joined Doc Caswell, going from vehicle to vehicle to check on everyone's condition. Around 10:25, the EOD element reported: They had completed their work. The IED had been an antipersonnel mine stacked on top of two antitank mines. Immediately following their report, the wrecker reported it was beginning to recover the first MRAP. At 11:15, the wrecker finished recovering the first MRAP. It would have to drag it, because the MRAP's rear tires would not spin. We had significant concerns that the MRAP would simply not budge and that we'd still be stuck out here all night.

The prospect of spending the night scared me big time. At night, we'd have the advantage; we were safe. But when that sun came up, they'd be back and in more force, and there was *no* guarantee we'd be as lucky as we had been today.

At 11:30 the 101st QRF commander; Captains Morriarty, Ricker, and Goodman; and Sergeant First Class Meyer established a movement plan to get us back to FOB Vulcan. They discussed actions on contact, disabled vehicles, medevacs, and the order of march. Immediately following this meeting, Captain Morriarty pulled us (the dismounted security element) off the ridgeline and sent us back to our respective vehicles.

I returned to our MRAP and asked Boggins and Alderson how they were doing. Boggins said that after 13 straight hours manning the gun, he needed a break.

Finally, at 1:00 a.m., our mass convoy left the area, with Captain Ricker taking over as TC for our MRAP.

Not 10 minutes into the movement, Murphy (as in "Murphy's Law") reared his ugly head for one more hour of pure frustration.

The ASV towing the MRAP lost all its hydraulic fluid and, in turn, needed to be towed.

"I give us 6 to 10 odds we get hit again tonight, 1 to 10 odds we actually make it out by morning, especially since we're with these morons [the 101st QRF, EOD, and Wrecker]," joked Captain Morriarty.

The 101st QRF commander ordered his ASV-2 to tow the ASV-1. For 40 nerve-racking minutes, we sat in the middle of a hostile village, inviting the enemy to shoot at us. At last, the convoy began to move again.

Not 10 minutes later, the wrecker called over the radio that it was stuck and that it needed the 101st QRF's MRAP to push it in order to get it moving again.

All I could think was, we're really doing this, putting all these people, these American soldiers, in danger because some lieutenant colonel at the 101st doesn't want us to blow up his damaged vehicle and leave its charred carcass behind.

Finally, around 2:00 a.m., we started to move again. At 2:15, our convoy reached Route One, turned north, and headed back home to FOB Vulcan and FOB Ghazni. Because the wrecker was not able to go any faster, the max speed of the convoy never exceeded 10 mph. As I looked out the back window of our MRAP, I could see black streak marks and grooves in the pavement left behind by the rear wheels of the towed MRAP.

An hour later, the convoy met another towing convoy (sent by FOB Ghazni). The damaged MRAP was put on a giant flatbed, which allowed the whole convoy to move faster. At this point, Sergeant First Class Alderson indicated he was too tired and nauseated to drive, so I replaced him as the driver of our MRAP. Captain Ricker thanked the 101st QRF for helping us out and ordered FOB Vulcan elements to break off from the 101st convoy and return home. At approximately 3:30 (12 hours and 20 minutes after we hit the initial IED, and 18 hours after we left on the mission) our MRAP, the M1151, and the three M1151s that responded as FOB Vulcan's QRF arrived home.

The next morning, I inspected our MRAP and the damage it took from the RPG round that initiated the ambush. Frighteningly, the RPG round actually penetrated its hull.

If Fareed, Doc Caswell, and I had not exited the MRAP prior to the RPG strike, we would have at the very least suffered severe injuries if not death. In a twist of wicked irony, smoking saved my life.

Tuesday, April 29, 2008

I barely slept after we got home, a restless, post-trauma sleep. I got up around 8:00 a.m. and immediately called my parents to tell them that I loved them.

My mother said she had been worried sick about me and was beyond relieved to hear from me. (She'd had no idea why she was so upset all day long. I later learned that she had awoken in the middle of the night and begun to pray for me. Comparing times, it was exactly the same time as when the attack began.)

I opted not to tell them what had happened, because I didn't want to worry them any further. I also decided I needed to get my head around everything that happened before I talked about it in any detail with anyone back home.

I spent the morning cleaning out our MRAP and resting in my bunk, reading articles online, downloading music, and trying to internalize everything that had happened.

I was a shattered mess. My hands still shook. Every knock or loud bang sent me back to panic land.

Around 3:00, First Sergeant Boggins came to my bunk and told me the combat stress counselor was in the chow hall waiting to talk to all of us involved in the attack.

For the next two hours, we vented. I nearly cried. Captain Morriarty erupted with the most violent anger I've ever seen from any man. He was livid about the decision to not blow up the damaged MRAP and get out of there; how we were sent no usable air support (the one airplane we saw was not American and did nothing to aid us, as the pilots—who were Dutch—didn't speak English); that we only had two pairs of NODs among our 14-man team; that the 101st QRF took three hours to reach us. Seeing him explode actually made me feel a lot better. I wasn't the only one feeling those emotions. It felt great to vent.

My moment of honor came when Captain Morriarty turned to the whole group and shared how I had told him I felt like a failure, mainly because I don't think I hit any of the enemy; I felt useless, and, because I felt useless, I felt like a coward.

Captain Morriarty turned toward me.

"Zeller, you're not a coward. You returned fire. You did everything I told you to do without question. You didn't turn and run, you didn't hide. You held your place and returned fire. You're no coward. You're brave."

I didn't feel brave, but hearing him say that sent my spirits soaring. I tried my very best to hold it back, but a tear managed to roll down my cheek.

Sergeant First Class Meyer (who survived the legendary "Black Hawk Down" and is one of the bravest and best soldiers I've ever had the honor and privilege of knowing) looked us all in the eye.

"You men performed as well, if not better, than any of the active-duty units I've been with over the years."

I later told my men just how much of an honor a comment like that is—its worth is beyond description.

I write of these events, because the story needs to be told. The heroics of people like Captains Morriarty and Ricker; First Sergeant Boggins; Sergeants First Class Meyer, Postman, and Alderson; Sergeant Blasker; Docs Caswell and Sullivan; Staff Sergeant Santino; Private First Class Torino; First Lieutenant Eastwood; Second Lieutenant Shen; our interpreter, Fareed; and the men of the two QRFs—these people deserve all the accolades known to humanity. These men, every one of them, are genuine heroes. Without question, I'd go anywhere and do anything with these guys. I also hope word gets back to the right people to ensure this *never* happens again.

The counselor evaluated me and decided he needs to see me for a few follow-up sessions, which makes me happy, as talking about all this really helps. At one point, he asked me if I could go back out on mission. I hesitated. Everything in my right mind said, "*Hell no!*"

I looked at him with shocked eyes, took a deep breath, and said, "Absolutely. If my guys go out, I have to be there with them. I can never ever leave these guys alone. . . ."

I trailed off and finished the rest of that sentence in my head, ". . . because they're family; I love them."

It's true. We all went through something so profound, so amazingly violent, so shocking that we're forever bound. I look at the guys around me who didn't go through it, and they just aren't the same, or maybe we're different. Most of the guys on our FOB have yet to be in combat, or a "tic," as we call it. As a result, I look at those not involved, those who weren't there, and all I see are ducks. I look at my men, and I see turtles.

That evening, for the first time in two days, I slept a sound, peaceful sleep.

Wednesday, April 30, 2008

I spent today monitoring the radios in our TOC and writing my sworn statement of Monday's attack. A sandstorm blew in, turning bright-blue day to gray-brown night. I'm intensely proud of my mission and the chance to help the Afghan people. I wouldn't change any of this for the world. I knew something like this would eventually happen, though I admit I was surprised it happened so soon into our tour. I could only pray it would be the last. I believe in God, and, as a result, I truly believe what will happen is in His hands from this point forward.

Whenever I get scared or down, all I have to do is think of my family, friends, and the Afghan kids. I did this for them. To me, that alone was worth all the risk in the world.

10

There's a Lot of Dumb in War

Wednesday, May 7, 2008

I gradually returned to my old self as I resolved not to let the horrors around me alter who I am. I made a trip up to Kabul, which was a very welcome respite. The drive to Kabul takes roughly three hours, depending on traffic and enemy activity. Thankfully, we didn't receive any contact on our drive up Afghanistan's fabled Highway One (the route from Kandahar to Kabul). The drive is actually gorgeous. Rugged mountains stand at stark attention like a row of soldiers, lining the road into Afghanistan's capital city. Sadly, all this spectacular scenery is ruined by the massive amount of pollution that hugs Kabul in a constant asthmatic grip. I think Kabul may even beat L.A. for the worst smog I've ever experienced.

Highway One is normally devoid of major traffic; you'll pass the occasional taxi or jingle truck (Afghan cargo trucks, decorated with all sorts of mirrors, mosaic paintings, neon lights, pictures of Bollywood actresses, etc.) and, my favorite, Afghan Greyhound. Afghan commercial buses are a sight to behold. We have a joke here: "How many Afghans can you fit into a vehicle?" The answer: "One more." The same holds true for cargo. Afghan buses, filled to the brim, roll up and down the highway, with piles of cars stacked sometimes two rows high upon the vehicle's roof. Yes, passenger cars hitch rides atop bus roofs. I have yet to see a crane in this country, so I haven't a clue as to how they actually move the cars up and down.

The ruins of an Afghan village in Khogiani district, Ghazni province. Note the rough terrain that rung the valley. The Taliban would attack us from this higher ground.

On our ride to Kabul, we passed an illegal ANP checkpoint that had traffic backed up for several miles. Being Americans, we can drive right through these illegal tolls without any worry. The poor Afghans, on the other hand, wait hours on end to finally make it to the checkpoint and engage in a futile attempt to lower the passage fee. The ironic thing is that as we roll through, the ANP stop what they're doing, smile, and wave. You can tell whether the checkpoint is legal by the look on the civilian drivers' faces and the time it's taking to get each vehicle through. If it's a checkpoint that is searching for insurgents and contraband, the line moves rather quickly, as cars are chosen at random for detailed screening. If it's illegal, the people all get out, sit on the sides of the road smoking cigarette after cigarette, and sometimes even make chai. Their faces are always dejected, one more injustice in a land rife with undue sorrow.

Entering Kabul, we ran straight into a massive traffic jam. There are no real driving laws in this country; it really is every vehicle for itself. In entering Kabul, you go through a ghetto of sorts, where the outgoing side of the road is paved and the incoming side of the road is a study in how to make perfect potholes. The guys I was traveling with opted for the paved side, which led straight into oncoming traffic. In traveling to Kabul, Sergeant Blasker and I had hitched a ride with another police mentor team. We were the second vehicle in our three-vehicle convoy. I felt myself becoming enraged as I watched how the other team drives. Sirens blazing, air horn blasting, these guys drove like the ultimate road-warrior assholes. We have a standing order not to drive in that manner unless our lives are in danger, yet, orders be damned, these men drove as if to ensure every Afghan around lived in sheer terror when they took to the road.

At first, I sat in my seat shaking my head at the absolute insanity of the whole ordeal, but after several near-collisions, I exploded. Slamming my foot down on a virtual air brake, I yelled to no one, "What in the *hell* do these idiots think they're doing?" Before anyone could answer, I watched in horror as the Hummer in front smacked into a van. In the van driver's defense, there was nothing he could do. Traffic in front of him stopped short. Had I been driving the lead vehicle, I simply would have waited for the van to find a way to get out of my way, but apparently for the soldiers I traveled with that day, waiting was not an option. The first collision with the van was minor, nothing more than a cracked rear taillight. The second collision, however, was plain asinine. The Hummer floored it and, with textbook precision, rammed the van out of its way and into the right-hand curb, where it came to rest within a meter of a storefront filled with people. As we drove by, I looked out my window to see if the van's driver was injured. Thankfully he wasn't, but I'll never forget his face, one of the angriest I've ever witnessed in my entire life. We're under orders to stop whenever we have a collision and give the driver of the unfortunate vehicle a receipt they can take to the nearest U.S. base to claim damages. Did we stop? Absolutely not.

(Over the radio) "Law Dog 3-7, this is Law Dog 3-6. You give them a little combat bump?"

(Law Dog 3-7 was the lead vehicle, Law-Dog 3-6 was the rear vehicle. We were Law-Dog 2-5.)

Law Dog 3-7: [Chuckling] "Roger that, Law-Dog 3-6."

Law-Dog 3-6: "Well better hurry it up, you've got 45 minutes to get Daddy to chow."

Law-Dog 3-7: "Roger that, Law-Dog 3-6."

"You've got to be [expletive] kidding me!" I exclaimed to the men in my vehicle. "We're doing this just so these jackasses don't miss breakfast? If *any* of you guys *ever* drive like this in one of my convoys, your asses will be mine, clear?"

We made it to Camp Phoenix, our base in Kabul, without any other accidents and sought out Captains Morriarty and Ricker, First Lieutenant Goodman, and Sergeant First Class Alderson. Visiting Camp Phoenix is like a vacation as far as residents of FOB Vulcan are concerned. The food is fantastic, movies are shown nightly at the FOB movie theater, and people walk around saluting each other like there isn't a war on (we don't salute at FOB Vulcan, as that's a guaranteed sniper check). In fact, the longer one stays at Phoenix, the longer one wonders if there really is a war on; it's as if its residents live on an entirely different plane of reality.

Once reunited with Captain Morriarty and Sergeant First Class Alderson, we became inseparable. Postcombat stress is best handled through companionship with your fellow warriors. Our own Band of Brothers, we sat outside that night and recalled in detail the events of our ordeal. We discussed our frustrations, our fears, laughed at how lucky we'd been, shared the fact that we're all having some trouble sleeping and that any loud bang causes our adrenaline to rush forth. With disdain, we looked around at all the "Fobbits" (people who spend an entire war living on a FOB, seldom, if ever, leaving the wire) and marveled at how different they all suddenly appeared. Three weeks prior, these had been our fellow soldiers, friends of years (decades for some), and yet now they were like strangers to us all. They simply couldn't relate—an abundance of ducks surrounding a group of turtles. Alderson remarked that within the first 24 hours of his arrival back at Camp Phoenix, he was ready to punch the next person who looked at him the wrong way.

We were celebrities of the worst kind. I couldn't walk more than 10 steps without someone coming up to me to ask me to recount my experience of actual combat, something these Fobbits will likely never experience. Countless times, I told our story, taking care to emphasize how proud I am of my 13 brothers in arms, how they did their jobs dutifully, and that, against all odds, we made it out basically unscathed. Inevitably, I'd get the über–gung ho GI who looked at us with an unhealthy degree of envy: combat chasers. These fools are actually jealous of us. My wish is that every single one of them gets out of this place alive, well, having never experienced the fear we had.

Thursday, May 8, 2008

Within 24 hours of our arrival at Phoenix, my soldiers and I linked up with Team One and headed back to Ghazni. Leaving Kabul, we passed the soccer stadium where the Taliban used to execute people in public during a match's halftime, and I felt an overwhelming sense of pride. If nothing else, at least we've ended that barbaric medieval horror. That afternoon and evening, Ghazni endured a much-needed soaking rain, and I thanked God for bringing the Afghan farmers at least a few more days of healthy crops; food really is one of the keys to winning this war.

Friday, May 16, 2008

I awoke at 2:30 a.m. to prepare our vehicle for the 4:00 a.m. convoy to Camp Phoenix in Kabul. After a series of delays, we rolled out of the FOB at 4:30, just as dawn broke over the horizon, painting the mountains of Ghazni in hues of purple, pink, and beige. A quiet solitude encompassed the land, as the Afghan masses soundly slept in their mud-brick homes. We left early in order to avoid Kabul's smothering traffic. Within 10 minutes of leaving the FOB, our MRAP began to overheat. For the next two hours, we'd stop every few miles to let it cool down before continuing on. Twice we futilely tried to tow it with a seven-ton cargo truck driven by two Afghan National Army soldiers. We finally hit Kabul smack-dab in the middle of morning rush hour, arriving at Phoenix nearly three hours later than expected.

As I waited my turn in the refueling line, a fat navy sailor, his gut benefiting from the fare of the Phoenix Chow Hall, approached my vehicle and in an unnecessarily gruff voice barked, "Where's your data plate for the vehicle?" Part of our preconvoy procedures is to check fluid levels, tire pressure, and engine issues, but never was I trained to ensure that the vehicle's data plate is actually in the vehicle. So, when I looked at him puzzlingly, and said, "Um . . . it isn't here?" he angrily shot back, "No! And without it you can't refuel! Furthermore, you need to move your vehicle over there and wait while I call to ensure you aren't driving a stolen vehicle."

Eventually the sergeant arrived, apologized for the delay, and got my vehicle refueled, and we headed off to rendezvous with Captain Morriarty.

As I walked into the transient housing tent, I couldn't help but grin at the site of Captain Morriarty and Sergeant First Class Alderson racking out in T-shirts, laptops perched atop their stomachs. Once settled in the tent, my soldiers and I sauntered off to the Camp Phoenix Post Exchange (PX) to hit up the ATM and buy some much needed items (Red Bull, beef jerky, magazines, DVDs). Standing in line for the ATM, I had my second near-pummeling-of-a-Fobbit of the day. Private First Class Torino (one of the Waghez Fourteen) stood in front of me, and we started to chitchat: "I think our AO is gonna start to get awfully hot in the next few weeks" (hot meaning active with enemy attacks). Before Torino could comment, a first lieutenant standing behind me (and clearly a Fobbit by the size of his KBR-fed gut), said, "Yeah the temperature is really starting to get up there."

Me: "No, I meant hot as in active with enemy activity."

Fobbit (disgusted at my apparent insensitivity): "What, you mean KIA [Kabul International Airport] getting rocketed last night wasn't hot enough for you?"

At first I took the bait and started to respond with what I considered hot (an event like our ambush), but then I realized there was no point in arguing with the Fobbit. It's not his fault he's living a different war.

With goodies and cash in hand, I met up with Sergeant First Class Postman and headed to the Phoenix Chow Hall to gorge on all the chicken strips with honey mustard I could stomach.

May 17: We ended up staying an extra day in Kabul, which I used to my full advantage. I ate, read, e-mailed, ate some more, napped, ate again, watched TV, and finally, around 11:00 p.m., treated my former soldier, Specialist Addison, and Doc Caswell to Pizza Hut. While chowing down on greasy American goodness, a group of my former soldiers led by First Sergeant Fast walked up. For the next hour, we laughed about how I cannot throw a hand grenade to save my life. During training, we found I simply have the world's worst aim. I chalk it up to years of playing rugby. Months ago, my former soldiers had presented me with a baseball and baseball glove, "so you can practice before we get deployed." Inscribed on the ball were all their signatures and messages of encouragement like "Throw toward enemy" or "If you need to use a grenade, remember these steps: Pull the pin, hold the pin, and hand to someone else to throw for you." As they left us to our pizza, they expressed their concern for our safety and pledged their indefinite offer of assistance. I went to bed that night with a massive smile on my face, glad to be once more in their company, if ever so briefly. War heightens one's sense of time . . . each moment holds an increasing significance and importance . . . the desire for one's future life-time becomes paramount . . . an unbridled longing serves as the unwavering guide toward one's homecoming . . . a coming out of darkness . . . a journey into paradise.

11

Memorial Day

Saturday, May 24, 2008

Several days ago, two officers, a navy lieutenant senior grade and an army first lieutenant, perished with their interpreter a few hours south of our base. They died horrifically in a massive explosion, victims of our enemy's most deadly weapon: the IED. Tragically but honorably, their names now join the elite ranks of our nation's most honored heroes, warriors who gave their lives so that others could live free.

I awoke early Saturday morning with a profound sadness in my heart: Today we would say good-bye forever to fallen comrades, friends, American brothers. Though I never personally met or knew these men, their deaths strike a very real chord concerning the threats we face: Death lurks around every corner, knowing only the boundaries of our enemy's resolve and creativity. As I dressed, I made sure to put on a clean uniform, a small, ultimately meaningless token to show my respect for these true heroes. With each battlefield injury, each combat engagement, and each fatality, I return to the predominant riddle of my own mortality: how odd it is to not know one's last day alive. These men woke on their final morning and had no idea that in a mere matter of hours, their lives would end in a horrific fireball, cut short by the flames and blast of a device crudely assembled hours prior by the hands of the most malicious of men. Undoubtedly, as in all wars, a weapon creates victims beyond their targets; three families (two American, one

---

The flag post at FOB Ghazni where we would hold every memorial ceremony for the fallen (note the American, Afghan, and Polish flags, all flying at equal heights).

Afghan) are forever incomplete, and a sense of loss will accompany them for the remainder of their days. For these people, Memorial Day will forever hold a new, unwanted meaning full of the most profound sorrow.

We arrived at FOB Ghazni 30 minutes before the ceremony began, taking our places in the ranks of assembled soldiers, sailors, airmen, Afghan allies, and civilians gathered to pay respect to the eternally departed. People came from as far away as the Pakistan border to say one final good-bye, to offer one final salute, to men they'd never met.

As I stood under the same hot, unforgiving Afghan sun that had only days ago sat silently over the very people we were celebrating, I could not help but again ponder my own demise. I decided that should I die, I wouldn't want to be remembered in such a way. I wondered how these men would react to their own memorial ceremony. I then realized that ceremonies to honor the dead are as much a means for the living to openly express grief. Moreover, this ceremony, so steeped in the most humble and dignified of traditions, is our nation's last official act to honor our bravest of citizens. Indeed, upon further reflection, I could think of no better way to honor their sacrifice.

For 30 minutes, we stood in ranks in complete silence, interrupted only by the music playing over the PA system (modern-day patriotic hymns from country-music stars ensconced in Nashville mansions) and the drumbeat of a lone helicopter arriving from an unknown mission. Five minutes prior to the ceremony, a contingent of Polish Honor Guards (we share our battle space with our Polish allies) marched in the utmost military precision to join us in ranks to pay their respects.

The ceremony began like all others in the military: the playing of our national anthem and an invocation offered up by an army chaplain. To honor our fallen Afghan comrade, the Afghan national anthem was also played. To honor the Afghan nation, all assembled brought themselves to the position of attention and held a steadfast hand salute through the playing of both nations' anthems, a sign of the highest respect. The invocation went as all others do, with heads bowed, somber silence reverberating across the sea of mournful bodies.

One by one, the commanders of the fallen got up to offer their respectful accounts of the dead. The PRT commander (for whom the men had worked) offered his memories of men dedicated to the mission, hardworking, honorable, fearless leaders, patriots to both nations. The navy officer had extended his tour, providing the PRT with invaluable insight of culture and key players as the new command rotated in months ago. The army officer had been handpicked for this mission months prior at Fort Bragg and had lived up to the promise as the perfect leader for a most difficult mission. The interpreter, the sole breadwinner for a family of 11 (8 siblings and 2 parents), had fled Afghanistan during the reign of the Taliban for the relative safety of Iran, only to return after the religious scourge had been seemingly eradicated from his beloved homeland. Proudly completing a high school education, the interpreter had hoped to continue his studies, but the demands of a huge and hungry family pressed him into service as an interpreter for U.S. forces (one of the best-paying legitimate jobs in all of Afghanistan).

Following the PRT commander, an Afghan dignitary and the local Afghan Army Commander paid their respects in quiet but meaningful speeches regarding the worthiness of the cause, the proud traditions of the Afghan people, and the solidarity they share with the United States.

Military memorial ceremonies work in such fashion: The overall commander speaks, the invited guests speak, and then one member of each man's unit speaks. The speeches by the survivors are the most emotional, the toughest to bear, and also the most genuine. They never cease to move me.

On this day, one speech in particular resonated with me profoundly. A sergeant from the army lieutenant's unit recounted how he was the consummate leader, a soldier's officer: first out front, leading by example, diligent to the core, caring never for himself, but always for his men. As we roll outside the wire, all units have a similar procedure to activate their electronic jammers (that allegedly disrupt the signal that sets off an IED).

Theirs went as follows:

"All Ghost Rider elements, place your dukes to green."

The sergeant, using the very words of his fallen leader, tearfully said good-bye in this way:

"All Ghost Rider elements, this is Ghost Rider-6 [the fallen soldier's radio call sign], place your dukes from standby to green. We'll follow you always and anywhere."

After the speeches, the chaplain offered a final benediction for the dead, asking God to grant their souls passage into paradise.

Following the benediction came the most emotionally difficult part of any military memorial, the Last Roll Call. Standing at rigid attention, a lone sergeant called out the names of each fallen man's unit. One by one, the living answered, "Here, Sergeant" when he called their name. Finally, with tragic inevitability, the sergeant called out the one name that would bring no response. "Lieutenant Smith!" Silence. "Lieutenant Smith!" Silence. "Lieutenant Smith!" Silence. With each silence, sorrow compounded the unbearable loss and grief, as if all in the audience wished, by some impossible miracle, that the fallen would rise from the dead and answer the call.

The profound unending silence was shattered by gunfire.

(In a hushed tone only heard by the firing detail): "Ready! Aim! Fire!"

Bang!

I jumped; the first bang always causes me to jump.

"Ready! Aim! Fire!"

Bang!

"Ready! Aim! Fire!"

Bang!

Silence. The metallic clicks of weapons being cleared, magazines being unloaded, and weapons returning to shouldered arm.

The starkest, most melancholic beauty of all: "Taps" played by a lone bugler.

"Day is done.
Gone the sun.
From the lakes,
From the hills,
From the sky.
All is well.
Safely rest.
God is nigh."

The words of "Taps" always ring in mournful reverie in my mind with each playing.

One by one, in groups of four, every man assembled passed in front of each memorial erected for the fallen: a rifle with bayonet standing alone, its muzzle pointed to the ground, a helmet atop the butt stock. Group by group, we marched up to each memorial; presented a long, drawn, slow salute; and got down on our knees. Removing our hats, we bowed in silent prayer, asking God to grant our brothers eternal peace and to comfort their families' unquenchable grief. Many removed their name tags or rank and placed it upon the box that held the weapon erect. At the first lieutenant's memorial, someone had left a captain's rank as a sign that in death he had achieved a rank long sought and deserved in life. Our prayers complete, silently each group stood and offered one final, slow, relentlessly sorrowful salute to our lost brothers. In military precision, each group performed a right face, marched the short steps to the next memorial, and repeated the final salute good-bye.

At each memorial, I offered up this silent prayer: "The Lord is your shepherd. He has led you through the valley of the shadow of death. Thou shall no more fear evil. Go with God. May he grant you eternal rest. Good-bye, my fallen brother."

Walking away, I realized that Memorial Day will forever hold new meaning for me. If nothing else, it is our sacred duty to remember these men, these patriots, each May when America is in full bloom with new life, for it is upon their sacrifice that our liberty stands, that our freedoms are anchored. Our debt of gratitude can never be repaid. That is why it is so important that on this day, we take time to remember those who gave us so much while asking nothing in return.

Today, Memorial Day, I give thanks and pay my respect to the men and women who gave their lives so that we all may live free. Sadly, there are three more men that we now must add to this most honored of lists, three men whom we are duty-bound never to forget.

12

Highs and Lows

Tuesday, May 27, 2008

Today I returned to real missions with my old team, Team Two. In my new role as head intelligence officer for our FOB, I perform a myriad of tasks: I mentor the Ghazni Provincial Intelligence Officer, I coordinate reporting from a plethora of assets, and I serve in various roles in our TOC, my favorite being senior collector. As a collector, I get to go out with each of our teams and "do my thing." Basically, while the teams mentor and train the Afghan National Police, I sit down with many different Afghans (regular police officers, soldiers, citizens, leaders, mullahs, village elders, children, etc.), drink chai, and talk. During these talks, I eventually acquire key information. Moreover, through these talks, I've learned abundantly about Afghan culture and significantly improved my Dari and Pashto.

This mission was particularly important to me for several reasons. First, ever since acquiring this new job, I'd had to fight to get outside the wire. I felt that if I did a great job on this mission, I'd prove my worth, word would get out that I am an asset, and I'd no longer have to fight to get out on missions. As we rolled out the gate and headed for Andar, I wondered if this would be my last real combat mission. Anxiety briefly tried to overwhelm my senses, but I channeled it into something positive, something I could control: determination to silence my critics.

I'm the sole intelligence guy on a FOB of infantrymen. I liken the relationship to being the kicker in football: Sometimes the game falls completely on my

Siddiq and I standing in front of the FOB Vulcan memorial wall.

shoulders, and depending on the way the ball goes, I'm either the hero or the scourge. This mission was literally my make-or-break moment.

Our mission was in the Andar district, where the subgovernor was holding his weekly security meeting with his staff and their U.S. mentors. My task during the meeting was simple: Observe, stay silent, stay out of the way, "be a fly on the wall." I feel as if I performed to perfection. Each time I do such a mission, I am astounded by how much one can learn about people just by watching their reactions, movements, breaths, eyes, and persona. I think I took a bold step forward in proving my worth. Indeed, it was far easier to remain the anonymous lieutenant when I was a member of Team Two. Now that I'm on the Provincial Team, I must acquire the permission of each team chief before I can roll with his respective team.

Wednesday, May 28, 2008

Sometimes war is a lot of waiting around for something to happen. I woke up, showered, walked into the TOC, and found chaos on the radio. Far away, on one of Afghanistan's endless mountain chains, a unit had hit an IED. Frantically, their leader was pleading for a medevac helicopter to hurry to their position: "I've got two urgent and three routine patients!" Translation: I've got two guys who will die in the next two hours if they don't get to a hospital and three guys whose injuries aren't life threatening. The fear in his voice was haunting. Helpless, terrified, his tone reflected a man in the extreme throes of desperation. He was doing all he could to make the impossible possible. Five minutes after his first desperate call came a mournful announcement: "Be advised, our patient status has changed, we are now one KIA [killed in action], one urgent, and three routine." Just like that, everyone with a radio in our AO had heard a man die. A brother lost to a cowardly device upon an unimportant piece of terrain, and a leader who tried in vain to do all he could to stave off the inevitable. His sadness traveled at the speed of heartbreak throughout our AO, rendering all who had heard his plea into profound silent reflection.

And then, just as quickly as it started, it was over. The remainder of the day, I felt as if I were only going through the motions, as if I am most alive only when my adrenaline flows.

13

The Andar Shura

Saturday, May 31, 2008

The Andar Shura. Judgment Day. My one and only real chance to prove my worth.

While during many rides to Andar, I sit in nervous purgatory, awaiting the inevitable IED or fire fight that'll ruin our day, this ride I sat in supreme confidence. Athletes talk about going into a game knowing something is different, that they're about to display a record-breaking performance, a feat of unbelievable skill and strength. My experience was no different. I was on my game. Michael Jordan in the finals, Babe Ruth at bat, I was in the zone of perfection.

We drove up to the Shura to find the subgovernor absent (President Karzai allegedly summoned him to Kabul). A sea of bearded, serious-looking men sat around the district center's courtyard. As we entered, their eyes locked onto us like lions moving in for the kill, piercing glares of disgust, trepidation, contempt, and confusion slicing through our useless body armor.

While the subgovernor had called the Shura, the Taliban had done everything in their power to ensure no elder attended, going as far as to kill two men in a neighboring village as a warning not to attend. Yet, despite the threat, more than 200 elders came. What we didn't know at the time, however, was that they were not there to discuss Andar's impending reconstruction. Rather, they came to formally complain about a recent raid on their village.

Eating a meal at the Andar district center with Afghan Police officials from the Ministry of the Interior. Clockwise from the left: Palmer, Alderson, three of the police officials, Farid, Morriarty, a police official, and Janis.

Leaving Captain Morriarty and his entourage to deal with the mess, Janis and I secluded ourselves in a side office and went to work. We met with numerous sources and solicited prodigious amounts of key information. The highlight of the day came when I met with Mamour, the elder of Mash village.

As Mamour walked into the room, I stood out of reverence, placed my right hand over my heart, and greeted him with the most respectful greeting I could muster in my limited Dari. His eyes bore into my soul, deeply suspicious of this infidel before him, and for the first time I felt like an unwanted invader. He walked into the room in disgust at best, but I vowed he'd walk out in neutrality at the least.

I offered him the common pleasantries, inquiring about his health, his family's well-being, his livelihood, and his good fortunes. Normally Afghans return these things in kind, if for no other reason than out of social habit. This man answered my questions and then sat and stared at me, his eyes challenging me.

Mustering all my skills and strength, I took a breath and was about to begin explaining why I had asked him to join us when he said (in Pashto), "I've spoken with hundreds of Americans who've filled thousands of notebooks full of empty promises and meaningless notes. Why should I think you are going to be any different?"

For the next hour, we had an impassioned debate as to how to best help Andar. He complained that the government didn't care for him and his people and that what they most needed was security right then and there. At first, all my attempts to get him to understand that security was coming failed. I sat there listening to him lecture me on how Andar needed a hospital, needed for the dam to come back on line, needed this and needed that. His vision of assistance rested on huge gigantic leaps forward, leaps that, although possible, could cause the government and coalition forces to lose whatever respect they engendered. Our vision is the exact opposite: baby steps. With each small victory, we build that much more trust. Each new school, each new well strengthens our relationships with the locals. When we deliver on promises, we win credibility and respect. When we fail, we lose the war.

I tried to explain to the man that security was coming but that we needed his people's help; we needed them to cooperate with government forces, to alleviate their fear of the Taliban, and to stand up for themselves against our common enemy. My pleas fell on deaf ears. Recognizing that my approach was failing miserably, it hit me: I needed to approach this from the perspective of an Afghan.

"Look. You're right. You've heard a lot of different Americans promise different things. But, I'm not those Americans. I'm different. I can't promise you that things will dramatically improve, but I can promise that with your cooperation and help, we'll try our best. I also realize that you and I both know that I'll leave this place in a matter of months, and you'll still be here. I realize this makes you highly skeptical about anything I have to say. But, if you'll hear me out and consider what I have to say, then that's all I can ask."

For the first time in our conversation, he looked keenly interested in what I had to say. I knew I had one chance to reach him, and that left me with my trump card: I invoked Islam.

"To you, America appears an all-powerful country. But, many years ago, this was not the case. We too once faced a tyranny that scared many into silent acceptance, just as the Taliban have done to you. But, we chose to stand up, to fight, to change things for ourselves. I'm asking you to bravely make that same choice. I know it won't be easy. But, let me ask you this, when the Prophet Mohammad, praise be unto his name, first heard the words of God spoken through the Angel Jabriel [Gabriel], was he not at first afraid? Yes, he was, but he made a choice to overcome his fear and listen. Then, when God commanded him to spread the word of the Holy Koran, he faced another choice. Many people would not listen. His enemies tried to kill him for doing God's will. He could have chosen to stop. He could have chosen to take the easier path and resist his calling. But he didn't. He *chose* to spread God's word. And despite the most impossible of odds, he succeeded, all because he *chose* to act. You face a similar choice. You can continue to fear the Taliban and let them rule over you with oppression, or you can choose to stand up and fight with your govern-ment. You want security, I get that. But while Afghanistan is a proud nation of honorable people, its government and security forces are like an infant. You have a choice. You can help this infant to grow, to become a man, or you can remain silent, and, who knows, maybe that infant will die at the hands of oppressive men. The choice is yours. All I can do is ask you for your help and meet whatever requests for aid you ask."

Janis stared at me. At first I feared I had made a *big* mistake in referring to the Koran and Mohammad. But then, Janis smiled in a way I've never seen before and passionately translated my words to the old man, who sat nodding in agreement but hesitant suspicion. Mulling over my words, he stared deep into my eyes, into my soul.

[Nodding] "Yes, I agree. But the fact remains, we still need security. I have told you all that I need. We shall see if you deliver." He spoke these words as if to say, "You've got one chance. I'm betting you'll never deliver on anything we need; I dare you to prove me wrong."

Of all the things he asked for, one is actually immediately feasible: fertilizer. Tomorrow's mission, I'm headed over to the Ghazni Provincial Reconstruction Center to find out how I can get several tons of fertilizer to Mash village, to an elder named Mamour—the first of many baby steps.

That night, as I recalled to Captain Morriarty what I had learned from my conversations, he sat in shock. When I finished, he exclaimed, "This is great! As far as I'm concerned, you're coming with me as often as you can." He'd later repeat the same praises to our entire FOB leadership. For the first time in two weeks, I felt vindicated; I had proven my worth.

14

Humanitarian Assistance

Sunday, June 1, 2008

In the afternoon, I went over to FOB Ghazni to discuss counterinsurgency strategy with a few other units. While there, I lobbied for simultaneous kinetic operations and humanitarian assistance missions. The thinking is as follows: You reward villages that cooperate with HA and punish those that assist our enemies with raids, detentions, and other kinetic operations. Hopefully word spreads, and because people prefer HA to scary soldiers bursting into their homes in the middle of the night, more and more villages agree to cooperate with the government.

A few days earlier, Captain Morriarty advised me to focus on small victories. I want to take over all HA ops from Doc Jones, but I know I can't just come out and do that; he'll push back and likely win. Doc Jones is scheduled to go on leave starting tomorrow. At our nightly meeting, he indicated he needed someone to manage his responsibilities while he's gone. I instantly volunteered for the duty. After the meeting, he begrudgingly handed over his set of keys—success! Internalizing my joy, I patiently listened as he "lectured" me about what would happen if I were "too liberal" with the HA. My goal is to empty the connexes of HA at least twice while he's gone and to do such a good job that our higher commanders request I continue to run the HA ops until we leave country.

Walking away from Doc Jones, I was all smiles. Janis approached me, and I happily informed him that from that point forward, if he ever needed HA, I would make sure it got handed out. As I walked away, Janis asked if he were accompanying me to

Handing out humanitarian assistance to villagers in Khogiani district, Ghazni province.

Kabul tomorrow morning. When I said I was going alone, he responded, "No. This cannot be. If you go, I go. You are my brother." His sentiments moved me beyond words. He knows the risks of going outside the wire. He knew that I was just going to Kabul to run a quick errand and that I didn't require my interpreter, and yet he insisted that from now on I never leave without him.

15

Blowing Off Steam

Afghanistan has morphed into a desolate desert landscape—barren, dry, and oppressively hot. The blinding, scorching sun sits high upon its throne in the sky, casting short squat shadows, baking the earth, robbing the people of essential food. Night comes like a welcomed guest, cooling the land, inviting people to venture outdoors and to bask in evening's gentle breezes. Afghanistan strikes me as a country in precipitous balance, a nation that spends the majority of its days in torrid summer and frigid winter, kept alive only by a fleeting spring and frail fall.

Saturday, June 7, 2008

I joined Janis in the evening for our nightly cup of chai. Over piping hot brew and delicious compressed milk Afghan candy, Janis shared his story. Born a Pashtun, his family fled Afghanistan's violence for Pakistan in the early 1990s. After the fall of the Taliban, they returned to help rebuild their cherished homeland. Janis, armed with a high school degree and a working knowledge of English, spent many days searching for work but found only odd jobs, mostly involving manual labor. Then the unthinkable happened: His sister, mother to six children, only 23 years old, fell ill with cancer. Medicine is both scarce and expensive here in Afghanistan and can often drain a family of whatever little savings they possess. Being the eldest son, with his father retired, Janis stepped dutifully into the role of sole breadwinner for both his and his sister's families (he describes his sister's husband as lazy and incapable of helping her financially). Ignoring the dangers to himself and his

Janis and I entertaining ourselves while trying to stay awake for a 4:00 a.m. ride from Camp Phoenix to FOB Vulcan.

family, Janis took a position as a U.S. Army interpreter: "I purposely asked for the toughest assignments, the most dangerous missions, because I knew this would bring in the most money, money I could use to buy my sister medicine and health care." Despite a valiant struggle, the cancer won, leaving Janis with six children and a lifetime's worth of responsibility.

The threats to an interpreter in Afghanistan are ever present, lurking like evil shadows. They are the worst armed (technically, they are forbidden from carrying weapons) and least protected (lacking body armor) participants in the war. Should the Taliban capture them, they are guaranteed slow, agonizing, brutal deaths. Often, the Taliban targets their families (with beatings, robberies, displacement, or killings) as a means of forcing them to quit. Janis recalled how the Taliban captured an interpreter last year on his way home to Kabul (each terp gets about a week's worth of leave every month). The Taliban castrated, beheaded, and disemboweled him, sending the pieces to his family and to his base's fellow interpreters as an example of what happens to "collaborators." Janis said they had found him by riding the taxis and buses that offer transport between Kabul and the numerous bases and cities dotting Afghanistan. I asked him if he had ever been almost caught. He replied, "Yes! This past time when I was coming back to Ghazni, the Taliban were riding on the bus questioning everyone. They asked me what I was doing going to Ghazni. I told them I am a student here and that I was returning for school. Had they caught me, they would have pulled me off the bus and cut my head off." I vowed from this point forward our terps would only go on leave if we could personally drive them to and from Kabul or fly them using the resupply flights that occur every few days.[1]

---

1 To read more about life as a terp, go to http://bit.ly/Idps9H.

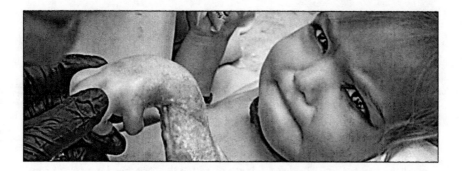

16

Shatara

Wednesday, June 11, 2008

"How would you like to save the country of Afghanistan one child at a time?" asked Captain Morriarty. Curious, I replied, "I'd love to; what can I do to help?" Captain Morriarty explained that he and his team had paid an unannounced visit to the Andar Medical Clinic. While touring the facility, they came across a 16-month-old girl named Shatara, who had fallen into a fire, leaving her with third-degree burns over half her body. Whoever had treated her had done such a poor job that her left arm had become horrifically infected. Sepsis had set in. Without immediate care, she was likely to die of massive infection within a matter of days.

For all the war, all the danger, all the sacrifices, this is why I love this job. This is what we're here to do: help the people. These are the missions I crave.

I sprang into action. "Ghazni TOC, Ghazni TOC, this is Law Dog TOC. My team in Andar has come across a 16-month-old girl with third-degree burns on nearly half her body. The medic on the ground says that if she doesn't get immediate treatment, she'll die. Team is going to immediately ground-medevac the girl to the Ghazni PRT, how copy?" I said over the radio.

"Roger, Law Dog TOC, I copy your Andar team bringing in a young girl with third-degree burns, stand by. . . . Law Dog TOC, be advised, we've launched a bird [medevac helicopter]. Bird will be on scene in approximately 10 mikes. How copy?"

Shatara (her name means "Star" in Dari) with second- and third-degree burns from falling into a bread-baking furnace.

They *never* launch a bird, unless it's for American or NATO forces. Ecstatic, I called Captain Morriarty and related the unbelievable. Thirty minutes later, I came crashing back to reality.

"Law Dog TOC, Law Dog TOC, this is Ghazni TOC [the 101st], be advised, our medic on the ground has seen the little girl and reported that her injuries are not life-threatening. No need to medevac at this time, how copy?"

Confused, I immediately called Captain Morriarty. "Sir, Ghazni TOC says they're not medevac'ing the girl by helicopter?"

"Yeah they just told me, Lieutenant. So what we're gonna do is medevac her by ground convoy to the PRT. Please call ahead and make sure they know we're coming. We're leaving time now."

I called Ghazni TOC to update them. "Ghazni TOC, this is Law Dog TOC, be advised at this time my team is ground medevac'ing the girl to the Ghazni PRT. Team requests medic be on scene at gate to take delivery of the patient and her father. Team should be arriving in the next 30 mikes, how copy?"

"Law Dog TOC, negative, you are to ground medevac the girl to Ghazni hospital. Do not bring her to the PRT."

At this point it's time I introduce a new villain into my story, Major Smith (name changed to protect the guilty), chief doctor of FOB Ghazni and one royal asshole.

After our April firefight in Waghez, our injured (those knocked out) had gone over to the PRT for medical examination. Upon reaching TMC (The Medical Center), Major Smith (the head doctor) instructed our wounded, several of whom were suffering severe concussions, to return the next day during "sick-call" hours. First rule of medical care: *Never* turn away a patient, especially when you're sitting on your ass with nothing to do (as he had been when our guys showed up for treatment). Suffice to say, Major Smith earned himself a FOB's worth of enemies when he turned our injured away.

Major Smith was so callous, so heartless as to turn away an injured little girl. I had to act; everyone was counting on me. There are moments in one's military career where you take matters into your hands, defining moments where you choose to do what's right by breaking the rules. Should you get caught, the punishments can be quite severe. For me, this was such a moment.

I picked up my cell phone and dialed the Ghazni TOC.

"This is Lieutenant Zeller over at FOB Vulcan. We just informed you that one of our teams is inbound with a patient and her father. You came back and said we were to go to Ghazni hospital. I just wanted to let you know that the girl has already been to Ghazni hospital. The doctors there told her parents they couldn't treat her and to seek out Americans." The truth: This entire story was a lie—the girl and her parents had never been to the hospital. I made the whole thing up in a desperate attempt to get FOB Ghazni to treat the little girl.

"Our doctor says the medic on the ground examined her and that her injuries aren't life-threatening. Also, we don't have a pediatric-care center here; she'll get better care at Ghazni hospital. You have your orders, do *not* bring her here." Click.

Speechless, fuming, ready to end my career by killing a superior officer, I stood in silent rage. There was nothing I could do.

"Law Dog 2-6, this is Law Dog TOC. Be advised, FOB Ghazni says it will refuse to accept your patient. They are ordering you to Ghazni hospital."

"You're kidding me! Don't they realize we're just down the road from them right now? We've already passed the hospital."

I called Ghazni TOC once again.

"Hey, Lieutenant Zeller again. Listen, our guys are basically at your gate, they've already passed the hospital."

"You have your orders, take her to Ghazni hospital." Click.

"Law Dog 2-6, this is Law Dog TOC. FOB Ghazni is adamant. They're refusing to accept your patient. You must continue to the Ghazni hospital." I felt like the world's biggest failure as I relayed this order.

"Roger. Do you know where the hospital is exactly?" asked Captain Morriarty over the radio.

"No, but I'm looking now. Stand by," I replied.

"Never mind, we'll do it ourselves, just like everything else," came Captain Morriarty's curt reply.

I turned to Captain Norris, who had just returned from FOB Ghazni, to vent my frustration and to update him on the situation. "Sir, FOB Ghazni turned our guys away! Can you believe that?"

"I saw pictures of the little girl. Her injuries weren't that bad. Doc Caswell grossly exaggerated the extent of her burns."

"Sir, I was an ambulance medic for three years. When my medic here tells me that the skin on her arm erupted with pus when they removed the bandages, that her skin is burnt black in places, that tells me her injuries *are* that bad!"

"Lieutenant, you don't know what you're talking about. I saw the pictures. You didn't. She'll be fine."

Two hours later, Team Two returned, fuming with palpable anger. As I walked up to Captain Morriarty, Doc Caswell came storming by: "Sir, I swear to God, I'm gonna fucking kill someone. I cannot believe what just happened."

At dinner, Doc Caswell, Jim (a DynCorp, the company contracted to physically train the Afghan National Police in police work, member of Team Two), and First Lieutenant Palmer regaled me with their day's experiences. The clinic was full of Taliban. The father took a *huge* risk by bringing his little girl to us.

The team had dropped off the girl, leaving her with doctors who promised to do all they could, but who also admitted there was little they could do, as their hospital lacked many antibiotics and the equipment to treat burns—so much for a "better level of care than we [FOB Ghazni] can provide."

As the team left, they promised the father they'd check up the next day to ensure the family had been transported by ambulance to Kabul (where there is a burn unit). Walking past the father, each member of the team reached into their wallets and handed over all the cash they had on hand, a little over $150, more than he'd earn in almost half a year.

The team then drove back to FOB Ghazni to refuel their vehicles and to stop by the Special Forces compound. Captain Morriarty, being ex–Special Forces, figured he could pull a favor and get the SF medics (the best in the business) to look at the little girl, the next best thing to American-level care at FOB Ghazni.

As the team passed through FOB Ghazni's gate, they encountered a crowd of medics. "Where's the little girl?" one exclaimed.

"We were told not to bring her here!" yelled a furious Captain Morriarty.

"No one bothered to tell us!"

The missed opportunity sent tempers skyrocketing; had they gotten her on the FOB, no one, not even the asshole Major Smith, could have turned her away.

I ground my fist into my thigh.

"Can I borrow your camera, Jim?"

"Sure, what do you need it for?"

"I'm going to prove to Captain Norris just how badly she was injured."

Storming into the TOC, I sat at my computer and uploaded the photos from Jim's camera. "Hey sir, can you come take a look at this?" I said to Captain Norris.

"Sure, what's up? I . . . uh . . . wow, okay, I did not see that picture. Yeah, those injuries look pretty bad."

"See that charred flesh that takes up the entire left half of her torso? That's a massive third-degree burn. You see that blistering around the burn? That's a rather large second-degree burn. And that pink around the second-degree burn—that's a first degree. She needed our help. She needed our care, and we failed."

"Well the report they got at FOB Ghazni was that the burns were weeks old, basically healed, and not life-threatening," Captain Norris forcefully replied.

"Sir, the burns alone are life-threatening. More importantly, the infection in her arm? That's what'll likely kill her."

"Yeah, well, Ghazni hospital has antibiotics. These people have got to start taking care of themselves. We can't save everyone and do *everything* for them!"

Major Garrison, not one to miss an argument or an opportunity to share his two cents, sauntered into the room. "Norris is right, Matt, these people have got to start doing things for themselves. Otherwise we're gonna be here for the next 20 years!"

The dam of my emotions burst. "Gentlemen! Don't you two or, for that matter, the idiots over at FOB Ghazni understand the principles of counterinsurgency? Today we had a *perfect* opportunity to win over a heart and mind, and we royally screwed that up! Had we been able to get his little girl the necessary care, had we delivered on our promises, word would have spread that the Americans really *do* care. Instead, we made ourselves look totally incompetent. Moreover, it's not just our duty, but our moral obligation to help those in need, *especially* when someone seeks *us* out, which is exactly what happened today."

"Matt, you're too emotionally involved. You aren't thinking clearly," said Major Garrison in his most parental and scolding tone.

"Sir, it is our responsibility, our duty, our moral obligation to do something. It's what makes us different from our enemies. *We give a damn!* Team Two and I seem to be the only ones with any moral clarity. There's a war on out there. People get killed for using government services like a hospital! No life is more valuable than others; this 'Americans first and only' attitude *has* to stop, or we're going to lose this thing!" I shouted.

The argument crashed to an abrupt silence.

"Christ, now I have a headache," an emotionally exhausted Major Garrison sighed.

He continued, "You're right, we can do better. The doctor at FOB Ghazni screwed up. I'll take it up with the 101st commander."

People wonder why the Taliban are resurgent; the more we fail on our promises, the more we let our selfish and thrifty attitude guide our actions, the more it hurts our overall efforts, prolonging the war and our stay. Had we made good on our promise to get her to an American doctor, word of our good will would have spread like wildfire. Now, our actions are just another blatant example of another broken American promise, just another American lie.

And yes, I lost my military bearing. I got emotional. Do I regret it? Not at all. If anything I do helps change the way we treat these people . . . well that's worth all the aggravation in the world. My only regret: I didn't get to yell all this to Major Smith.

A grad school mentor of mine, General Montgomery Meigs, once told me, "If you do what's right, you'll sleep at night." Profound wisdom.

Thursday, June 12, 2008

Team Two visited the little girl in the hospital. She hasn't been treated at all. There are no plans to move her to Kabul, as the doctors originally promised. Her situation remains critical.

17

Hospital of Death

Friday, June 13, 2008

I volunteered to do our team's assessment of Ghazni hospital, which gave me the opportunity to check up on Shatara. I spent several years in high school serving as a volunteer ambulance medic. I've seen people die, horrific gunshot wounds where blood literally pours out, and massive trauma, but nothing in my life could have prepared me for the misery and deplorable conditions I witnessed today. Ghazni hospital redefines poverty, sorrow, and pure unadulterated optimism. Despite a complete lack of antibiotics, massive blood shortages, decades-old medical equipment, and intermittent (at best) electricity, the hospital staff struck me as some of the most cheerful and positive people I've ever met.

Seated beneath two shade trees, basking in a pleasant morning light, Ghazni hospital is a decades-old building that at first glance appears quite new due to fresh paint. I expected to smell the familiar stench of rotting flesh, death, and disease, as I entered the building. Instead, the atmosphere reminded me of an old parlor or the crypt of a medieval church. The air was stale, the lighting dim, and eerie silence crept throughout the seemingly empty halls.

Passing by people squatting on surprisingly clean floors, their eyes staring at us with the routine piercing suspicious glare, we made our way up to the second floor: the children's wing. A crowd of elderly men sat in front of the double doors that separated the children's wing from the rest of the hospital. Mothers typically care for

The Ghazni hospital. Note the burn marks above most windows—they come from coal and wood fires used to heat individual rooms in the winter.

their children in lieu of nurses in Afghan medical facilities. Best guess was that these men were relatives of patients, who chose to remain out of the children's wing, for fear of encountering a female to whom they were not related. Brushing by the men, ignoring every cultural norm, we pushed through the double doors and proceeded down a very dark hallway, stopping at the last door on our right. I then realized that the hospital must keep the lights off during the day to conserve precious power.

Approaching the door, I heard the horrific cry of a child in pain, that piercing wail that screams agony, vulnerability, and helplessness. Peering into a crowded room reeking of feces, I saw a burka-clad woman gently lift a naked baby girl into a large bowl that served as a bathtub (and likely cooking pot and laundry). Her eyes squinting from tears, her cries pleading for a better life, our little patient struggled in her mother's arms as water gently caressed her horrifically burned body. Her torso looked like one gigantic scar; a wrinkled mass of putrid, infected flesh, ringed in bright pink. Pus dripped from holes in her bandaged left arm, revealing pieces of charred, gray-black flesh.

I turned away.

It's just not fair. This poor little girl, not yet two years old, was already deeply damaged. Without medical treatment, she'd likely die a slow, painful death. At best, with treatment, in this society, her scars will guarantee her a lifetime of ridicule and scorn, as no man will likely ever marry her. And the pain, the unbearable pain, she must feel. The Special Forces medics who came with us instructed our interpreters to let the mother know they were going to do all they could to save her little girl, now our little girl.

I turned one last time to see the medic cradling this vulnerable child in his arms. The juxtaposition was striking: Here stood a man capable of so much violence, one of America's elite killers, and yet at that moment, his tenderness radiated throughout the room. As gentle as an angel, he went to work, determined to ease her suffering and to heal her wounds.

With nothing more to do, I turned away and headed back down the hallway toward the central staircase. My mission was clear: I needed to learn as much as I could about this hospital and do whatever it took to ensure the level of care provided rose above the absolute bottom.

Back on the first floor, I bumped into a doctor, who directed me to wait outside the recovery room while he fetched the hospital's chief surgeon. Seconds later, a spry man bounded toward me: "It is *so* nice to meet you. My name is Doctor Mohammad, and I am the chief surgeon of the hospital. We are so glad you have come to visit us."

"Doctor, my name is Lieutenant Zeller, and it's our pleasure to be here. I'm with the Provincial Police Mentor team, and one of our responsibilities is to visit key infrastructure sites throughout Ghazni and assess their needs and capabilities. I hope you don't mind if we look around your facility. Also, we've brought some of our medics to operate on the little girl with burns upstairs."

"Wonderful, this is simply wonderful! We are so glad you are here. Unfortunately, today is Friday, Jumna, our Holy Day, our day of rest, and as such, most of the staff, including the hospital administrator, are home with their families."

"Can we still have a tour of the hospital?"

"Sure! Of course! If you follow me, we can start with the recovery room."

Stale air poured out of the recovery room as we entered through two aging double doors. Fighting my urge to cover my nose and mouth at the awful stench, I confidently strode forward, hoping my confident strides would mask my revulsion. Patients lay quietly, futilely defending themselves from hordes of flies. Women scurried to cover themselves, lest one of the "infidels" see their wrinkled, tattooed faces. Dr. Mohammad led me around from bed to bed, describing the extent of each patient's ailment and the treatment he or she had received. I stopped at the bed of a little boy no older than eight, his arms held vertically in crumbling plaster casts (Afghan traction). The room lacked life monitors, IVs, saline solution, or even a mosquito net to keep insects away, yet the boy smiled as I took his picture, likely the first of his entire life. I gently leaned down to the brave child and whispered in hushed tones, "Don't worry, it'll be okay, you're going to be fine." Though we were separated by a gulf of language and culture, the message found a way to cross the void as he smiled and flashed me a thumbs up.

Dr. Mohammad led our entourage through a series of rooms in the "male wing" of the hospital, stopping at each room to explain every patient's condition and treatment regimen. Each room was a repeat of the last: an Afghan soldier shot in the leg, a policeman shot in the torso, a child who had fallen from a great height (breaking both his legs), an elderly man suffering from dysentery. At one point we stopped at the bed of a man who had just had his appendix removed the day before. Smiling, I lifted up my shirt to reveal my own appendectomy scar. "Don't worry buddy, it gets better. The worst is over." As I pointed to my scar, he grinned, flashing rotting yellow teeth.

"Hey, Matt, you better come see this," one of our DynCorp police trainers, Jim, said.

Nothing could have prepared me for what I saw next. I entered the sparse corner room to find a small boy, no older than eight, covered in a mosquito net, with a catheter protruding out of his left side, emptying into a makeshift colostomy bag. A large soiled bandage covered his lower left abdomen. "Kid's father says Americans shot his son and killed his wife approximately 20 days ago," Jim exhaled. His words were like a gut punch and rendered me speechless. I couldn't breathe. I didn't want to believe the news: "Jim, find out everything you can about what happened and get back to me. Let's make sure we do whatever we can to right this."

Doctor Mohammad led us next to the hospital's blood bank, a closetlike room filled with ancient hand-me-down medical equipment and a refrigerator with shelves organized by blood type. I noted aloud that the hospital was dangerously low (one pint) on supplies of O-negative. At this point the hospital administrator joined us: "Yes, yes, we have a very bad problem with stocking our blood. Many times, the doctors, including myself, come here to give our own blood in order to strengthen our supply." Although the hospital's destitute nature saddened me, I was relieved to have a task that took my attention away from the injured little boy.

As we walked out of the blood bank, Jim ran up: "Matt, we're gonna need pictures of this kid. The father's story sounds awfully credible, and what really makes me believe him is that he has yet to ask for anything from us."

I returned with Jim to take pictures of the boy's injuries. I held up the camera and asked the boy's father in broken Dari for permission to photograph his son. He stood there, his gaze pleading with us, his sworn enemies, to save his little boy.

"Where are the doctors or nurses? Why aren't they here checking up on you?" I asked the father through our interpreter. "The hospital staff does not care about us," the man replied.

The man then leaned over his son's frail body and removed the bandages. We gagged. The boy looked as if something had bitten a large chunk of flesh out of his back. The bullet had torn through his body, shredding organs as it went, and exited with explosive force out his back, leaving a four-inch-round wound filled with pus. As I snapped several photos, I was glad I had visual proof I could use as evidence in any future run-in with Major Smith and his minions who claim Ghazni hospital provides adequate levels of care. I turned to the father and stuck out my hand. Shaking it, I offered my deepest apologies and promised we'd get to the bottom of what happened. As we left the room, our interpreter told us the father's story:

Twenty days prior, the boy, his father, and his mother had been out at night, walking back home, when they saw strange lights accompanied by a loud noise in the sky. The object landed close by, further sparking the boy's curiosity. He ran toward the unfamiliar, excited to investigate. Shots rang out. The boy's mother ran to help her injured son. Shots rang out again. In a horrific 60 seconds, three lives were forever changed. In the weeks that followed, the father, a shell of his vibrant former self, had buried his wife and sold all his earthly possessions to pay for his son's operation and medicine. He had run out of money two days before we arrived at the hospital, leaving both without food or medicine.

After hearing this story, I reached into my wallet and pulled out all the money I had (sadly only $5) and handed it to our terp: "Give this to the father, and let him know we're gonna do all we can. I am so sorry this happened."

Jim and I walked down the suddenly very long hallway corridor, back toward Doctor Mohammad and the hospital administrator. "Jim, I cannot believe this happened."

"I can. Sounds like a night raid done by special ops. If I had to guess, the family saw a helicopter coming in to drop off the soldiers for a night raid. Having never seen a helicopter before, the boy didn't know he shouldn't approach it. He probably ran right at the security perimeter. He probably was carrying a stick, which at night, through the scopes, looks an awful lot like a rifle or RPG. Thinking they were about to get attacked, the guys on the perimeter shot first. Sad to say but it happens all the time. What we need to do now is make sure we do all we can to ease their suffering."

We rejoined Doctor Mohammad and the hospital administrator and headed to the hospital lab, which, like the rest of the facility, was stocked with ancient medical equipment. I mentally noted that the lab reeked of cigarette smoke and had windows covered with torn screens.

"Doctor, do you have an isolation ward?"

"Sadly, we do not."

"Well what do you do with people who have TB?"

"If we suspect a patient has TB, we bring them to that room [pointing to a corner down the hall] and run tests. If they are positive, we send them to the TB hospital on the other side of the city."

"Do you use this room for anything else?"

"Yes. It is used as an additional recovery room and also serves as our intensive care facility."

I found the room surprisingly well equipped with some of the most modern medical equipment the hospital owned: a life-signs monitor, clean linens, and a locked drug cabinet next to an ancient EKG machine.

"Doctor, I've noticed this is the only room with medicine in it. Where do you keep your narcotics?"

"Our pharmacist keeps them in his office."

"May I see it?"

"Ah. That will be a problem, as today is Jumna, and thus he is off duty. He is the only one with the key."

I couldn't hide my shock any longer. "So what happens when you need to get drugs and he's away?"

"Well, this usually only happens on Jumna. . . ."

"Well, Doctor, what happens if, God forbid, you need to get drugs on Jumna?"

"The night before Jumna, we take out all the drugs we need for the next day."

"What happens if that isn't enough? Say you get a massive casualty situation, and you have more patients than drugs on hand—then what do you do?"

"Well, in that case, we call all the doctors back to the hospital, including the pharmacist."

At least they had a plan in place.

"We'll see the children's ward next."

We entered a large room with high concrete ceilings and walls of crumbling plaster. Women hurriedly shielded their faces with their brilliant-colored scarves and vibrant green and purple gowns. Trying to appear as unintimidating as possible, I slowly approached a child and her mother seated on a bed. Raising my camera, I tried my best to dissuade their unease by smiling as I hurriedly snapped several photos. Flies buzzed all around me, thriving in an environment rich with bacteria, filth, and disease.

"Next we'll see the infants' wing. Here we have an incubator for newborns," the hospital administrator proudly proclaimed, pointing to the (once again) ancient incubators. I leaned down to check the date on the equipment; it was a late 1970s model.

A large commotion erupted behind us. A woman, ignoring her loose burka and the view it afforded us, ran down the hallway, an entourage of family in tow, cradling an infant girl. The child's limbs flopped lifelessly in her arms, its eyes fixed, staring off into the unknown. It was clear to all but the mother that she was gone.

"Ah. They're taking her [the baby] to the assessment room. Hopefully we'll know her status shortly. This way to our malnutrition room," the hospital administrator (who had to know the girl was dead) said nonchalantly.

"What is the state of your malnutrition program, Doctor?" I asked, doing my best to steel myself for the inevitable shriek I expected to erupt at any moment from the frantic mother.

"Well, before Doctor Smith arrived, it was most successful. The former doctor, Doctor Williams—do you know him?" Afghans always ask if you know the previous American they worked with; I don't think they quite comprehend America's massive population.

"No, I don't."

"Ah, a pity, as Doctor Williams is a great man. He started this malnutrition program several months ago. He spent several days each week here training our staff, supplied us with extra medicine, and provided us with high-energy biscuits for the malnutrition program. Unfortunately he left, and Doctor Smith, his replacement, has been most unhelpful. He has stopped supporting the program, causing us to run out of high-energy biscuits. Can you help us get more?"

"We'll do our best to make sure you receive the support you need."

A woman's cry pierced the tranquil silence of the corridor. The doctors had just informed the mother that her baby girl had died. I turned to find Captain Morriarty still staring at the assessment room where the doctors had taken the child. He must have been thinking of his own young son, his imagination running wild with unthinkable scenarios.

"Next we will see the generators," the hospital administrator said even more nonchalantly than before, as if what had just transpired was so routine that it didn't warrant any attention.

Doctor Mohammad and the hospital administrator led us out to a beautiful courtyard filled with meticulously kept flower and tree gardens, a refuge of shade and tranquility in the midst of dust, disease, and death.

"We're passing the hospital's laundry facilities," Doctor Mohammad said, pointing to a well, a pot of water, and two clotheslines strung between two walls.

"Is all the hospital's laundry done out here?" I asked.

"Yes. We do our best to sterilize the linens, but lacking enough supplies, we often have to quickly reuse sheets," the hospital administer sighed—yet one more deficit he faces.

The hospital has three generators, two of which are broken. The third, which is also the least powerful, is kept running by an elderly mechanic who seemingly also lives in the generator shed. I made note of the parts the generators lacked, vowing, if nothing else, I'd get them back online.

The hospital administrator gave us a very brief tour of the addiction facility located in a walled-in compound behind the generator shack. Interestingly, he did not invite us to meet any of the addiction patients. Up until this point, he had been only too happy to show off every other patient in the hospital. Glancing back as we left the addiction compound, I caught a glimpse of what looked like cells carved into a mud-brick building, and I shuddered at the thought that addiction is treated in such a manner.

Our tour ended with a review of the emergency room. I observed happily that the ER was the best-equipped room in the entire hospital, with life-signs monitors, modern defibrillators, and the most sterile conditions in the entire hospital. Doctor Mohammad proudly posed for a picture in the middle of the room as the hospital administrator told me how the ER also serves as the operating room.

Our tour complete, we moved to the hospital administrator's office, which, by the looks of its tiled walls, had once been a bathroom or examination room. Speaking about the needs of the hospital, the administrator and Doctor Mohammad told me how they could not return home during the summer, as "the Taliban will kill us for working with the government." I was also shocked to learn that the hospital charges for all examinations, X-rays, and basic care. While the doctors claim the charges are miniscule, the amounts they quoted are more than most people here earn in one day.

"What happens when people can't pay?" I asked.

"In those cases, we perform the services for free," Dr. Mohammad replied.

Throughout this conversation, the gentlemen educated me about the inadequacy of Afghanistan's medical supply system. Ghazni hospital serves not only as the provincial hospital but also as the regional hospital (covering nine other provinces). The Afghan Ministry of Health supplies the hospital with equipment and medicine based on an arbitrary list that does not take projected number of patients, current patients, or current supplies into account. The list does not even begin to cover the hospital's basic needs, a situation made all too evident by the dreadful level of care I witnessed.

I had heard enough. It was time to leave. Standing, I bade the men farewell. They looked at me hopefully, as if they thought I had the power to answer their prayers.

As I exited the building, Jim approached me and updated me on the little girl with horrific burns.

"The SF medics did all they could, but at this point she needs a skin graft, a serious regimen of antibiotics, and an appointment with a plastic surgeon."

"Okay, how do we get all that?"

"Well, I'm not promising anything, but I think I've got a way to get her and her whole family to a burn center in the U.S. If it happens, the center will fly them over, do the procedures, and send them back here all free of charge. I'll know in a few days if it's a go for sure."

That night, I lay awake, tossing and turning with the gravity of the hospital's situation and my fear that our efforts would prove inadequate.[1]

---

1 June excerpts on the website include my work as Humanitarian Assistance Coordinator, my efforts to make sense out of the violence and chaos, an attack during our trip to Kabul, and equipment failures; see http://bit.ly/KjE9rX.

18

A Brother's Suicide

Saturday, July 5, 2008

Death, always an inevitable tragedy in war, manifests itself in unthinkable ways. Most people associate death during war with combat. But we seldom consider another pervasive killer: suicide.

Famished, I walked into the chow hall to grab a quick lunch. As I perused the meal's selections, Specialist Guzman ran into the room. "Hey, did any of you guys know First Lieutenant Foldes?"

"Yeah, he was on my team at Fort Riley. Why do you ask?" As the words fell out of my mouth, I could tell by the look on Guzman's face that something troubled him.

Guzman struggled to find the words: "He's dead."

My legs buckled. I slumped into a booth.

"He . . . he . . . he killed himself."

Guzman's words had shocked life back into me. Where before I was numb, I suddenly became acutely aware of everything around me.

First Lieutenant Clint Eastwood joined the conversation: "From what I understand, he did it in the chow hall at Camp Phoenix."

I couldn't handle the news. Each new revelation shocked me more than the last. He's dead. He committed suicide. He did it in a chow hall. The circumstances of his death were the antithesis of the man he was in life.

Shocked, I silently stood and trudged out of the chow hall.

For the next few hours, I walked around in a daze. I sought out Sergeant First Class Postman. Choking back tears, we recalled the amazing man we were privileged to have known: always positive, a perfect gentleman. His mantra at training: "Just remember, today's a great day to be a soldier!" He personified optimism, strength, and confidence. He was the one guy everyone could always count on. A physical fitness stud. Charming, reserved, dignified, and successful, he had had a brilliant career ahead of him in both the civilian and military worlds.

Suicide is a permanent solution to a temporary problem. I can't fathom why he did it. I wish to God I had been there in his final moments to do anything, everything, to stop him.

The night before we left Syracuse for Fort Riley, we stood in the middle of the hotel bar in uniform for a group photo. As the bartender took the photo, I remember thinking, "I wonder how many people around me will still be alive when this is all said and done?" If I only could have known.

Later that afternoon, I sought out Guzman in his bunk. Guzman and Foldes had been in the same unit back in New York. We talked about his life, his indomitable spirit, and his dedication to the cause. Guzman recalled how earlier in his army career, he (Guzman) had attempted to earn the German Armed Forces Proficiency Badge. To win the distinction, one must go through a grueling physical trial consisting of a swim, a 5km run, a 100m sprint, a shot put, a shooting range, a first-aid test, and a 30km march. All the events are either timed or must be completed to a certain standard (like hitting five out of five targets). Guzman had succeeded at all the events save one: the swim. When Foldes found out about Guzman's swimming struggles, he volunteered to teach him how to swim, on his own time. For several weeks, Guzman would head down to a swimming pool in Manhattan, where Foldes would personally coach him. Guzman found the process grueling, and even though he wanted to quit numerous times, Foldes never gave up on him. That's the kind of guy Foldes was: Even when you had lost faith in yourself, he kept his. He saw the best in people, and he endeavored to help all those around him maximize their potential.

As Guzman got up to go on mission, I left him with a final thought: "Guzman, you know what you've got to do now, don't you?"

"No, Sir, what's that?"

"You've got to go out and earn that German Armed Forces Proficiency Badge for Foldes. And, you've got to stay positive. You remember the man he was in life. You make your success become a part of his enduring legacy."

With a nod, Guzman signaled his agreement, turned, straightened his slumped shoulders, and headed out the door to continue with the mission, just as a soldier does, and just as Foldes would have done.

These past few weeks saw a dramatic ebb and flow in activity. Early July continued June's unfortunate trend of ever-more-daring and destructive fighting. Yet, by the middle of the month, attacks in our area of operations ceased without explanation. Before we had time to properly analyze our newfound quiet, intelligence threats directly against our base coincided with a renewed Taliban vigor. The war returned, the enemy was emboldened, our resolve was unwavering and firm, and fighting raged all around us.

I had quite the experience over the course of July's stiflingly dry, hot days. Captain Goodman had to go home on emergency leave, which sent Captain Norris (my immediate boss) to temporarily take over his team. In his absence, I absorbed his S3 (operations and planning) duties into my intelligence responsibilities. I spent my days firmly planted on our FOB, running our unit's operations as well as our intelligence activities. I ran our air-movement operations (helicopters), shuttling supplies and personnel to troops in the field. I made sure our soldiers going on and returning from rest and relaxation (R&R) leave had flights to and from our base as appropriate. I monitored both the ANP operations and intelligence activities as needed, meeting with a series of key Afghan officials on a daily basis.

19

Inside the Wire

A pitch black void. I sit up in my plywood bed, my mattress soft from the foam pad that cushions protruding springs. The hum of the air conditioner and the shadowed outline of my M4 focus my reality—still in Afghanistan, another night down, another day to go.

I rub my eyes, willing them to focus in the dark. 0800. I've only slept four hours, just enough to temporarily stave off my exhaustion. My body lurches to the right as I gracelessly drop off my bed. I reach for the uniform draped over the seldom-used metal desk chair. I smell the fabric: still no discernible stench, still good to wear. I smell myself: still no discernible stench, still good to go. I can't remember the last time I had a proper shower; between all the work and unforeseen crises, there simply isn't enough time.

Silently, alone with my thoughts, I put on my uniform, tie my boots, and strap my M9 holster around my right leg. Exiting my room, I take my antimalaria medicine and grab my sunglasses in preparation for the blinding Afghan sun; the transition from the barrack's eternal blackness to the scorching Afghan day can induce nightmarish headaches.

I wince in preparation for the blast of heat and intense light and open the door. I cross the threshold from Arctic to oven, a wakeup call better than any cold shower.

Walking into the chow hall, I grab a Diet Pepsi and water and make my way back to the TOC.

The mornings change, but the crises remain the same.

Such-and-such unit is under attack, so-and-so needs a helicopter ride to here or there, person A needs information B, ASAP, what's the status of location X or unit

The inside of our compound at FOB Ghazni during the beginning of a dust storm.

Z, did you hear about the explosion down south? Did you know that the Taliban attacked the base up north? Quick! Get the location up on imagery! We need to know what's going on!

I take breaks around mealtime; lunch and dinner bring a few minutes' respite. Inevitably, just as I'm making progress on problem C, someone from the ANP, ANA, or NDS shows up (two hours late) for a meeting.

I walk out. We shake hands; if we've known each other for some time, we hug. I inquire, in Dari, about their health and family's well-being. I offer drinks. I escort them into our meeting room. They sip their apple juice, I slam my Diet Pepsi, they complain about such-and-such and how I must absolutely fix it at that very moment, and I nod and listen intently. Once they've said their piece, I take about a minute to digest everything I've heard. Ideas begin to dance in my head. I visualize solutions, ranking them in order of potential success, feasibility, and efficiency. I present my ideas, and they nod and listen intently. They agree with everything I say; they never disagree, and not because I'm a genius—it's the Afghan nature.

We shake hands. They promise to report back as soon as they've implemented the solution. I escort them back out into the stiflingly hot day. We shake hands again. They turn, I turn, and we go our separate ways.

I'm not even in my seat when the next crisis hits.

At some point, I grab a quick dinner—boiled mystery meat again.

Turning to our navy cook, I ask, "Hey, Red, what is this?"

"Food," he nonchalantly replies.

I choke down a few bites, walk out of the chow hall, and offer the dogs my scraps. I take a few moments to play with them, to pet their heads, and to remind them how much we all love their company.

I return to the TOC.

The cycle repeats endlessly until 1830, when our entire FOB gets together to do our battle update briefs. The meeting adjourns; I contemplate a trip to the gym and go if I can escape the TOC before another crisis arises.

Exhausted from the day and my workout, I take slow steps back to my b-hut. I look up and stare at nature's masterful canopy; I feel infinitely small. I shake off the urge to contemplate life, the ridiculousness of this war when compared to the vastness of the universe, because I've got guard duty in three hours. No time to philosophize. I grab my body armor, night-vision goggles, and M4 assault rifle and return to the TOC.

At 0100, I suit up in 70 pounds of body armor and head out for two hours of guard duty. I walk our perimeter and stop at each fighting position for 5 or 10 minutes. I gaze out at the lime-green environment displayed through my NODs and watch the world outside our prison. I've grown accustomed to the sounds and sights of the world outside the wire. A lone vehicle drives through the deserted streets of Ghazni. I prepare myself to unleash hell at a moment's notice. I move on to the next position and acclimate myself to its surroundings; the dogs follow me, my faithful fellow sentries.

At 0300, I brief the incoming guard team on the current situation: status normal, all quiet on the Ghazni front. Coffee is on in the chow hall, radio Ghazni and Gardez (our higher headquarters) every hour, be sure to spend 5 or 10 minutes at each fighting position, see you in the a.m.

I return to my bunk, remove my body armor, place my M4 and M9 within reaching distance, curl up in bed, turn on my laptop, and check my e-mail. Around 0400, I drift off into a few precious hours of sleep; another day is over, another day dawns in just four hours.[1]

---

1 To read more about my intelligence work, the longest 72 hours of my life, and our efforts to work with the population, go to http://bit.ly/IdpHBL.

20

Ajiristan

Tuesday, July 15, 2008

Captain Norris is desperate to go on a mission to our most-remote and seldom-visited district: Ajiristan. For the life of me, I cannot figure out why he wants to go there so badly, but he won't give the cause up. For a few days, we've had an on-again off-again mission planned to visit the district center, to reinforce the ANP who occupy it, and to help improve their defenses and quality of life. The district center is a good 25-hour drive; an hourlong helicopter ride provides the only plausible way to reach it in a timely manner. For days I've tried to talk Captain Norris out of the mission, and today I enlisted Captain Goodman to assist me in my argument. We both claimed that because we can't effectively secure our immediate area, flying out to the middle of nowhere to temporarily secure our remotest district makes no sense. Eventually, we won Major Garrison over to our side, and the mission seemed to die, much to Captain Norris's disappointment.

Monday, July 21, 2008

Still recovering from my previous sleep deprivation, I slept another 16 hours before I roused myself for continued service. As I entered the TOC, I found out

---

A CH-47 "Chinook" helicopter landing at FOB Four Corners in Andar district, Ghazni province.

that the Taliban overran the Ajiristan (our most-remote district) District Center over the night. The ANP based at the center fought valiantly for hours and hours, only abandoning the center when they ran out of ammo. We had tried futilely to resupply the DC for weeks, but each attempt ended in failure. The local national air resupply (we call it Jingle Air, an homage to the cargo trucks we've nicknamed jingle trucks) refuses to fly out there, the ANA's helicopters claim it's too dangerous, and coalition aircraft refuse to fly without coalition personnel to guide its landing. Thus, no one resupplies the ANP at Ajiristan for several weeks, the Taliban launch a major assault, and the ANP fight until they run out of ammo and flee for their lives.

And why did the Taliban decide to attack the ANP at the Ajiristan DC? Why now? Because those untrained, nonmentored ANP just happened to capture Mullah Janna, a senior Taliban commander and the movement's direct link to al-Qaeda, a militant with a $1 million bounty on his head, a fighter whom we hadn't had a solid lead on in over three years. These men, these brave, brave ANP, on their own, captured a Tier One target, who we promptly picked up and then left the ANP to fend for themselves. And people wonder why the Taliban are so resurgent; when we fail to resupply our allies with even the most basic of necessities, we cannot hope to retain popular support.

Thursday, July 24, 2008

I walked into the TOC to find Captain Goodman and Captain Norris running around in a frenzy.

"Captain Goodman is going home today on emergency leave. I'm taking over for him as Team Chief for Team One," a visibly excited Captain Norris replied. He has spent most of the deployment on our FOB employed as our S3 (head of operations).

"Wow sir, looks like you're finally going to get your wish and earn your CIB," I half-chuckled.

"Yeah, maybe," Captain Norris said with a laugh that quickly died as the reality of combat and potential death sank in. I needed to break the tension, if nothing else then for his peace of mind.

"So sir, does this mean I'll be taking over for you as the S3?"

"I guess it does," he said with a sigh of relief.

For a half-hour I drank from the fire hose of knowledge unleashed by Captain Norris, a wealth of S3 experience that stems from nearly three years as an assistant S3 for our brigade headquarters.

After my S3 baptism by fire, I sat back down at my desk and gathered my thoughts. The S3 is one of the first to arrive on shift and almost always the last to leave. Without the S3, operations are not planned, soldiers do not get placed on flights, coordination between other units in the AO breaks down; literally, the S3 is the axis around which all U.S. operations move, the most vital cog in the U.S. Army war machine. We have a saying: "Intelligence drives operations," meaning the S2s brief what they think the enemy will do next and the S3s build their plans to mitigate any enemy advantages while attempting to assure U.S. victory. Now as the S2 and acting S3, I'd be solely responsible for intelligence collection and analysis *and* operations planning; I could do the entire war-gaming phase of mission development (the stage in which S2 enemy analysis is incorporated into S3 friendly-forces operations planning) on my own. It's the dream of every single army intelligence officer to be in my position: the sole provider of both enemy predictions and recommendations for friendly-forces actions to the unit commander. In a word, I'd just become Major Garrison's consigliore.

I spent the remainder of the day building an imagery targeting package for Captain Norris, with satellite photos of buildings and villages known to house bad guys, which he would use in Team One's upcoming operation.

That night, Lightning Main (our higher HQ) continued its unendingly comical and pathetic "Ajiristan" inquiries: "What is the current situation in Ajiristan?" "What is FOB Vulcan planning to do about it?" Lightning Main has told us repeatedly in the past that we are "not a maneuver unit," meaning we cannot launch independent offensive operations to seize territory. Our job is to advise and to train the Afghan National Army and Afghan National Police. If the ANA and ANP want to launch an offensive operation, we can guide them and accompany them, but we are not allowed to do such operations independent of the ANA and ANP. Every night, I'd answer the inane questions with sarcastic responses.

"What is the current situation in Ajiristan?"

"The Taliban still control the district center."

"What are you planning to do about it?"

"Not a thing."

At this point in our radio ballet, I pictured the men and women who man the Lightning Main TOC staring at their radio in disbelief.

The fact that we're technically OPCON'd (operationally assigned) to the 101st only makes these questions even more pathetically humorous. Under the terms of the OPCON, only the 101st has the manpower and ultimate authority to mount an operation to retake the Ajiristan District Center. Lightning Main knows this, so if it wants the District Center recaptured, it could coordinate an operation through the 101st. If the situation in Ajiristan changed (if the Taliban magically gave up and left, or the ANA and ANP decided to act on their own, or the 101st decided to retake it on its own), we'd immediately report it to Lightning Main. The constant questions served as Lightning's lone measure of pretending to have control over us. Given its track record of completely ignoring our requests for more men, gear, ammunition, fuel, and equipment, it should come as no surprise that we regard it as completely useless.

Tuesday, August 12, 2008

Today, Captain Norris, after aggressively lobbying, finally got his wish for a mission to Ajiristan. Several days ago, elements from the 101st and other U.S. units recaptured the Ajiristan DC from the Taliban without firing a shot; the enemy had fled before they arrived. After 48 hours on the ground, the 101st decided to leave, thinking the ANP and ANA would remain to hold the DC. The Afghans had other plans. The ANP said they refused to stay out at the DC without the ANA. The ANA refused to stay without American forces, and before anyone knew it, we all realized that the DC would fall back into Taliban hands almost as quickly as we had taken it.

At midnight, some genius colonels decided that in order to get the ANA to stay (which would prompt the ANP to stay), they'd send three U.S. mentors out to the DC for a week. These "leaders" believed that the 101st had killed a great many Taliban in retaking the DC, that the DC compound was in perfect shape (with a lot of defenses in place) and thus easily defended, and that the Taliban had initially overrun the DC when the ANP willingly abandoned it without a fight. In truth, the 101st hadn't seen a single Taliban and had found and left the DC in complete disarray, with breaches in the walls and only a single strand of barbed wire around the premises; the ANP had only abandoned it to the Taliban after they ran out of ammunition during a four-hour firefight. I should note that the ANP likely would have never abandoned the DC had the Afghan government or U.S. forces properly and regularly resupplied its compliment of ANP, but because the Afghan government, "Jingle Air," and the U.S. military refused to fly air resupply missions for months, here we are.

Fearing our higher HQ was setting up our soldiers for a Kunar-style catastrophe, Major Garrison successfully lobbied to send 11 additional soldiers from our teams to assist the initial 3. For the rest of the day, our FOB scrambled to prepare Team One and Team War Eagle (the ANA mentors) for their "weeklong" mission to Ajiristan. Very quickly, we realized we lacked enough ammunition and supplies to sustain them for a week's worth of operations. We requested that the 101st leave behind extra ammunition and supplies at the DC as it traded positions with our guys. The 101st assured us it would, but it didn't.

Two CH-64 helicopters ferried our brave men out to Ajiristan, where they instantly realized they'd been severely screwed: the DC was nearly destroyed, 11 of* the 38 ANP were high on a mixture of opium and hashish, and the 101st had taken all its ammunition and supplies.

The horrifically ironic part of this whole ordeal was that 30 minutes after our soldiers took off for Ajiristan, a helicopter landed on our FOB with a resupply of ammunition, a resupply we requested two months ago and just *now* received—yet another shining example of our higher HQ's utter incompetence.

Monday, August 18, 2008

In the most extreme form of army cruelty I've ever seen, 30 minutes before the Ajiristan teams were to be flown out via helicopter, our higher HQ and the 101st cancelled their exfil and informed them that they'll be remaining in Ajiristan for at least another week. That evening, as we sat down to begin our BUB, the radio crackled to life: "Ghazni TOC, Ghazni TOC, this is Ajiristan DC. Request medevac at this time. We have a young Afghan girl here with shrapnel wounds from a mortar to her leg."

It turns out that the Ajiristan team had returned to the DC, reestablished its defensive posture, and registered its mortars by firing a few volleys to test their accuracy. Unfortunately, one round went behind a mountain and allegedly impacted right near the girl, wounding her leg. For the next 24 hours, the Ajiristan team repeatedly, almost on the hour, requested Ghazni TOC (1/506th) to medevac the girl and her father out of Ajiristan. While they waited, "Doc" Sullivan kept her stable and as comfortable as possible with gentle care and a healthy, continuous dose of morphine.

Saturday, August 23, 2008

Our higher HQ extended the originally six-day Ajiristan mission to the 31st. Sadly, all that those of us back on the FOB could do to assuage the Ajiristan crew's frustration was to publicly advocate on their behalf during our regular radio traffic with our higher HQ, conversations that I found intolerable and extremely aggravating.

Sunday, August 24, 2008

Finally, a day of good news. Our overall commander, Major General Cone, declared today that Police Mentor Teams involved in Focused District Development (FDD, the program designed to make an Afghan district's police force operations ready independent of U.S. mentorship) can only be used for FDD purposes. In layman's terms, what his announcement means is that because all our teams are involved in the FDD program, we can never again be tasked to do another mission like the one to Ajiristan. He handed down this directive once he found out that the Deh Yak crew had not been able to mentor their district's police for almost three weeks due to the fact that they're currently stuck in Ajiristan. Personally, I think Major Goodman's (he got promoted while on leave) daily report finally got through to someone with actual decision-making power. Every night since the Ajiristan mission began, Major Goodman has sent up a report in which he declares that the mission's purpose is to "indefinitely delay the inevitable loss of the district to the Taliban."

Monday, August 25, 2008

A planned resupply flight of the Ajiristan team failed to leave for the umpteenth time today. For several days now, the Ajiristan team has reported in with an increasingly dire situation: dwindling water, food, and radio-battery supplies. At this point, the team reported it was "black," completely out of drinkable water. Each day a flight had been scheduled by our higher HQ and the 1/506th, who ultimately controlled the helicopters. Each day our team had left the relative security provided by the makeshift outpost to secure a landing zone in the middle of Taliban country. Each day they had sat there for hours waiting for a flight that never came, only to find out that the flight had either inexplicably turned around or never even took off hours after they had secured the landing zone. Yet, in the truest sense of military professionalism, the team took each day's rejection in stride and responded with an emphatic but calm request to improve their worsening situation.

Wednesday, August 27, 2008

Today marked a new low in the long list of complaints against our higher HQ and its inability to support us. As one will recall, the Ajiristan crew was originally told the mission would last six days at the most. Weeks past that deadline, our brave crew radioed back that they're running extremely low on water and food, basic life necessities. For several days, Captain Norris patiently radioed back the team's supply consumption report and finished each transmission with a request for the next available resupply flight. At the end of today's report, the weeks of lying and zero support from our higher HQ took their toll: "Vulcan TOC, this is Ajiristan TOC, be advised, we will be black on water by this evening, request immediate resupply flight, over."

"Roger, Ajiristan TOC, good copy. Will inform Ghazni TOC and request immediate resupply flight, over."

"Black" is a category of supply. Green = good or full. Amber = some used, but enough to get by. Red = dangerously low, need resupply ASAP. Black = gone, nothing left. Water and ammo are two items that, next to medevacs, pretty much take priority when it comes to helicopter missions. Going black on water is just as urgent as going black on ammo. One can have all the ammo in the world, but if soldiers are dehydrated and passing out due to lack of water, that ammo is pretty much worthless. When a unit reports black on water, priorities shift, and water moves. We had always suspected our higher HQ (ARSIC-E and the 101st) had no qualms about putting us in the most precarious of situations with little regard for our safety.

We relayed Captain Norris's plea for water to Ghazni TOC, and the radio crackled to silence. Finally, after what felt like an eternity, an exasperated voice spoke: "Vulcan TOC, this is Ghazni TOC, be advised, there are no more resupply flights available for today. Ajiristan TOC will have to find a way to ration their additional supplies."

Captain Norris had transmitted his daily pleas (including today's) over the tactical satellite radio, a radio that pretty much everyone in our area of the country could monitor, including the 101st in Ghazni and our higher HQ (ARSIC-E) in Gardez. They had heard those pleas in real time for the past few days. Everyone knew that they desperately needed a resupply flight, and yet nothing but days' worth of excuses materialized. Everyone knew that our higher HQ had sent the Ajiristan crew out with only enough supplies to last a little over a week and that they had already been severely rationing their food and water to extend those initial supplies to the present. Everyone also knew that the team had been sent out without water purification chemicals, such as iodine, and would now have to risk drinking from the local streams and wells that normally brought dysentery, once they ran out of their original supply of bottled water. I could only imagine how Captain Norris and the Ajiristan crew must have bristled as they heard Ghazni TOC's directive come across the radio. They were alone, and they'd continue to be alone for the indefinite future. When they returned days later, on a flight that was twice canceled before it finally arrived, they appeared ghosts of their former selves. Each man had lost an average of 15 pounds, most had some level of dysentery, at least one officer had gone temporarily insane, and all vowed never to return to Ajiristan for as long as they lived.

In a case of tragic irony, their mission ended up being entirely worthless. As one will recall, the Taliban originally seized the district center (they had already controlled the entire district around that one village, but the Afghan government seems to only freak out when they lose the lone outpost—but I digress), we bombed it for two weeks, and the 101st sent a detachment of American soldiers, ANA, and ANP to retake it (without a shot fired). The 101st soldiers planned to leave after being on the ground for a day, the ANA claimed they wouldn't stay without the Americans, and the ANP claimed they wouldn't stay without the ANA. Our higher HQ volunteered our Team One (without consulting any of us) to the 101st to replace them, which would prompt the ANA to stay, prompting the ANP to stay. Our higher HQ lied and said the mission would only take six days.

Three weeks later, a two-star general got wind of all this and ordered Team One to be extracted ("Mentors should be used to mentor the Afghans, *not* hold territory indefinitely," a rare occasion where someone with common sense called a shot). When Team One left, the ANA left as well, just as they had said they would three weeks earlier, leaving Ajiristan to be held by 20 ANP (17 Pashtuns and 3 Hazara). The Pashtun, realizing the Taliban would eventually attack and kill them all, deemed the situation hopeless and in a rather diabolical move, convinced the three Hazaras to take a nap while they "pulled guard." While the Hazara slept, the Pashtun abandoned the police station, never to be heard from again. When the Hazara awoke hours later, they found themselves alone, in an area dominated by Pashtuns (who speak Pashto, while the Hazara speak Dari). The Hazara quickly sized up the situation and promptly abandoned the district center. Within four hours of Team One's departure, we received intel that the Taliban had retaken the district center (and its brand new complement of American-supplied weapons, communications gear, and fortifications) without firing a shot.

21

Two Sides to Every Story

Sunday, July 20, 2008

That afternoon I sat in the TOC when the radio crackled to life. For the next two hours I listened to a remote base helplessly report in detail a brutal enemy mortar barrage. "Base . . . base . . . this is OP1 . . . incoming enemy mortars at this time. Mortar rounds just impacted one of our b-huts, destroying the building. No injuries at this time. Break. Incoming enemy mortars at this time. Mortar rounds just impacted our fuel point, causing a massive explosion and uncontrolled fire. Mortar rounds just impacted the TOC. Break. Minor injuries to two U.S. personnel at this time. No need to medevac." And so it went for seemingly forever. Finally, after painstakingly ensuring, checking, rechecking, and rechecking again that they had identified the Taliban's mortar position (so as to not fire on innocent civilians), the base fired artillery rounds back, suppressing the enemy's attack within several salvos.

The next day, I read in the news that the Taliban claimed the base had fired on and killed innocent civilians in an unprovoked U.S. attack. In truth, the Taliban suffered such severe losses that the only way to mitigate the defeat was for them to claim another U.S. atrocity. It's the typical Taliban modus operandi: They lose fighters; strip the bodies of Taliban garb, gear, and weapons; call the press; and claim the dead are innocents flagrantly and callously murdered by U.S. forces, a

Our Afghan National Army soldiers standing victoriously over the dead bodies of two Taliban fighters they killed earlier that morning. The Kandak commander, Colonel Nasser, had just given a press conference during which he said, "This is what happens when you fuck with my unit."

brilliant and nearly flawless propaganda strategy that we often cannot effectively rebut.

That night nature treated us to a wondrous heat lightning storm, magnified through the forest green perspectives of my night-vision goggles. Through my NODs I saw bolts of raw energy dance playfully across the sky, each bolt lasting a magnificent second before it faded away from existence just as quickly as it had arrived. It is during times like these that I, for the briefest of moments, forget the carnage around me, forget entirely about the war, and lose myself in a singular spectacle of unimaginable beauty.[1]

---

1 Read more about how our higher command hampered our efforts at http://bit.ly/J1o5fI. To learn more about my favorite Afghan intelligence officer, Siddiq, go to http://bit.ly/IgUNxk.

22

TIC Magnet and the Taliban Strike Back

Monday, July 28, 2008

The Deh Yak team got into another firefight today. They were on their way out of a village they had just searched with the ANP when one of their MRAPs rolled over while attempting to go around a bend on a dirt road (the "road" gave out and slid away down an embankment). The teams ended up waiting several hours for the recovery assets to arrive, during which time the enemy chose to attack them. An hour-long firefight ensued, resulting in a lot of frayed nerves.

I got word from Captain Norris that Colonel Wilde had relieved Captain Ricker as Team Four's chief for "failure to obey orders." The news stopped me mid-stride. I stood and blankly stared off into oblivion. "Sir . . . you're kidding me," I finally managed to say.

"Afraid not. It's bullshit, but what can we do? We've got to drive on, we've still got missions to do," Captain Norris said, returning his attention to the ongoing operation.

"Speaking of today's mission, Sir, after your firefight, do you finally feel as if you've earned your CIB?"

"Oh yeah, without a doubt," Captain Norris half-chuckled in an attempt to cover up the obvious concern that at any moment he or his men could have died.

An Afghan Police station in Andar district, Ghazni province. Note the near-total devastation caused by many a Taliban attack. We found three poorly equipped men and a boy manning it. They pleaded with us not to leave.

"What's your plan for tomorrow, Sir?" I asked.

"Baker Company wants to go to Sangor village, as that's where the Taliban attacked us from today," he replied, trailing off as he replayed the battle in his mind.

"Sir, with all due respect, Sangor isn't the village you should hit. You need to go after the village immediately to Sangor's south: Alu Kheyl. The only reason the Taliban attacked you from Sangor is because it was the village closest to where you were today. You need to hit Alu Kheyl. Haji Mohammad, the Taliban commander in Deh Yak, lives there, and one of my informants tells me he led the group that attacked you today. You obviously got too close for his comfort," I said.

"Yeah I know, I recommended the exact same course of action to the Baker Company guys [the 101st element joining our units during the weeklong mission]. They rejected it. They want to go to Sangor," he sighed.

"What route do you plan to use to get to Sangor?" I asked, pulling out a map of the area.

"Well, the plan Baker Company and I worked up today has us moving up this paved road to this intersection," Captain Norris said, pointing to the map. "From the intersection, we'll turn left and head north, approaching Sangor from the south," he said, moving his finger up the route they intended to use.

"Sir, you do realize that you'll pass right by Alu Kheyl if you take this route. Haji Mohammad and his men are going to think you're coming for them and are going to open up with everything they've got, and the whole mission to Sangor will never happen," I said, incredulously.

"Yeah, that could happen. We'll just have to see. But for now, this seems to be Baker Company's show; we planned the mission today, they plan tomorrow's," he said, exasperated and clearly trying to end the conversation.

Tuesday, July 29, 2008

Team One has dubbed Captain Norris a "TIC magnet." TIC stands for "Troops in Contact," a firefight. Thus far, he has only gone on four missions with Team One, and each time they have ended up in a firefight.

As planned, Team One, their ANP, an accompanying company of ANA, and Baker Company rolled toward Sangor from the south. As they passed Alu Kheyl village, a torrent of fire erupted all around them: Haji Mohammad and his men, just as I had predicted. For the next four hours, Team One, Baker Company, and their complement of ANA and ANP fought gallantly against a well-armed enemy force, calling in numerous artillery barrages from 155mm howitzers. Private First Class Rivera recalls firing at least 12 high-explosive (HE) grenade rounds from his

M203, an amazing feat considering he served as a driver that day and thus had the fewest chances to fire his weapon.

Eventually, our forces' ammunition dwindled to critically low levels, prompting them to call in the U.S. Air Force to drop a 500-pound bomb on the compound our reconnaissance aircraft had observed housing a multitude of fighters. The deafening roar of the F-15's twin jet engines announced the impending strike, as the fighter swooped in for the bomb run. Arcing down from its lofty perch, the fighter carved a magnificent approach, silhouetted by the brilliant afternoon sun. It released its payload, and the bomb came screaming in like a freight train traveling at supersonic speed. The explosion, a momentary cloud of fire, concussion blast, and massive energy, removed the compound and an estimated 37 enemy fighters from existence. Where once a massive mud-brick compound stood, now only rubble and the occasional body part remained.

As I listened to the events unfold over the radio, I found myself exuberant. I had been right, and not just right, but *spot on.* I allowed myself a momentary pat on the back. Thirty-seven enemy dead, two enemy fighters captured. Even better, enemy fire had not injured or killed a single U.S. soldier—a near-total victory, darkened only by the death of an ANA soldier due to enemy fire. Team One escorted the dead ANA soldier's body back to our FOB, a somber convoy considering the tremendous tactical victory they achieved.

Later in the afternoon, I met with the ANP finance officer, the man responsible for ensuring that all ANP in Ghazni receive their monthly pay. The man wields considerable power, given the level of endemic corruption in the ANP. Prior to the American Army's taking over the ANP's training and development, the payment cycle hypothetically worked as follows: The Ministry of the Interior received the monthly payment in cash from the Ministry of Finance. The MOI then sent each province its allotted share of the payment, again in cash. The provincial ANP HQ distributed the cash among the district chiefs, who in turn, handed it out to their assigned men. In truth, at any and every level of physical cash transfer, graft ensued. On average, in any given month, the individual ANP only received about one-third of his allotted pay, if he received it at all. Most ANP claimed the government owed them on average at least three months of pay.

We recognized instantly that this system failed completely and only served to line the pockets of extremely corrupt men. We devised a new system. The ANP men were given bank accounts, a first for most. We then coaxed the MOI into transferring all the pay via electronic transfer, which significantly reduced the level and opportunity for graft and outright theft. Though a vast improvement, the new system had two major flaws. First, only the major cities (Kabul, Jalalabad, Kandahar, etc.) had banks from which the ANP could withdraw their pay, forcing many ANP to take time off and to travel great distances. Second, any ANP who signed up with the service prior to this year likely had yet to open a bank account. ANP who signed up after this year automatically received a bank account. To rectify this pay problem, any ANP without bank accounts were given them as they went through FDD (Focused District Development) training. In Ghazni, 3 of our 19 districts had either completed or were currently undergoing FDD training. The remaining 16 districts still received the majority of their pay by physical delivery. Until all the districts complete FDD training, the pay problems will continue.

Team Two's and Team Four's ANP are currently undergoing FDD training in Kunduz and Jalalabad, respectively. Their ANP have yet to receive their bank accounts (it takes about a month for the MOI to process them into the system that transfers their pay to electronic fund transfer). The Ghazni ANP finance officer has to travel to Kunduz *and* Jalalabad once a month to physically deliver the cash needed to pay these ANP. Captain Morriarty had called me at least once a day for the past three days complaining that his ANP claimed they had yet to be paid for this month or for the past three. He feared his ANP would mutiny and quit in droves if they didn't receive their pay within days. Normally, Captain Morriarty would express this concern to our S1 mentor (the U.S. officer who mentors the ANP finance and personnel officers). As I'm still playing jack-of-all-trades, the duty fell to me. Thankfully, the ANP finance officer already knew of the situation and had implemented a plan to fix it. Within a week, our ANP at training in Kunduz and Jalalabad were paid, and we averted another crisis.

Wednesday, July 30, 2008

The Taliban have recently taken to blowing up large sections (bridges or culverts) of Highway One. Today's strike occurred against one of the 101st's MRAPs as it traversed a culvert. The bomb was nearly identical to one used against an MRAP in Kandahar back in June, a blast that killed all five U.S. soldiers riding in the vehicle. Fortunately, in this incident the trigger man detonated the IED too early, and the explosion only took out the entire engine block rather than the crew compartment. Nevertheless, the blast injured four U.S. soldiers and initiated a three-hour firefight between U.S. and Taliban forces.

As if that weren't enough for one day, a massive explosion erupted a few kilometers to our east: The Taliban had blown up a bridge on the main road to Andar. As the bridge blew, Taliban forces just south of FOB Ghazni began shelling the base with inaccurate rocket fire in an attempt to slow any response to the bridge attack.

When we first arrived in Afghanistan, I briefed our teams that the Taliban announced their 2008 strategy months in advance: They planned to sever the main highways, effectively cutting off government services from reaching most areas outside Kabul. Today, the Taliban clearly began an offensive aimed toward achieving their strategic goals.

In the evening, General Khan Mohammad (the Ghazni Provincial ANP chief) and Haji Fasil stopped by to announce they had sent forces after the Taliban who had fired rockets on FOB Ghazni. I hadn't seen Fasil since I confronted him with corruption charges about a month ago. As he walked into our TOC, I expected his smile to quickly melt away and for him to glare. The exact opposite occurred; he smiled, ran up to me, and gave me a gigantic hug and kissed me once on each cheek. I had accused this man of directly supporting the enemy and running a massive drug-smuggling syndicate in our last encounter, and here he was, carrying on as if we were the dearest of friends.

As quickly as Haji Fasil and General Khan arrived, they departed, leaving me profoundly confused.

23

Arnold

Thursday, July 31, 2008

The highlight of the day was Major Garrison's phone call from Gardez.

"I've got news. I'm bringing back a second lieutenant to work directly under you. Lieutenant, this is a great opportunity for you. You'll have the chance to mentor and to mold a brand-new, just-out-of-school second lieutenant. You can show him what real intelligence work looks like in a combat environment and school him on what commanders most need. It's a phenomenal opportunity, and I know you're up to the job. I'll see you in a few days. Out." Click. Deafening silence.

The news rendered me speechless. Since April, I've asked for an assistant. I thought I had asked for too much when I requested that Specialist Addison be transferred from Kabul to our FOB in Ghazni. And yet, here I was, soon to have my own second lieutenant working under my tutelage.

To be honest, once I gained composure and processed the information, I had mixed feelings. I was relieved to finally have help, because now I could accomplish many of the goals I had set aside until I could find the free time. I was excited to *finally* have an officer my age, of my army profession (intelligence), to help me achieve those goals so long ignored. I feared ending up with a "by-the-book" officer who would question my every move. I consider myself an officer who often completely ignores "the book" and does whatever is needed to accomplish the mission. As a result of my sometimes unorthodox methods and blatant disregard for

---

Lieutenant Arnold and the Afghan Police counternarcotic officer, who Arnold later found out was a hashish addict.

protocols that hamper my progress, I have a tendency to butt heads with those who exalt "the book" and all its "infinite wisdom." I only prayed that my new assistant wasn't one of those anal assholes.

Sunday, August 3, 2008

Riding an old Soviet helicopter refurbished by the Afghan National Army, Major Garrison, our new cooks, and my new assistant, Second Lieutenant Craig Arnold, finally arrived from Gardez today. Our entire FOB delightedly welcomed the new cooks, as our current navy cook ran out of creativity and energy weeks ago; we've eaten the same three meals (boiled pot roast, turkey circles, or pork chops) for every lunch and dinner for about the past month.

Second Lieutenant Arnold instantly strikes me as an energetic, enthusiastic go-getter determined to make a difference, to work hard, to do a phenomenal job, and to support the teams in any way he can. I find we have a lot in common, and he reminds me of myself at his age (23). I've instantly taken to him and predict we'll end up lifelong friends as a result of this experience. Best of all, he isn't a "by-the-book" officer and seems very willing to accept the fact that, given our remote location and unsupported disposition (our higher command routinely neglects us), we tend to routinely "improvise" well beyond protocol. I can't wait to start mentoring him; he possesses the potential to be a phenomenal intelligence officer.

That night I sat him down, explained in depth how I run my intelligence operations, and counseled him on the three questions and one piece of advice all good intelligence officers need to be able to answer for commanders: 1. What's happening? 2. Why is it happening? 3. What will happen next? and 4. Recommendations on what we can do to mitigate or to counter the enemy's current and future operations. I found him extremely receptive to my guidance and eager to get to work. I feel as if one of my prayers was finally answered.

As we walked out of the TOC, gunfire erupted on our FOB's western wall. Within seconds, soldiers dressed in their full complement of body armor and weapons ("full battle rattle") poured out of their b-huts and manned their fighting positions, scanning the exterior perimeter through their night-vision goggles, ready and willing to shoot dead any enemy fighter stupid enough to challenge them. Twenty tense minutes passed before the word came down that the ANA had repelled the enemy "attack," the first of several enemy "probes" (tests) against our FOB defenses that came throughout the next weeks.

Tuesday, August 5, 2008

Today I continued Second Lieutenant Arnold's training with his first intelligence meeting with an Afghan informant. We also met with both the ANP and ANA S2s in our weekly intelligence synchronization meeting. I think I finally have the two forces (ANA and ANP) trusting each other to the extent that they'll share information freely; before, they wouldn't even speak to one another. After the meeting, the ANA S2 pulled us aside and briefed us on an audacious sting operation he currently has planned. Weeks ago, he captured a Taliban cell phone and has used it to contact one of the Taliban's main weapons suppliers in Ghazni. Pretending to be a farmer who found artillery shells in his fields, the ANA S2 told the Taliban he wants to sell the shells before "the Americans search my house, find the weapons, and arrest me for being an enemy." The ruse seems to have worked thus far, as the Taliban have agreed to an initial meeting. The ANA S2 asked for my advice. I told him that since he's Hazara (most Taliban are Pashto), he'll need to do some serious acting to convince them of his "loyalty" to the cause. I suggested he use the fact that he's missing a leg (due to a landmine he stepped on back in February) to his advantage: "Tell them you lost your leg fighting the Americans and now hate the coalition and Afghan government." He agreed my suggestion was a great idea that he'd most certainly use.

Thursday, August 7, 2008

After Team One's epic battle in Alu Kheyl, I called my good NDS friend, Siddiq, to gather any information he had concerning the attack. Specifically, I wanted to know if our efforts had killed Haji Mohammad; Siddiq informed me his sources said they had. I immediately passed this information to the 101st, who asked how we had acquired it. "One of our NDS partners in Waghez told us," I replied. Little did I know that that one sentence nearly destroyed our best intelligence relationship, as the 1/506th immediately informed the Ghazni NDS chief that one of his deputies worked with us without his authorization. Siddiq was called all the way to Kabul to face his highest superiors, who informed him that if he ever worked with us again without explicit permission, he'd end up in prison. I decided the only way to make things right with Siddiq was to pass him to the Special Forces intelligence soldiers who could pay him for his work, a move he took as a sign of our deep respect for his assistance.

As the Afghan afternoon drifted into the cool comfortable evening, the ANA S2 called Arnold and me over to his office to discuss his ongoing sting operation. As we talked, I noticed he kept referring to a "master list" that broke down the Taliban leadership and structure by district. I decided I had to have the list.

"Can I have that list?"

"Ney, ney [no, no]."

"Do you know what a patriot is? A patriot gives his all for his people and his country. You lost your leg for your nation. You continue to serve, without question. You, sir, are a patriot. I love the Afghan people. I want to help the Afghan people. I know you've sacrificed a great deal to get the information on that list, but let's be honest—what more can you do? If you give me a copy of that list, I can pass it on to people who I can assure you will use it to kill and to capture a great many number of Taliban in Ghazni. Your efforts will not be in vain. Your government will have spent its money wisely. By letting this list sit in your office, unused, all that effort will end up wasted."

"Okay. I'll make a copy, and you can have it."

"Thanks my friend."

As Second Lieutenant Arnold and I walked out of his office, I remarked, "Thank God he gave it to us willingly; now I don't have to go back when he's gone and steal it. It just goes to show that everyone has their pressure points; you just have to know where to push. Appeal to his efforts, hype his accomplishments, and present the potential for failure, and he'll likely cooperate," I said as Arnold nodded attentively.

Thursday, August 14, 2008

Early in the afternoon, Major Garrison handed Arnold and me an urgent assignment: create a briefing that encompasses all of Ghazni's 19 district centers, 5 ANP substations in Ghazni City, and a database of every police chief and subgovernor's contact information, and get it done ASAP, in addition to our weekly intelligence summary. Nine frustrating and mentally exhausting hours later, we finished with an exasperated sigh of extreme relief. Stepping outside for a celebratory smoke, Second Lieutenant Arnold continued to beat himself up over a mistake he had made on a task I had assigned him.

"Don't worry about it. It ended up being a minor hiccup. You're doing a great job. As far as I'm concerned, you're a Godsend," I reassured him.

Inhaling on his cigarette, he thanked me for the vote of confidence and seemed to cheer up. After working with him for several days, I'm extremely impressed with his work ethic, intelligence, and reliability. He's become an invaluable member of our team and my right-hand man. I'm blessed to have him and have no doubt he's got a rich and rewarding career ahead of him.

24

Combat Groceries

Friday, August 8, 2008

Captain Fraser (a member of my Fort Riley training team) joined our family today as our new ANP S1 mentor. Early in the morning, we drove over to FOB Ghazni to pick him up and to introduce ourselves to the commanders of the incoming Polish Battle Group who will replace the 101st in the coming weeks.

As we rolled out through our gate, I heard salsa music blaring. Looking back, I saw Captain Norris (a Cuban American) and Specialist Guzman (a Dominican American) dancing away inside the turret of their vehicle. Guzman had hooked up his iPod to the Hummer's external PA system, blasting salsa music the entire trip to FOB Ghazni. As we drove down the road, our Latin convoy turned many heads of very confused Afghans who couldn't make heads or tails of our motley crew. For the briefest of moments, it felt as if we were on a midsummer's road trip with our best friends, partying down the wide open road.

We parked our vehicles and sought out the Polish and Captain Fraser. Major Garrison, Second Lieutenant Arnold, and I found "the Pols" hanging outside a seldom-used tent, looking very bored and forgotten. We spent about 30 minutes exchanging pleasantries and doing the inevitable "how do you say this, how do you say that" in each other's languages. Eventually, we received word Captain Fraser had arrived at our convoy, bid the Pols farewell, and exited their tent.

Taking a pit stop at clearly the nicest and most modern gas station—hell, the only gas station—we ever saw, on Highway One between Ghazni and Kabul.

I walked up to our awaiting vehicles to find a smiling Captain Fraser. Extending a firm handshake, we exchanged pleasantries, and I welcomed him to our Ghazni family.

Saturday, August 9, 2008

Captain Norris officially became Team One's team chief, which means when Major Goodman gets back from leave, he'll be my immediate boss.

Sunday, August 10, 2008

Here we go again. Two times last night, we took enemy fire to our FOB's external walls. The Taliban continue to probe our defenses and to harass our sentries, illusive ghosts firing from the shadows.

Monday, August 11, 2008

Once a week, we travel over to FOB Ghazni to draw our weekly food rations. This entire process serves as a prime example of our camaraderie and teamwork, for it requires an all-hands effort. The five-ton cargo truck rumbles to a stop just outside the food storage CONEX containers. Men stream forth from all points around the FOB. Officers, enlisted, soldiers of every and all rank stop work and line up in bucket-brigade formation to move box after box off the truck. Red, our senior cook, calls out each item's destination. "T-bone steaks! Cold!" (indicating it has to go to the freezer). "Potatoes! Kitchen!" (indicating they go directly to the kitchen). "Soda! Chill!" (indicating it goes to the refrigerator CONEX). Each man echoes the item and its destination as he passes it to the next man down the line.

When soldiers arrive on our FOB and witness this process, they often remark at how they are totally caught off guard: "Sir, I've never seen anything like that in my military career. I mean, even the most senior officers here help out with whatever needs to be done. It makes us really feel like everybody is part of a team here, that everyone pulls their fair share."

25

Mail

Wednesday, August 13, 2008

Some people drink. Some play sports. Whatever your poison, we all have our outlets. For soldiers deployed to combat, denied sex, alcohol, and most forms of entertainment, we turn to mail. Mail brings news and tastes of the outside world. Mail can mean the difference between a great and an awful day. Mail is our lifeblood, a reminder that we aren't forgotten, that people really do care.

Mail also has its evils. Mail brings "Dear John." Mail announces divorces via subpoenas and lawyers' notices. Not receiving mail is the greatest evil of all: Does anyone really care about me? One can see the full gamut of emotion right after mail call simply by looking at the faces of those around. Every letter tells a story, every package delivers love, and the absence of both leaves a soldier longing for connection.

Early after lunch, Second Lieutenant Arnold and I sat in the TOC, planning a few projects we hope to complete in the near future. Suddenly, the walls shook, and shock waves raged through our bodies. A VBIED (vehicle-borne improvised explosive device) had just detonated outside FOB Ghazni, a huge explosion considering the fact that FOB Ghazni sits two miles south of our FOB. Thankfully, the blast injured no one (Afghan, U.S., or coalition) and caused only superficial damage to the FOB walls.

Later in the evening, a massive firefight erupted about a kilometer outside our FOB walls, inside Ghazni city. RPGs and tracer rounds flew into the sky in dramatic

---

My bunk on FOB Vulcan.

numbers as explosions echoed like thunderclaps through the canyons of the city's concrete and mud-walled buildings. Within moments, gunfire erupted with horrific staccato as a blitz of rounds impacted along our FOB walls. Once again, our eager sentries were denied clear targets, rendering our weapons silent.

After these late-night attacks, I'd stumble through the darkness of our blackout FOB back to my bunk, my mind focused on processing everything that had occurred—another day left at war and a day closer to home. Often, I unwound by watching movies; I lost myself in their storylines, characters, and worlds, escaping to faraway lands, distant cities, and abandoned times. At each movie's conclusion, I sighed at the realization that I was still there, alone in my bunk, still trapped at war, with many months to go, an end I could neither see nor imagine.

26

Listening to Friends Die

Friday, August 15, 2008

For the second time on this deployment, I listened to U.S. soldiers die over the radio.

"Wardak TAC! Wardak TAC! This is Dog 3-7. We just hit an IED and are in heavy enemy contact at this time. I'm requesting an immediate medevac for four U.S. soldiers," a sergeant shouted over the radio.

"Roger, copy in contact at this time, requesting medevac," the base's radio operator replied.

"Hey you need to hurry on that medevac, two of these guys may not make it unless it gets here ASAP," the increasingly aggravated sergeant said.

Ten minutes later, the radio crackled to life. "Wardak TAC, this is Dog 3-7, be advised, one of my WIA [wounded in action] is now KIA [killed in action]. I need that medevac now!" the raging sergeant commanded.

"Wardak TAC, this is Dog 3-7, ETA on the medevac?"

"Dog 3-7 this is Wardak TAC, we're still working on it."

"I've got three guys down and one KIA, I'm still in contact, I need you to fucking get me an ETA on the medevac!"

Another endless 10 minutes passed.

The Andar District Center. It was a year old at the time of this photo (2008) but looked significantly older.

"Wardak TAC this is Dog 3-7, be advised I now have two KIA; my two WIA still need an immediate medevac!" the sergeant said, resigned to the fate of losing two men.

Almost an hour after his initial plea, the medevac arrived to shuttle the two WIA and two KIA back to BAF for treatment and for repatriation back to the U.S., respectively. The firefight raged for another three hours.

27

Promotions Without Rank

Autumn descends across the desert,
and the stifling Afghan summer fades into a distant dream.

Saturday, August 16, 2008

In the afternoon, as I walked back to the TOC, I saw a small child sleeping on a piece of cardboard box in front of our freezer CONEX. I ran back to my room, grabbed a plastic bag, and filled it with crayons, candy, pens, and paper. I made my way back to the child and as silently as I could, crept up to his sleeping frame. I knelt down and gently placed the bag at his side. As I walked away, I saw him open his eyes and watch me with sheer terror. Then he looked down and saw the bag; slowly, his terror gave way, and he gave me an exuberant grin. Tearing into the bag he called his father (one of our welders) over to proudly display his new possessions. The father thanked me profusely with a hand held steadfastly over his heart. I walked into the chow hall, grabbed several cold waters from our refrigerator, went back outside, and handed them to the father and his co-worker.

The Deh Yak District Center, temporarily staffed by the Afghan National Civil Order Police.

Sunday, August 17, 2008

Today, Second Lieutenant Arnold and I spent the day making IDs for our Afghan FOB workers, one of the many projects I'm now accomplishing thanks to Second Lieutenant Arnold's assistance. I'm particularly proud of how they turned out, and all the soldiers seem to get a kick out of them due to a security feature I included: a "watermark" image of Chuck Norris, holding an Uzi.

Monday, August 18, 2008

Per Major Goodman's orders, I awoke at 0530 to hand out the badges to our FOB workers. Two hours later and much to my consternation at losing that precious additional sleep, the FOB workers arrived. I decided to test my Dari abilities and opted to hand out the badges without the aid of an interpreter. One by one, the workers entered our office building, and I asked, "*Nam-eh chi ast?* [What's your name?]" After getting their names, I'd ask, "*Mobile eh dari?* [Do you have a cell phone?]" Those who did have phones would hand them over as I handed them their badges. With all the workers properly badged, I walked outside to enjoy a rare moment of quiet solitude as the Afghan sun began her oppressive ascent into the morning sky. I found the full complement of workers gathered around, smiling profusely as they admired one another's badges. One worker, seated upon a pile of sandbags, called me over and pointed to his badge's picture. Even without speaking proficient Dari, I knew what he was saying: He didn't like his ID picture, which is most likely a first, considering these are probably the first pictures of themselves, not to mention their first IDs. Bemused at how life continues to reveal these human commonalities, I pulled out my army ID, pointed at it, and puffed out my cheeks to appear as bloated as I look in the picture. They all got the gist and laughed heartily. Ever since I handed out their IDs, the workers stop to wave and to say "hello" to me.

Tuesday, August 19, 2008

Major Goodman informed me that I've done such a great job as the "acting-S3" that I'll now be both the FOB S2 *and* the S3. I'm honored my bosses think I'm doing a great job and feel that I should continue to amass responsibility. At the same time, however, I fear that I've amassed so much responsibility that I'm integral to the FOB's successful operations, meaning that should I need to take any time off, there will be a period of excessive inefficiency as the remaining personnel try to learn my responsibilities. I've vowed to train Second Lieutenant Arnold with a renewed vigor so the FOB's operations will not suffer when I take some time off.

28

Bashi Habib—Grandfatherly Warlord

Thursday, August 21, 2008

Today I had the first of what would be many meetings with a very interesting man: Bashi Habib. Bashi is a spry, cheerful man who possesses a grandfatherly charm that masks his ruthlessness and his manipulative ways, making him a masterful Afghan politician. In a land where only the strongest and often most ruthless survive, he counts himself among the richest men. Over his 70-plus years, he's built a comfortable existence through a combination of charm and brutal violence. He has used his vast wealth, natural charm, and cunning brilliance to advance his position in life, usually through massive gift giving; in our case, he gave each of us a traditional Hazara woman's formal gown for our wives and girlfriends. Sitting with him, staring into his disarmingly soft, gentle eyes, I imagined he must have conducted this very meeting countless times throughout the years with the Russians, the warlords, the Taliban, the nascent Karzai government, and now us, the latest crop of American forces to rotate through Ghazni.

Yet, for all his grandfatherly charm, Bashi Habib has an often whispered about but seldom openly acknowledged dark and evil side. In his previous manifestations, he was a powerful warlord who ruled over a vast swath of Hazara territory. Though he's mostly given up his militia, he's rumored to have personally killed 57 people after an attack on a family wedding in 2007. What makes him truly terrifying and yet so utterly fascinating is that there's no sign that the torment of a very violent life weighs at all on his mind. Sitting there, observing his jovial calm and

Major Garrison meeting with Bashi Habib on FOB Vulcan.

politician's charm, I couldn't help but like him. I found his engaging elder statesman "act" captivating.

The meeting itself was more formality than substantively productive. I called him "Agha" (an honorific), which delighted him, and in turn he embraced me as his "American son." We drank chai and talked of our families, and by the end of the meeting he agreed to provide us with intelligence sources to spy on the Taliban in exchange for our potentially building a girls' high school in a Jaghori district (where he was subgovernor at the time). We never finalized the contract to build the school, but the last estimate was that should the coalition build it, 2,700 Afghan girls would receive a formal high school education, a prospect I found extremely rewarding.

My experiences with Bashi personify a critical lesson of Afghanistan: Sometimes one has to overlook a person's past evils in order to achieve profound good.

29

You Can't Make This Shit Up

Monday, August 25, 2008

Today Arnold and I met with the Qarabagh informant provided by Bashi Habib. Over the next three months, we'd meet with him a handful of times before we came to determine that he was nothing more than an information peddler, someone who tries to sell useless information to as many coalition units as possible. Although we had suspected the veracity of his information from day one, we confirmed our suspicions in a moment of humorous dumb luck. As we escorted him off our base, another U.S. unit arrived to stop by to pick up a blown-up MRAP. As they drove in, one of their intelligence officers thought he recognized the man as one of his sources. Upon seeing this other U.S. officer, our source instantly turned away from him and refused to look in his direction until after he was sure that he had left. Then, in a moment of incomprehensible stupidity, the source went to that unit's compound and attempted to sell them the same information we had ultimately refused. While he sat in their compound, the other U.S. intelligence officer called me and asked me to call the source's cell phone. I dialed. Before the source could react, the officer leapt forward and ripped the phone out of his hands. I could barely contain my laughter when the other U.S. intelligence officer answered, as I pictured the absolutely dumbfounded look that must have fallen across our mutual source's face.

One of our fuel resupply trucks burning after coming under Taliban attack.

Tuesday, August 26, 2008

Colonel Nasser (our Afghan Army battalion commander) reported that our FOB was probed again last night and faces an imminent attack. We merry band of 20 maintain our vigilant state of high alert.

Thursday, August 28, 2008

I slept in for the first time in God knows how long and spent the majority of the day doing mindless intel analysis and arguing with our FOB's development officer, a U.S. Navy lieutenant commander who I originally liked but have come to abhor, as I find his arrogance simply intolerable. For example, we've had a number of fuel trucks (civilian trucks contracted to deliver us fuel) attacked, blown up, and hijacked. At one point, we lost so many fuel shipments to Taliban attacks that we ran out of fuel and our generator died, leaving our FOB without power. The Taliban actually win twice every time they successfully attack one of our fuel convoys. First, they project their power to the Afghan people and further erode the belief that our military might offers adequate protection. Second, they supply the Taliban with fuel, fuel they can use for their own movement and sell back to the Afghan population at prices substantially below the market.

In order to deny the Taliban these seemingly endless double victories (at one point, we were losing a fuel shipment every day), I suggested we put our FOB on solar power; it's good for the environment and denies our enemies targets. Moreover, we're in the desert; the sun is literally out and blazing every day for more than 14 hours at a time. When I suggested this, he gave me some speech about how solar energy isn't feasible for the military (a Marine general in Iraq used it to great avail), and it is too expensive to get the panels into Afghanistan (a lie—we give out solar panels to Afghan villages as part of HA projects).

We never got solar panels, but the Taliban got tons of free, U.S.-taxpayer purchased fuel!

Friday, August 29, 2008

The army has decided that all MRAPs currently in Afghanistan should be turned in as soon as possible to be swapped with MRAPs currently in Iraq, because those are "lighter and less prone to rollovers" (more suitable for our terrain, as we have a few hills called the Hindu Kush). We ended up swapping our RG-31s for the more heavily armored Cougar variant of MRAP, which was the bread and butter of the USMC in Iraq. We all quickly became fans of its seemingly impenetrable armor and reliable engine (it doesn't overheat and die when going uphill).

I've lost count of the number of times we wanted to arrest the Andar subgovernor. Within two weeks of arriving in Ghazni, we suspected he was working with a Taliban faction in Andar. Within two months of our arrival, he framed the Andar police chief after the Taliban stole two police vehicles; we eventually cleared that chief's name and found him a new, safer job. He even attempted to fire the next police chief, Nabi Patang, within a week of his appointment, because Nabi refused to help him aid the Taliban.

Today, he allegedly pulled out his pistol and put it to the head of the contractor we had hired to rebuild the Andar district center, telling him that unless he paid him the bribe he deserved, he'd kill him on the spot. What makes this even more of an issue is that the Andar police are currently in Kunduz going through FDD training (just like the Deh Yak police did in Jalalabad). When an ANP unit goes off to training, the ANCOP (Afghan National Civil Order Police) take over their district for the duration of the unit's training. The ANCOP are like a well-trained SWAT unit. We were once told that one ANCOP soldier is the equivalent of five regular Afghan police. Their tactical movements are strong, they seem to interact well with their locals, and they only answer to authorities in Kabul (they are not easily influenced by local powerbrokers). The Andar subgovernor seems to have done something to this particular ANCOP unit, for instead of aggressively patrolling the district, they remain hunkered down in the district center.

30

Comings and Goings

Sunday, August 31, 2008

The Taliban attacked Ghazni tonight with a mortar barrage. I suspect our FOB was the target, given that the rounds all landed near our FOB and got progressively closer, but we'll never know for sure. Although the attack didn't come close to hitting us, it did strike well within the city proper and injured three people, including one little girl who sustained severe and life-altering injuries.

Wednesday, September 3, 2008

So far I've miraculously escaped the myriad of illnesses that seem to plague everyone at some point during their tour. I did not get "the Kabul Crud" when I first arrived in April, and I religiously avoided any Afghan food made with dairy and thus avoided "Mohammad's Revenge." Today I finally caught the Ghazni flu. I spent the next two days in bed resting, an odd luxury my body desperately needed after months of little sleep, long hours, and hard work.

Standing in Andar district with a NDS officer and a little girl, to whom I gave Oreos and a pen; note how she cowers away from me.

Thursday, September 4, 2008

Four months prior to our arrival in Afghanistan, the soldiers of Teams One and Three landed in Kabul. They endured one of the coldest winters on record and by the time of our arrival were tough grizzled veterans with a bond I both envied and initially found impenetrable. I was certain that as turtles, they saw us as ducks, rookies, Fucking New Guys (FNGs), and found our arrival as deeply unnerving as the departure of the South Carolina teams (who had preceded them by almost 10 months). The army's rotation policy, especially with the mentor teams, means that every four to six months, a series of veteran soldiers are replaced. Moreover, this rotation policy means you have new guys every few months, but they are always (in theory) paired up with someone with experience on the ground.

Teams One and Three were members of our brigade's advance party, a detachment our higher command sent ahead as guinea pigs, and their experience in training and actually deploying to and from Afghanistan provided valuable lessons learned for the brigade writ large. More importantly, they filled a gap in coverage that had long ago been created by some unforeseen screwup in soldier rotation, a gap that exists to this day. They're family, and their departure is bittersweet. On the one hand, I celebrate the fact that guys I care for so greatly will soon be home safe. Selfishly, however, I yearn for them to stay.

I look at the new arrivals, their innocent faces, unsure of where they are or what this place is like. I see beyond the bravado they attempt to use to mask their concern and fear. A handful of them are Iraq vets, but this is not Iraq, and I wish they'd stop trying to compare the two. In truth, they haven't a clue, not a single one of them. None of them was in Waghez with us. None of them got stranded at FOB Airborne. None of them was in Tangi Valley, or Ajiristan, or Southern Deh Yak. I don't want to learn the new guys' names, and I find myself fighting my brain's attempts to remember their unfamiliar faces. The FOB, our home, our sanctuary inside hell, suddenly feels alien, a totally new and unrecognizable place.

I find myself giving them the same speeches and advice passed on by the South Carolina guys when we first arrived: "Yes, you'll get your CIB. We've all been in a firefight at least once. And don't wish for it, it sucks when it's really happening." "Yes, you can trust the terps. Don't mistreat them, they're just a part of the team as any of us; yes, they are armed, get used to it, they'll likely save your life just like they've saved all of ours." "Yes, the Internet sucks here. After this tour, you'll never complain about Internet speed again." I'm the veteran, and they're the rookies, turtle vs. ducks.

Monday, September 8, 2008

We received three new interpreters today, and already our terps are suspicious of them. At first, I chalked up the complaints to the fact that the newbies aren't showing our veteran terps the deference they feel they deserve. Then Janis complained, and if I've learned one thing this tour, it's to trust Janis.

"Janis, why are you suspicious of them?"

"Matt, they are not good. They are very young, very arrogant. One claims to be former ANA, but I do not believe him. He says he lived in Pakistan for a long time."

"Okay, Janis, let's go meet them."

He was right. They're really young. One is Hazara and stinks to high heaven; he also cannot speak Pashto (which is a big problem, as a huge portion of Ghazni only speak Pashto). One is extremely arrogant. The other won't say a word to me and seems incredibly nervous; Janis informs me he is the one who claims to be a former ANA soldier. I tell Janis I'll look into it but to keep an eye on all of them.

Tuesday, September 9, 2008

Janis and Eshan came to me after breakfast and renewed their complaints against the new terps. The Hazara needs to shower; he's already earned the nickname "Stinky," and he's only been here 24 hours. The arrogant one needs to be put in his place. And the "former ANA" cannot speak Dari and cannot recall the names of his Kankak or company commanders while he was in the ANA, facts that arouse immediate suspicion, as most ANA can speak both Dari and Pashto and *all* soldiers can at least recount those two facts when questioned. Moreover, the "former ANA" allegedly threatened our veteran terps last night. Apparently, as the veteran terps explained how things work, the "former ANA" told them he didn't have to listen to them (he does) and that if they tried anything, he'd make a phone call and have them all killed, a subtle allusion to some nefarious Taliban connection he could exercise when needed. I decided to send the ANA S2 to interview this new terp to see maybe if he'd be more comfortable talking to a "fellow ANA" than to our terps. The interview did not go well. First off, the ANA S2 can only speak Dari (he's Hazara, so it'd be uncommon for him to speak Pashto). Habib had to translate what the ANA S2 said into Pashto so that the new terp could understand and then translate the new terp's responses into Dari so that the ANA S2 could understand.

The ANA S2 concluded there was no way the new terp could be former ANA and was extremely concerned he may be a Taliban plant; he allegedly has only been a terp for two months and spent a great deal of time in the tribal regions of Pakistan. I immediately brought these concerns to Major Garrison, who promptly blew me off: "Matt, you're too concerned about these things; you're probably blowing this way out of proportion."

I stood there speechless. I was his intelligence officer, and if he wasn't willing to at least consider my concerns, especially when I presented credible evidence, then there was only one recourse left: He had to fire me, or I had to resign. "Sir, I believe I've lost your faith and confidence. If you cannot or will not consider my concerns, especially when I present evidence, then I don't know how I can continue to serve you." He sat there stunned. Leaning forward in his chair, Major Garrison turned off his officer's persona for a moment and went into quiet mentor mode. "Matt, you're the smartest and best intelligence officer I've encountered in 20 years in the military. Your products and work are of the highest quality. You have my faith and confidence. Sometimes you just get too emotional about issues. You need to separate your emotions from these things." And, for the most part, he's right. You'll get all my concerns, but I'll also likely become deeply attached to the issue. The old saying "it's nothing personal, it's just business"—I struggle with keeping it just business. In this case, Major Garrison was wrong. The terps, the ANA S2, Craig, and I all had concerns about this new terp, and only Major Garrison could do something about it. In the end, he promised he'd keep an open mind and have the teams keep an eye on that terp but also pointed out that we were extremely short staffed with terps, and until he screwed up, we needed him more than we needed to get rid of him. In the end, First Sergeant Rock gave him a stern talking to and let him know that it was unacceptable to threaten the other terps and that if he ever did anything like that again, he'd be fired at the least and arrested at worst. He behaved the rest of our tour.

And Stinky learned to shower, but only after I started greeting him each morning with "Wa Lamba," which means "Take Shower."

31

Ghazni's Rotten Politics

Wednesday, August 27, 2008

With Team One still in Ajiristan, Deh Yak collapsed. Before they had left, Deh Yak had a functioning police force that had begun to reestablish an Afghan government presence in the Taliban-held southern portions of the district. In truth, Deh Yak was our unit's greatest success, but with Team One gone, the district subgovernor, Haji Fasil, and the provincial governor, Doctor Usman Usmani, had found an opportunity to regain control.

Ever since our arrival and Doctor Usmani's appointment as Ghazni governor, he and Haji Fasil had tried to replace Captain Faiz Mohammad as Deh Yak's police chief. First, they had sent Doctor Usmani's cousin, Major Torelli, up to Jalalabad, where Deh Yak's police force had gone to train during their two months of FDD training. Torelli produced questionable papers claiming he had been sent by the Afghan Ministry of Interior to replace Faiz. Torelli, a Pashtun, assumed command and instantly began to segregate the diverse police force into ethnically homogenous subunits. He emphasized prayer observance over training and attempted to breed strife between the Pashtuns and the non-Pashtuns of the force. Faiz, a Tajik, had taken a different approach to commanding the unit. He had constructed an ethnically heterogeneous force that rewarded competence over ethic and tribal loyalty. An aggressive and bold tactician, Faiz loved to fight the Taliban and inspired confidence in his police force by personally leading them in battle. Upon returning

Posing with Ghazni Governor Usmani after the infamous governor's dinner. Clockwise from the left: Me, Governor Usmani, Bashi Habib, Janis, Fareed, and Palmer.

to Deh Yak after their two months of training in Jalalabad, Torelli stole two police trucks, several machine guns, and ammunition, and he fled the district to Ghazni city with 10 men who were loyal to him, where he took up a comfy office job. Faiz ended up returning to his job as police chief, but Usmani and Fasil never took their eyes off him.

Ever since the Torelli incident, we had tried to find out why Governor Usmani and Haji Fasil wanted Faiz replaced. He was loyal to the Afghan government, had the respect of his men, took the fight to the enemy, and had no apparent ambitions beyond being police chief of Deh Yak (he wasn't gunning for any of the other jobs Usmani and Fasil could give away to support their broad patronage network). What we didn't know at the time was that Faiz's decision to erect a police checkpoint on the outskirts of his home village, Rabat, weeks prior would be the impetus for the aggressive campaign to replace him.

Tajiks inhabit the majority of northern Deh Yak and have concentrated themselves into a series of large villages, the largest being Rabat. Rabat sits on a plain at the edge of rocky mountains that run all the way to the outskirts of Kabul. Pashtuns inhabit southern Deh Yak, an area we long suspected of harboring low- to mid-level Taliban commanders. Our intelligence indicated that Haji Fasil had made a deal with the local Taliban: Keep Deh Yak quiet, and he wouldn't go after them. Our arrival and Faiz's aggressiveness, however, likely disrupted that agreement, as we and Faiz sought to place police checkpoints throughout southern Deh Yak. In retaliation for these checkpoints, the Taliban began threatening Rabat, hoping Faiz would back off. Rather than capitulating, he erected a police checkpoint in the village, armed a few of the villagers as a self-defense force, and then went on a two-week-long mission throughout southern Deh Yak in which he attempted to capture or to kill the local Taliban commander, Haji Mohammad. That mission had ended prematurely when Team One had been abruptly ordered to Ajiristan.

The governor and Haji Fasil had launched a serious campaign to discredit and to replace Faiz. Major Garrison thought we had nipped it in the bud days earlier when the provincial authorities assured us that nothing would happen in Deh Yak without Team One's being present. When I got a phone call from a crying and frantic Faiz, I was quite shocked to learn that he had just been fired and replaced with a man who had just days before been a gate guard at the provincial police HQ in Ghazni City.

Livid, I hissed to Habib, "Who is doing this? Who is with him from the Provincial ANP right now?"

Habib informed me that Faiz claimed both General Khan and his deputy, Colonel Zaman, were at Deh Yak and had personally delivered the news to Faiz.

"Habib, you tell them if they aren't here within the hour, I am cutting off all development and construction projects!" Habib, barely containing his glee, rapidly translated as I spoke. "Dammit! Give me the fucking phone!" I said as I snatched the phone from Habib's hands. "Now you listen to me, if you don't reinstate Faiz right now, we are stopping all new construction on the district centers, the police stations, everything! You can pay for it yourself as far as I'm concerned! *Get your ass to my FOB with now!*" I screamed, with no regard to the fact that they couldn't understand a word of my English; my anger and the tone of my voice transcended any linguistic borders.

I threw the phone back to Habib and went off to find Major Garrison and Major Goodman, who were busy trying to get Ajiristan water. I informed them that General Khan and Colonel Zaman were on their way, that they had tried to fire Faiz, and that I had just ripped them each a new asshole. Major Garrison sighed, generally overwhelmed with the nonending crises that wouldn't cease. Major Goodman just smiled.

Faiz arrived within 20 minutes of our initial conversation and instantly began pleading his case. It all came down to the Rabat checkpoint. In trying to protect his village, Faiz had inadvertently uncovered a massive chromite smuggling operation: Governor Usmani, Haji Fasil, and General Khan had been smuggling chromite from a mine just north of Rabat. Faiz's checkpoint sat on the only road to Rabat, which also happened to be the only road to and from the mine. Faiz had refused to be a part of the corruption, and that made him a liability. The governor and Fasil had used Team One's absence to draft a diabolical scheme designed to destroy Faiz's reputation with the community, us, and the Afghan government. First, they paid villagers in southern Deh Yak to claim that Faiz had raped their women. Then, Governor Usmani ordered General Khan to have his operations officer draft a report to the Ministry of Interior claiming Faiz was a Taliban plant within the ANP. Upon receiving the report, the MOI ordered Faiz's immediate removal and an investigation into the charges against him. Finally, Haji Fasil had paid Khan a hefty bribe to appoint the former ANP HQ gate guard, a man they could control and who wouldn't interfere with their chromite smuggling, as Faiz's successor. We had known for quite some time that the governor, Haji Fasil, and Khan were running a large smuggling operation, but we had only suspected it involved drugs and wood. With Faiz's insights, everything fell into place: the initial attempts to replace him with Torelli (the governor's cousin), the opposition to the Rabat checkpoint, and the opposition to the operations in southern Deh Yak (they had angered the Taliban, who felt the Afghan government was no longer honoring its part of the deal). Faiz was a competent commander and a tough fighter, and as he sat sobbing in our conference room, I felt determined to fight for him. Everything was on the line for him: his job, his family, his home village, his honor. In seeking to protect their smuggling operation, these Afghan officials were willing to destroy even the best of the men sworn to protect them.

After an hour of waiting, Colonel Zaman arrived looking visibly shaken. Moments later, General Khan came running toward us, beads of sweat streaming down his face, nervous, exhausted, and nearly tripping over himself as his short legs shuffled across our gravel parking lot. One could tell he was nervous that he had ruined relations with us. He was tired—tired of the scheming, tired of the job, tired of it all. As I escorted him into Major Garrison's office to resolve the situation, I knew I would never see him again. He retired within days.

Major Garrison, First Sergeant Rock, and Major Goodman talked with General Khan, Colonel Zaman, and Faiz for hours. At first, Khan and Zaman agreed to reinstate Faiz. Khan even admitted that Faiz's checkpoint interfered with his chromite smuggling. For months he had denied every allegation of corruption; he even seemed to revel in the cat-and-mouse game we'd played. Now, the old man was exhausted and bested. The governor and Haji Fasil had overreached, we had caught them, and he was tired of covering for them. The meeting moved to adjourn with an agreement to reinstate Faiz, when Bashi Habib appeared seemingly out of nowhere. Bashi, the old Hazara warlord and, in the eyes of the governor, our personal friend and favored Afghan elder had come to broker an agreement and to act as the governor's representative in this matter. Bashi quickly claimed that honoring the agreement we had brokered would insult the governor, who had not had a representative involved until now. With Bashi's involvement, the new agreement would let Faiz keep his job until Team One returned to investigate the manner thoroughly.

Saturday, August 30, 2008

The Pai looch. Every Afghan provincial police department has a Criminal Investigative Division (CID, similar to internal affairs in a U.S. police department) charged with investigating official misconduct and corruption. Craig recently established a friendship with the Ghazni CID officer, a relationship that paid dividends today. He arrived at our FOB in a panic, his fear palpable. With the pleasantries established, he dropped his bombshell: The Ghazni Governor has a list of eight names (he, the CID officer, is one of them) targeted for assassination.

It all began with an assassination attempt on the governor as he traveled from Ghazni to Kabul back in July. While on the road in Wardak, a Taliban ambush shot up his convoy but missed killing him. Convinced his ANP detail was incapable of protecting him or possibly involved with the plot, the governor returned to Ghazni via helicopter, refused further police protection, and hired his own force: the dreaded Pai looch. In Pashto, Pai looch means "those who walk without shoes" and is a derogatory term Afghans used to describe the Taliban who often have hard, calloused feet due to a lack of shoes. In a move of sheer genius, the governor hired the Pai looch as Afghan police, ordered them assigned to his protection detail, and then made it clear that they answered only to him. As mentors, we were powerless to hire, to fire, or to arrest Afghan police, so the CID officer's insights were invaluable.

We first encountered the Pai looch a few weeks back, when we noticed men in black guarding the governor's office and mansion, buildings normally guarded by the ANP. At the time, we dismissed it as either ANP without uniforms or undisciplined ANP (the Ghazni force is up next for FDD training). The CID officer provided valuable insight into their true nature. After the July ambush, the governor had authorized the creation of an Afghan Police Quick Reaction Force, a force he personally staffed. The Pai looch are allegedly men from Kandahar (the governor's home province), and the rumor on the Afghan street is that they're all Taliban. Besides their lack of ANP uniforms, they have the long flowing beards synonymous with the Taliban of old and are further identifiable by a tattoo of the five-side of a die on their wrist.

The CID officer shook as he explained the governor's malfeasance. The governor had spent the past two months assessing the loyalty of the current provincial and district governments (particularly the police force). Those deemed not loyal were to be fired if possible, or "removed" (killed) by the Pai looch.

Another piece of the Ghazni puzzle had just fallen into place. Faiz and his Rabat checkpoint stood in the way of the chromite smuggling out of northern Deh Yak, and they had twice tried to fire him; the provincial NDS chief had been removed within a month of Governor Usmani's arrival; and just days ago, after General Khan had retired, Colonel Zaman had been appointed Khan's replacement, only to have that promotion put on hold after the governor secretly lobbied Kabul to have him either fired or transferred out of Ghazni (so that Governor Usmani could choose his own police chief).

We left the meeting with a profound new insight into Ghazni and the governor's corruption and concern about his Pai looch assassins. The list of the damned mirrored our list of men we could trust in the Ghazni government: Faiz of Deh Yak, the CID officer, Zaman, the provincial finance officer, and the NDS interim chief. As we walked away contemplating everything he had just told us, I turned to Craig to discuss our plan of action and met his eyes, which spoke volumes: The governor had to be stopped, and the Pai looch was where our investigation should start.

32

Reflections on 9/11

Thursday, September 11, 2008

It was a gorgeous Tuesday morning with nary a cloud in the radiant September sky. I woke up nearly late for my "History of the Silk Road" class (the irony that I'm currently serving in a land once part of the Silk Road is not lost on me) and sprinted half a mile across campus. I can't recall what we covered in class that day, though I do remember being tremendously bored. Class ended around 10:15, leaving me with about four hours before my next class. I leisurely walked back to my dorm, stopping at the campus mail center along the way. I wore a button-down shirt, shorts, and flip-flops, standard autumn attire for a Hamilton College student. I turned into the mail center and strode toward my mailbox, paying little attention to the crowd of people huddled around a TV in the hallway. Oddly enough, the presence of the TV was my first clue that something was amiss. The mail center never had a TV in the hallway before today. For whatever reason—I still can't explain why seven years later—I turned to see what on TV had the crowd so enraptured. I think it took about five minutes for the pictures on the screen to cross the threshold into reality. Tuned to ABC, the image displayed was split: On the left stood a lone tower of the World Trade Center billowing with smoke, and on the right a hazy picture showed a building with the words "Pentagon, Washington DC" written at the bottom of the image. Peter Jennings announced, "We're getting word now that the second tower will likely collapse at any moment." "*What?* Second tower? Where's the first?" I cried out. A lone distraught voice responded between tears, "It's gone." Over the next 10 minutes, through images alone, I learned the horrible fate of that morning, of planes colliding into buildings and announcing the end of our age of innocence.

At first, before I saw the images of passenger jets being turned into weapons, I thought the attack was an errant missile strike by a malfunctioning Russian or Chinese military unit. Islamic terrorism didn't even enter my mind. Even now, seven years later, try as I might, I cannot successfully recall that initial level of blissful ignorance. Perhaps I'm inexcusably biased, but for me, "terrorism" has become synonymous with militant Islamic fundamentalism. Prior to that Tuesday, whenever I heard the word, my initial images split between the Palestinian-Israeli conflict and domestic white supremacist groups. Today, I instantly see a bearded Saudi man.

As the second tower tumbled before my tear-filled eyes, I slipped into a prolonged daze. For the next several weeks, I walked around school not living my life but simply going through the motions. Everything and everyone in the new America seemed related to the attacks. We had entered a new and frightening time: the Post-9/11 Age. What I remember most about those first few days was the profound silence during the day due to a lack of commercial aircraft in the sky and the never-ending television coverage dominating every single network, including MTV and ESPN. Like so many others, I spent countless hours in front of continuous news coverage of our strange new world.

I began contemplating leaving school and joining the military. 9/11 was my generation's Pearl Harbor. I come from a family of proud military service on both my mother's and father's sides. At least one family member has served in every major American war dating back to the War for Independence. An innate obligation to serve began to boil. I suddenly found my life profoundly unfair. I was too lucky—I had benefited too much from a nation I had given nothing to in return.

My debt to society was too great to simply muddle through college and end up another wealthy lawyer. I couldn't justify my privileged life. I had attended the best schools, grown up safely in middle-class America, traveled the world, and enjoyed all the pleasures freedom brings, and for what? Ultimately, what good did *any* of that bring? As the days passed through my sophomore fall, I struggled to answer those questions that nagged and tore at my soul.

"Mom, Dad, I've got to do something about this. I just can't, I don't see how I can continue to do this. What good is my being here at college doing? How am I contributing? America doesn't need another kid with a liberal-arts degree on his way to law school, it needs soldiers, it needs fighters. When the Japanese bombed Pearl Harbor, did Grandpa wait to be drafted? No. He joined immediately, because our freedoms were under attack. He fulfilled his obligation, his duty to serve. I've got to do the same. I cannot just rely on others to carry this burden. Though I might be far from it, America needs her best and brightest.

"I keep thinking about all the people who perished in those towers. Some of them were tremendously successful and lived very wealthy lives. When all was said and done, did *any* of their contributions matter? Just because they made un-Godly sums of money and found incredible success in their professions, did they leave the world a better place? Something I keep imagining is this scenario of all these rich and powerful men and women trapped in the towers, panicking. All their money and success and power that mattered up until those final moments couldn't buy or change their fate. I keep seeing this image of these successful people collapsing into their own self-despair, only to be calmed by a janitor, the man earning the lowest wage of any in their doomed group. Here's this guy, and until today, *none* of these people paid him any mind, and yet now, he's the hero. He's the one who knows the stairwells and the building's design better than any of them. He's the one keeping them calm and attempting to lead them to safety. Here's a guy who spent his final moments making a difference. And no amount of money or college education had *anything* to do with how he lived his final moments. I just can't see how *any* of what I'm doing at college matters. I'm not making a difference. I'm not contributing to the cause. We were attacked, and rather than joining up as duty demands, I'm sitting here at school worrying about tests and papers that will never save a life or ever mean a damn thing in the grand scheme of anything. Mom, Dad, I'm seriously considering leaving school after this semester and joining the military."

My father expressed his desire to join in my place and his regret that his age made that impossible. My mother begged me to reconsider my decision. I couldn't. In addition to my innate desire to serve, I could no longer ignore an image: the children I hope to have one day. I vowed that I never want my future children to know the fear I felt on that Tuesday seven years ago. I want them to grow up blissfully ignorant, to only know a September 10, 2001, world. If all I did was go to college, graduate, proceed on to law school, earn the American Dream, and never serve, how could I look at them as a man and know that I stood by and let others do the heavy lifting to ensure their freedoms? The thought sickened me.

Early December 2001

My best friend, Patrick, and I had traveled to the local mall to purchase presents for our "Secret Santa" group. The mall had three legs of stores attached to a central food court. Patrick and I agreed to give each other 15 minutes to buy our gifts before meeting back in the food court. Being a more efficient shopper, I purchased my gift in record-breaking time and found myself strolling around the food court, admiring the Christmas decorations. That's when I saw them: three soldiers manning a recruitment booth, each standing tall and proud in his uniform. I headed straight for them and sparked up conversation with a young private: "Hi, my name's Matt, and I'm thinking of joining up. What are the chances I could join and guarantee a spot in Officer Candidate School?" (I had recently watched *An Officer and a Gentleman* and knew that enlisted soldiers could potentially earn their commission after successful completion of a grueling course in addition to basic training.) As the private struggled to answer my question (he was more familiar with the enlisted soldier route), the head recruiting sergeant, Sergeant Davis, walked up and said, "I'll take it from here, Private." After we exchanged pleasantries, I repeated my inquiry. Smiling, Sergeant Davis told me OCS wouldn't be a problem if I had the requisite college credits and achieved a certain standard on an army aptitude test. Within minutes, I had agreed to take the test and begin enlistment procedures; or, as Patrick likes to tell the story, "I left him alone for 10 minutes, and he enlisted to the first recruiter he saw."

A month later, on January 16, 2002, I officially enlisted into the U.S. Army National Guard as Private First Class Matthew Zeller. Four months later, I jumped the whole OCS process and joined an ROTC unit through Syracuse University, a path better suited to allow me to finish college on time *and* to achieve my goal of earning an officer's commission by graduation. And seven years later, here I am, doing what I set out to do. I'm proud of my service and my participation in this conflict. For me, Afghanistan was always the just and necessary war. When I think of our enemies here, I inevitably remember 9/11. I remember the crippling fear I felt that day. I remember the visceral hatred that welled inside my body. I remember the absolute sorrow that overcame me as I drove down the Riverside Highway, rounded the bend at 125th Street, and stared out at an alien skyline a month after the attacks. I take all these memories and emotions, and I use them daily to remind myself of our purpose here: to right an unspeakable wrong. To prove to America's enemies that we will not go quietly into the night, that our torch of liberty burns eternal. And to one day face the children I hope to have, to look into their innocent eyes, and to know that I did something meaningful and tangible to ensure their liberty.

On this seven-year anniversary of that fateful day, I ask you do three things. First, please take a moment to reflect on all that we've lost and experienced since that day. Second, ask yourself what you've done to make a difference. My greatest qualm with our government since 9/11 was that instead of being asked to make sacrifices, we were instructed to go shopping. And for the most part, I feel that's what we've done. We as a society have yet to truly endeavor to leave the world a better place than we found it. We will only continue to be a great nation so long as each of us, not just those in uniform, contributes to our betterment. In that spirit, I ask one final thing: that you commit yourself to something that will help leave our world better than we found it. Whether you send pens to Afghan children, join the military, volunteer with the local fire department, donate to charity, whatever, I ask that you commit yourself to something truly altruistic. Seven years ago today, in the ashes of our greatest modern devastation, we rose together as a nation and bonded in the rarest of ways; for the first time in a generation, we spoke and acted as one people, indivisible, with universal beliefs of liberty and justice for all, resolved to right an egregious wrong. Today, I ask that we renew that vow.

Somewhere on our journey from that Tuesday to this Thursday, we lost that common spirit. If we are to win this struggle against freedom and liberty (make no mistake, that is what this struggle in Afghanistan is *all* about), we need to unite like that once again. Today we continue to struggle not just for Afghanistan's security but for our very way of life. Our enemies here do not just want us out of this nation; they want our existence eradicated from the planet. Our worldview is simply incompatible with theirs. Sadly, our conflict is beyond diplomacy; we cannot negotiate with people who abhor our very essence. We must stand firm in our resolve to see Afghanistan succeed; otherwise we will subject ourselves to countless more autumn tragedies. We must find a way to silence today's enemies while ensuring that their children do not become tomorrow's terrorists. We can do this, but only if we commit ourselves to the task as one united people. Although we are of many creeds and cultures, we are in the end, above all else, one people united: Americans. And we can do anything if we set our minds to it, for our potential knows only the bounds of our dreams. Thus, today I ask you to reflect, to remember, and to renew our common vow—that together we will not let the events of that Tuesday ultimately define our destiny. We are Americans; it's time we start acting like it.

33

Why We're Losing, Part 1

Saturday, September 13, 2008

My grandfather fought in WWII. A Dartmouth grad, from a wealthy family, he likely could have avoided the war had he wanted. He didn't. Instead, he chose to join the navy almost immediately following the Pearl Harbor attack. As family legend has it, he left home in 1941 and didn't return until 1945. Countless other Americans have similar tales, stories of men and women leaving when the war commenced and only returning home once it was won. America doesn't fight wars like that anymore. For the soldiers of wars prior to Vietnam, war was one's life. You survived by either winning or not dying, but you were in it until its end or yours. Not anymore. Today, war is a temporary occupation. We rotate in and out of war; we don't remain until the thing is won, just until our tour is done. I think it's one of the reasons why soldiers joke that modern war is a lot like prison: We live behind barbed wire, our neighbors would gladly kill us if given the chance, we can't drink, we can't have sex, and we can only leave when we have permission, but we're also heavily armed. The incentive for a soldier faced with indefinite deployment is to fight as hard as possible, to take key and necessary risks, and to do whatever it takes to win, because winning means going home alive. But, if you know that your tour only lasts so long, that home comes regardless of the outcome of the fight, then your incentive isn't so much as to win as it is to survive. We call such thinking "short-time syndrome," and people who exhibit it "short-timers."

An MRAP that hit an IED and had its external/extra fuel canisters catch on fire and burn the entire vehicle. Note the escape hatches open on top—thankfully, everyone survived.

Short-timers pass on dangerous missions, avoid unnecessary risks, and spend a lot of time on the FOB. And no matter how honorable or brave the soldier, everyone eventually goes through it, and therein lies the problem with our current deployment regimen. If survival inevitably becomes your incentive, then you ultimately fail to complete your mission. The problems that arise during war do not adhere to your deployment schedule; they march to the meter of chaos. When you first arrive, you're a combat baby, learning how to crawl in your area of operations. By mid-tour, you've hopefully grown into a star athlete, capable of going the distance and doing what it takes to win the day-to-day struggle: mission first, soldiers always. But by the time short-time syndrome hits, you start factoring in different variables into your decision-making process: Is it really *that* important that we drive out to the dangerous district today? Honestly, am I best suited to solve this problem, or could the next guy do it better, because it's going to continue long past the time I'm scheduled to leave? Indeed, problems that arise during the onslaught of "short-time syndrome" almost always get passed on to the replacements. At the end of the day, one question that has nagged since the moment your boots first touched Afghan soil finds a way to severely alter your risk-assessment process: Is doing this/solving this problem/going on this mission worth the risk of getting someone killed or injured when we're so close to getting out of here alive? The moment you let that question influence your thinking is the moment you're officially a "short-timer," because inevitably the answer will be, "No, this isn't worth getting my guys hurt or killed, especially after all the crap we've been through." What we all fail to say aloud is that we're really screwing the next guy, the infant who suddenly inherited a problem we "combat adults" could barely handle.

Americans clearly won't favor indefinite deployments unless we're in another World War II–type conflict (win, or cease to exist as a nation). Thus, we're left with defined deployments that have (in theory) fixed start and end dates. I've already discussed how the current deployment process induces short-time syndrome, but I'll briefly mention one additional and catastrophic quagmire it causes: 100 percent organizational turnover every 365 days.

With each deployment rotation, almost every single person in a unit is replaced, from the commander to the cooks. Processes that have been perfected, problems solved, none of that matters once the new guys arrive and take over with their way of doing things. Thus, with every new rotation, not only are routines and regimens refined but also all the subject matter experts (SMEs, pronounced "smees" in military-speak) end up being replaced with combat infants. During my tour of duty, I watched two iterations of U.S. mentors, a U.S. army battalion, and two iterations of Polish battle groups rotate through Ghazni. Every iteration resulted in the same process. Old guys get short-time syndrome. Problems begin to stagnate and to manifest. New guys arrive. Old guys do their best to bring new guys up to speed in what little time they have together, but the new guys are still combat babies and struggle just to keep up, losing critical information during the transfer of responsibility. Old guys leave, passing on problems to the grossly inadequate new guys. The new guys spend the next two months recovering from their initial mistakes and rapidly growing up from combat babies into counterinsurgency grad students. One day the formerly new, now-soon-to-be-old guys wake up and realize that their rotation draws high, and the process repeats indefinitely. Complete organizational turnover every 365 days. In essence, we haven't been fighting in Afghanistan for eight years; we've been fighting in Afghanistan for a year and have repeated the experience eight times over and counting.

The answer to this problem is frighteningly simple: Assign units ownership of a specific area and deploy them back to that area for each rotation until the war ends. Year one: Deploy to area X. Year two: Recover back home. Year three: Redeploy to area X. Repeat until victory. The benefit of this deployment scheme is the following. First, units own a specific area. They have an incentive to see that area improve and the overall mission to succeed. When they leave, they aren't just passing on the problems to the new guy—they're passing on the problems to the guys who will be watching the shop until they return a year later. They have a vested interest in seeing that follow-on unit succeed, because if it doesn't, they'll be inheriting a whole slew of problems (some old, but some certainly new) at the next deployment. They realize they could be deployed and redeployed indefinitely and thus recognize that the way to break the cycle is to achieve success and to establish an area where their presence is no longer needed.

Second, subject-matter expertise is maximized. I just spent the last year becoming quite knowledgeable about all things Ghazni, Afghanistan. If the army decides to redeploy me, I ought to go back to Ghazni; it'll take me less time than others who've never been there to get back up to speed, and the learning curve won't be nearly as steep as if I'm sent to an area about which I know very little.

Finally, over the course of repeated deployments, units will develop a familiarity and rapport with the locals that can only be obtained overtime. The reason why the surge in Iraq worked so well was because many units on the ground ended up doing 15- to 24-month-long tours and thus had enough time to develop and to foster key relationships and to learn the necessary info critical for success. Deployments that partner units with specific areas could achieve the similar results without requiring prolonged or indefinite deployments, though there will always be a loss of knowledge, given personnel changes and the fact that the longer one is away from the fight, the less one knows what actually is going on. This may not be a perfect solution, but I think it's far better than what we have right now, a never-ending cycle of units leaving just at the point where they had become most effective.

34

Watches Without Time

Sunday, September 14, 2008

Today we held our weekly intelligence synchronization meeting with our Polish and Afghan allies and the remainder of U.S. forces left in Ghazni. Sync meetings actually involve multiple meetings. We purposely schedule the arrival of the other U.S. units ahead of everyone else so we can have the U.S. only meeting where we share all the info we have (most meetings are limited in the sense that we have certain info we can't share with the Polish or the Afghans). Once everyone has arrived, we have the actual sync meeting, something we've all found to be an invaluable experience, as it's helped all of us to gain a more complete idea of what is occurring in Ghazni (we each have a piece of the puzzle, and only together can we complete it). After the meeting, we have the meetings-after-the-meeting. Since we still don't fully trust the ANP, we have a meeting afterward where the NDS and ANA share info that they want us to know but not share with the ANP for fear it'll be leaked to the Taliban (who are rumored to have numerous spies within the ANP's ranks). After the non-ANP meeting, we have the non-Afghan meeting, where we and the Polish share info that we want each other to know but cannot share with the Afghans (mainly because it involves the very people who attend the weekly sync meetings or their superiors). The irony of all these meetings is that I'm sure everyone, including the Afghans, realizes that they occur, but we all act is if they're conducted in absolute secrecy. I'd be

An up-armored HMMMV that had its engine block destroyed and pushed into the front seat of the vehicle by an IED, killing the driver and passenger instantly.

very surprised if the Afghans don't have their own "Afghans-only" meeting after leaving the Polish and us.

Today's sync meeting went extremely well, as we all agreed that the Ghazni governor has become the central problem within the province; some (Arnold and I) even feel he's surpassed the Taliban as the main threat to the province's development and stability. The charges against him are substantial: He's extremely corrupt (smuggling drugs and stolen minerals), and, more importantly, he has his own police force and death squad who run illegal tolls and assassinate all who stand in the governor's way. Imagine if the police in the United States beat you and stole your money, and anyone you approached in the government to seek reciprocity either is in on the corruption, ends up dead for trying to assist you, or does nothing out of fear of reprisal. You'd hate your government and the goons who kept them in power. Now add a foreign military force that appears to back those corrupt officials, and you'd really hate them, because without their guns, planes, artillery, and helicopters, you'd be able to rise up and resist the government you hate so much. I'm beginning to worry that with each act of government injustice, blatant official corruption, and person the Pai looch beat or kill, this mind-set is slowly becoming the norm for Afghans. I fear the day when Afghans no longer distinguish between us and their corrupt officials and only see us as the very goons who keep these hated people in power; the day this happens is the day we've lost the war.

One of the major problems with the governor is that he thinks he can get away with all his illegal behavior, because no matter how blatant his corruption, no one from the coalition has attempted to stop him. I blame the governor, but even more, I blame the 101st battalion commander. The lieutenant colonel has fostered an environment in which the governor isn't merely tolerated, he's celebrated. The 101st has refused to investigate all the allegations we've brought against the governor.

The lieutenant colonel's relationship with the governor is a phenomenal case study as to why we're losing the Afghan war. His soldiers are superb, tough, aggressive fighters. His command staff will follow his orders without question. He hasn't a clue how to use any of them. His entire battalion lacks a defining purpose. Not a single person can answer the following question with a declarative statement: What are you trying to do here? Kill Taliban? Protect the Afghan population? Our mission is clear; we're here to train the Afghan police and army to be more proficient forces. As I see it, inherent in our mission is the need to fight official corruption; the Afghan security forces can only hold credibility with the Afghan population if the Afghans trust them to be fair and just enforcers of the law. Once we've lost favor with the Afghan people, we've inevitably lost them to the Taliban. The Taliban could literally sit back and let the Afghan government win the war for them: Its corruption is driving people into the arms of the resistance.

The title of this book, *Watches without Time*, is the manifestation of our current efforts in Ghazni and Afghanistan writ large. There's a tale of an American soldier interrogating an illiterate Taliban fighter just captured after a firefight. The American asks the Afghan Taliban why he continues to fight:

> American: You cannot possibly hope to win. We have fighter jets, bombs, drones, artillery, armored vehicles, helicopters; we're better trained, better equipped. You cannot possibly think you can beat us, can you?
>
> Afghan Taliban: It is true, you Americans have all the watches, but we have all the time.

The Taliban prisoner provides a perfect summary of our efforts in Afghanistan from 2001 to the present. A watch is an amazingly complex piece of technology that reflects a society's level of progress and development. But if a watch doesn't tell time, if there is no strategy that dictates how one should use that watch, then a watch is nothing more than an incredibly complex piece of technology that doesn't serve a purpose. For eight years and counting, we've lacked a strategy that dictates how we should use all this amazing technology; we've lacked a goal to which we can apply our strength and resources. Thus, in the current conflict, we Americans and our allies, with all our technological military might and marvel, are the watches without time.

35

Roller Coaster of Emotions

Wednesday, September 17, 2008

On a routine mission over to FOB Ghazni, my vehicle caught fire. It all happened rather suddenly, rolling along, situation normal, when next thing you know, there's a shit-ton of smoke engulfing our crew compartment, choking and blinding us. Sergeant First Class Fischer slammed on the brakes and steered the vehicle to the side of the road, and we all "exfilled" (army-speak for "hauled ass out"). As I tried to catch my breath, my combat instincts took over: Calm down, gain control of your faculties, scan your area for threats, make sure everyone is out of the vehicle, and extinguish the fire. As the Afghans drove by, laughing at our misfortune and cursing our general presence (our relations with the locals have begun to deteriorate), we quickly extinguished the electrical fire, hooked up the vehicle to an impromptu towing rig, and dragged the useless Hummer the rest of the way to FOB Ghazni. The vehicle is busted and will have to be fixed over the course of a few days, meaning we're once again down a vehicle. Losing a vehicle to maintenance will severely affect our abilities to conduct missions, especially given the six-vehicle-minimum movement requirements.

Haji Fasil stopped by the FOB again for another round of my chastising him. He once again has meddled with our efforts to reform the Deh Yak ANP. This time I all but accused him of running drugs, smuggling chromite, and aiding and abiding the Taliban, and he didn't even bother to protest. He suggested the team and I accompany him to dinner with the provincial governor on Sunday;

One of our terps, who we suspected was a Taliban infiltrator, Haji Fasil, and Janis.

I readily agreed, as this finally gives us an opportunity to clear a *lot* of issues up with his boss.

As the day ended, I volunteered Arnold and me for a large HA mission in Deh Yak on September 29. On the one hand, I'm thrilled to be going out on this; HA missions recharge my spirits and morale. On the other hand, I'm nervous as shit about going back out on a potentially long and dangerous mission. We're planning on going all over Deh Yak over the course of several days as a follow-up to all the recent fighting that has taken place between us and the Taliban.

36

Why We're Losing, Part 2

Saturday, September 20, 2008

Today was a microcosm of all that is wrong with our efforts in Afghanistan.

For several months, in my capacity as our team's operations officer, I've planned for several large missions scheduled to take place simultaneously on September 21, 2008. One of these missions involves an air assault into Waghez. We've been all set to kick off at midnight for several of these missions, and then late this evening we got "the word." President Karzai or some other grand pooh-bah made September 21, 2008, a national stand-down day for safety or "UN Peace Day," canceling all pre-planned missions. In addition to suffering from a serious lack of communication between units (our higher never tells us what's going on, otherwise logic dictates someone somewhere should have put a halt to our planning efforts so we didn't waste our time), we also suffer from a tragic lack of resources. Our Waghez mission required the dedication and use of at least two CH-47 helicopters and fighter jets to guard their movement. There simply aren't enough helicopters and fighter jets in Afghanistan to go around, so use of these critically important assets takes a great deal of forward planning and scheduling.

We are stuck on our FOBs, forbidden from interacting with the local population unless we travel in massively armored vehicles and go out dressed like storm-troopers from *Star Wars*. We cannot spend more than a few nights away from the security of our FOBs, and even then we have to be encamped at some Afghan

The Andar Police detachment organizing themselves for their return to Andar after returning from two months of basic training in Konduz province.

outpost, usually away from the local population. In essence, we secure only the area around which we're presently standing and spend too little time with our Afghan counterparts to effectively mentor or to develop them into anything that could possibly be considered an effective fighting force or replacement for our efforts. And to top it all off, every time we do try to do something good, our higher HQ stands firmly in the way, be it through lack of planning, communicating, or ill-informed, misguided policies that completely restrict our ability to conduct any meaningful kind of counterinsurgency mission. It's no wonder the Afghan people have no faith in us or our Afghan counterparts. We arrive in their villages for hours at a time, ask them the same inane questions they've heard from countless Americans, and then leave. Upon our departure, the Taliban or whatever community authority holds sway in the village returns to "govern" or to administer village life, and things continue on as if we don't exist. The Afghan people time and time again want peace, security, and an improvement from their current disposition. We'll never bring them any of that unless we actually embed with them, live continuously among them, and deliver on their requests in a timely and efficient manner. I fear this war is lost should we continue on our current trajectory, as our presence does nothing but fuel insurgency and instability. We aren't around long enough or consistently enough to actually be of any value to these people and seem to only invite Taliban reprisal and attacks on the areas we visit.

Sunday, September 21, 2008

UN Peace Day. The Waghez DC was attacked while hundreds of Afghan men toting Mullah Omar lunchboxes went out and planted countless IEDs. Several ANP and ANA outposts farther south were attacked, and since we can't go out, the wounded cannot be medevac'd for treatment. All of this because we were confined to our bases countrywide. Literally, if Osama Bin Laden had been outside my FOB gate, all I could have done was give him the finger and ask him to come back tomorrow. Utter bullshit.

Monday, September 22, 2008

After yesterday's debacle, we received permission to conduct all the missions we had had on hold due to UN Peace Day's no-movement policy. Early this morning, I called up the governor, profusely apologized for not attending his banquet in our honor, and accepted his offer to join him for dinner this evening. Relations with the governor smoothed over, I sent the Andar ANP team on its way to Andar to drop off the district's ANP force for the first time since returning from two months of training.

For the past two months, the Andar ANP have gone through a basic training–style course in Kunduz, taught by DynCorp contractors and overseen by Captain Morriarty, Sergeant First Class Alderson, and Sergeant Blasker. The ANP apparently took very well to the training, and Team Two is excited to bring them back to their district to see what they can accomplish in our remaining months. During the course of training, the ANP repeatedly expressed their concerns over returning to the district. Specifically, they're nervous about getting into a firefight alone with the Taliban, a fear Sergeant First Class Alderson and Captain Morriarty have tried to alleviate by highlighting the fact that for the first few weeks of their return, Team Two will be living with the ANP. Training was supposed to professionalize the force, and their slow reintroduction to the Andar population is meant to be a means of making the district's relationship with the police force more positive. Should the Andar ANP get into a firefight with the Taliban immediately upon their return, it would be very bad for their credibility with the local population, who would see such an attack as a sign of Taliban strength and ANP weakness. Moreover, after all the reassuring Team Two has done of the Andar ANP, should that firefight occur in our absence, all the credibility and trust that currently exists between Team Two and the Andar ANP will likely disintegrate.

Teams Two and Three (Team Three, the ANCOP mentors who cover down on a district while that district's ANP are at training) departed for Andar early this morning in high spirits, ready to aggressively tackle their upcoming weeklong mission. On their way to their first objective (the farthest outpost in Andar, known as the Bande-Sarde Dam OP), Lightning Main radioed the teams and ordered them to immediately return to the nearest base. Why, you ask? UN Peace Day Part II: Son of Peace Day.

At midnight, Lightning Main approved the mission to Andar. At 0430, the teams left for Andar. At 0630, Lightning Main changed its mind, radioed the teams, and then ordered them to drop everything they were doing, leave their ANP without any warning or notice, and travel to the closest FOB to await further instruction.

Teams Two and Three protested the order, citing their approved mission and the fact that they couldn't just stop what they were doing, but to no avail. The Taliban attacked the Andar ANP immediately after the teams left. Lightning Main refused to give them permission to drive the two kilometers down the road to come to the Andar ANP's aid; they were on their own, and all our credibility was gone.

Thankfully, the Andar ANP kicked some serious ass on their own, gaining a much-needed win and morale boost, yet a win that came at a loss of confidence and trust in our abilities to keep our word. To add insult to injury, we had to once again cancel our dinner with the governor (two days in a row), a major cultural snafu. Any position of strength we had in our talk has been eroded due to the number of times we've effectively snubbed his hospitality and invitations. All the issues I wanted to tackle will come at a point of significant weakness, as we've insulted his honor by inexplicably canceling two days in a row.

After the events of the past two days, I am convinced that we have a more coherent strategy on how to lose this war than to win it.

37

A Case Study in Corruption—
Ghazni Governor Usmani

Tuesday, September 23, 2008

After two days of setbacks, we finally had our dinner with the Ghazni governor, Doctor Usman Usmani—a singular, if not defining, moment in my Afghan tour of duty.

It seemed odd to attend a state dinner in combat attire. Usmani is essentially the equivalent of a state governor in the U.S., and yet I'm wearing my combat uniform, body armor, and full complement of weapons. Going to dinner with the man who is supposed to be in charge (who in reality depends on our presence for his survival) dressed as if we're going into battle: Nothing says "occupying power" more.

First, a brief lesson on the Afghan system of government. Afghanistan is divided into 34 provinces ("states" in the U.S.), which are each administered or "governed" by a provincial governor. These provinces are divided into districts ("counties" in the U.S.), which are subsequently governed by "district administrators," also referred to as "subgovernors." The Afghan population does not directly elect any of these officials. At the end of the day, they are all either indirectly or directly appointed by President Karzai. Karzai appoints the provincial governors, who in theory serve at his pleasure. Karzai even appoints (or instructs the provincial governors on whom to appoint) some of the district-level subgovernors. The result of

Waiting for Governor Usmani to arrive for our meeting with him at the start of the infamous governor's dinner.

this system is that almost none of these officials is actually beholden to the constituents he "serves." Their job survival is predicated on doing what is best for their immediate boss and, ultimately, what is best for Karzai.

Doctor Usman Usmani is the second provincial governor we've had during our tour of duty. Karzai removed the first within a month of our arrival. Doctor Usmani, a native of Kandahar, allegedly a "credible" Afghan surgeon, who claims to be Karzai's cousin, replaced him almost immediately after his dismissal.

Doctor Usmani arrived this past spring, saying all the right things. He talked about engaging with the people, meeting with elders, winning over locals, governing in consult with religious leaders, but in order to do this, of course, he needed an immediate donation so he could begin buying goodwill.

Since that first encounter with our team, relations with the governor have deteriorated. It all began with a fateful midsummer trip the governor took to Kabul, during which the "Taliban" ambushed his convoy somewhere around Salar village, in Wardak province. Governor Usmani survived the ambush and arrived safely in Kabul but deeply frightened, to the point that he refused to ever drive to Kabul again and demanded that ISAF fly him back to Ghazni. Somehow he made it back to Ghazni and immediately set out to improve his own security. Using the ANP, he created a "rapid reaction force" for the provincial-level ANP force that in theory was supposed to action intelligence as it arrived in a joint Afghan-ISAF information center. In truth, he used this force to put his private security detail on the Afghan government payroll so he didn't have to pay them out of his own pocket. And who did he choose to staff this security force? The Taliban. Yes, the Afghan governor of Ghazni province hired authentic Taliban fighters to staff his personal security detail.

They were pretty easy to spot from the start, dressed in flowing black robes, long bushy beards, and menacing stares. But stereotypes of dress and grooming aside, what made them stand out was the fact that they all had the same tattoo of a die with five "pips" (spots) on their left hands, below the thumb, where the fingers meet the wrist. I know that this is a Taliban tattoo, because several Taliban detainees admitted such to me after we captured them on the battlefield.

The locals have taken to calling the Governor's personal security detail the "Pai looch" (pronounced "Pie Looch"), which in Pashto means "those who walk without shoes," a derogatory slang term used to identify someone as "Taliban." These Pai looch have taken to terrorizing the local population, erecting illegal checkpoints on the roads and at the entrances to the local bazaar that they use to extract illegal tolls from an already extremely poor population.

Hence tonight's dinner: a good old-fashioned sit-down is the only way we're going to make any progress. Major Garrison came down with a bad stomach bug, and Major Goodman trusted me enough to handle this one on my own, so I went as the senior officer for the whole delegation. My initial plan was to sit and let Sergeant First Class Rucker and the DynCorp mentors for Deh Yak do most of the talking; our goal, at the least, was to get the governor to reinstate Faiz as Deh Yak's police chief.

Which brings me back to preparing to go to this shindig: Wearing my combat uniform felt quite imperialist, as if I, a 27-year old army first lieutenant, could just stroll in with my pistol strapped to my side, my rifle slung over my shoulder, and dictate terms to an Afghan provincial governor.

We drove to the governor's office as the sun set over Ghazni city, tinting the rundown buildings and crumbling roads a warm orange. Upon our arrival at his office complex, our convoy was stopped by an AK-47–toting man dressed in flowing black robes with a thick black beard and menacing scowl. Janis and I jumped out of the vehicle and informed him that we were here to have dinner with the governor as his guests. The man, confused, informed us that the governor had gone home for the day, and perhaps we should try him at his mansion up the street. Thanking him for the information, I turned with Janis and walked back to our Hummer. "Hey Janis, one more thing, ask him what he is; is he ANP, ANA, NDS?" "Or Pai looch?" Janis said, winking at me as a sign he saw where I was going with this. "You got it," I said, smiling back at my dear friend.

Janis and the man spoke for about 10 seconds before Janis turned back to me and walked toward our vehicle, grinning from ear to ear. "The man says he is Pai looch and the governor's personal security detail. He says he does not work for the ANP, ANA, or NDS. I didn't even have to ask if he was Pai looch, he said that's what he was himself."

We drove the half-mile to the governor's mansion, a colossal urban complex made of worn brick and cracked, cheap concrete. Colored puke yellow by the Afghan dirt used to make the structure's bricks, and poorly maintained, the building was extraordinarily upscale and large when compared to the living standards of most Afghans in Ghazni. Upon our arrival, a contingent of black-robed, AK-47–toting men met us at the gate and halfheartedly tried to tell us where to park our vehicles before they realized that we were going to park them wherever the hell we wanted. As Craig and I got out of our vehicle, I had Janis ask them who they were: "ANP, ANA, or NDS." It came as no surprise to anyone when they all self-identified as "Pai looch."

As we took off our body armor and arranged a security rotation for the vehicles (the gunners would remain behind to keep an eye on the untrustworthy Pai looch), Haji Fasil came strolling out of the governor's mansion as if he owned the place, with Bashi Habib in tow. Confused as to why we were visiting, I informed Haji and Bashi that the governor had invited us for dinner the past two nights and that we had arranged to visit with him this evening. The looks on their faces told me all I needed to know: The governor hadn't a clue that we were coming tonight. Another cultural no-no: Don't show up uninvited with a large entourage after you've twice turned down an offer to attend dinner.

Nevertheless, it is extremely egregious for an Afghan to turn away guests. Haji Fasil quickly dispatched an aid to inform the governor of our arrival and to cobble together a makeshift banquet in our honor. As we walked, he apologized if the feast wasn't up to our expectations, as they had not expected us. I assured him we didn't mind and were happy to be welcomed as guests. All the while, I wondered what in the hell he was doing essentially living at the governor's compound and not out in his own district.

Entering the governor's compound, I was taken aback. Never judge the interior of an Afghan's home by the appearance of the building's exterior. I expected to find cracked walls, peeling paint, rotting floors, and sparse furnishings. Instead, I found ornate and expensive Afghan rugs covering nearly every inch of the marbled floor. The walls were adorned with numerous pieces of art, none as prominent as a portrait of Karzai placed behind what was clearly the governor's chair or "throne" seated in the main room's "power corner." Well-cushioned and comfortable couches and chairs lined the walls, creating an environment of comfortable affluence and outright lavishness. While the governor talked a great game about being a man of the people, railing on and on over the past months about how he wanted to meet their needs and provide for them as if they were his own children, he lived in a level of comfort and wealth of which most of his "children" couldn't begin to dream. While he sat perched upon his silk-carpeted throne with Karzai's image staring down behind him, an entire orphanage and children's school sat a mere four blocks away in absolute despair. Kids ran around without proper clothing, dozens stuffed into rooms that realistically should only hold four at a time, walls falling apart, no power, no running water, and a lone stove to provide heat for the winter. The man was a hypocrite in everything he said and did. I didn't realize it at the time, but my anger was going to get the better of me, and we were going to have it out on everything: his corruption, the Pai looch, Faiz's firing, drug running, extortion, theft, graft—it was all fair game. Moreover, it angered me that this asshole was somehow the focus of our unit's efforts when we should have been devoting all our attention to the children four blocks away who were Afghanistan's real future.

After waiting a nerve-wracking 10 minutes (the whole entourage had begun to quietly question if I had taken them on a wild goose chase and that the governor wouldn't show), the governor walked in, looking as if he had been aroused unexpectedly from a nap. He made an effort to walk around the entire room and shake everyone's hands, thanking us for coming. In the seating order of the meeting, I ended up being seated immediately to the governor's left, with Bashi Habib sitting in between the two of us (a seat of immense honor and power in Afghan culture). Sergeant First Class Rucker sat immediately to the governor's right, as we had all agreed he would run the meeting. Janis sat, as always, immediately to my left and would act as the official translator for the meeting (more for the sake of the other Afghans in the room, as the governor speaks near-fluent English).

Once the governor had exchanged brief greetings with the group and chai had been served to all who desired it, he asked us, "Why are you here?" as opposed to going through the usual pleasantries. The guy clearly wanted us in and out as quickly as possible and was not amused at our unannounced visit. The sergeant thanked the governor for hosting us and stated we had come to discuss his dismissal of Faiz Mohammad as Deh Yak's ANP chief. The governor, seizing the moment, reminded us that he hadn't expected us to come tonight and thus could not guarantee a meal fitting of the occasion. He then glibly addressed the issue of Faiz's dismissal by saying, "I'm the governor of this province. You are guests in my country; you do not get to decide who is and who is not police chief of a district. Moving on, what's next?" His frank response admittedly caught all of us off guard. Pausing, Sergeant First Class Rucker turned his head to me and smiled as if to say, "Okay, your turn."

Sensing that the group expected me to talk, the governor turned at me and stared impatiently, awaiting my move, his fingers furiously playing with a set of wooden prayer beads.

"Well your honor, first, let me thank you for your hospitality and hosting us tonight. I realize there's been a mix-up, and I take full responsibility for not making it clear to your staff that we had accepted your offer for tonight. I thought I had communicated that effectively; I obviously did not. Nevertheless, you've graciously hosted us, and for that we're thankful. I also apologize for being unable to honor your invitations over the past several days. Unforeseen orders from our commanders prevented us from attending. I'm sure you understand and thank you for your patience."

He waved his right hand dismissively as if to say, "Say no more, moving on," in response.

"Your honor, the reason why we're coming to you this evening is more than just our concerns with your decision to dismiss Captain Faiz Mohammad as Deh Yak's ANP chief. Over the past several months of your tenure in office and our stay in Ghazni, we've increasingly been exposed to accusations of misconduct and illegal activities done on your behalf in your name. I should note, we're not accusing you of anything—far from it. We're merely coming to you as friends to let you know what we're hearing from your constituents, to ensure you're aware of the public's sentiment and what obstacles you might face in light of these accusations."

He immediately perked up, stopped fussing with his prayer beads, and glared at me, trying to get me to back down. His very presence angered me, and the fact that I had to show him any deference caused me to rage inside, but I could show none of my true feelings. We were in a game of emotional chess, waiting to see who would crack first. I silently stared right back, unmoved by his sudden change in demeanor.

"What accusations do you have? Who has made these? Tell me now! This is a very serious matter!" exclaimed the governor, seemingly the first to blink.

Calmly I replied, "Well, Agha, the accusations come from your constituents and from our own experience. I agree this is a very serious matter, and that's why we needed to come have this talk. I think we should start with your decision to dismiss

Faiz Mohammad. I realize the decision is yours and that this is your country; however I feel as if you were misinformed and led astray," I said as I shot a piercing glare at Haji Fasil, who sheepishly sat in a corner adjacent from the governor.

"Faiz Mohammad was a very bad man. I have evidence. He beat the people. He ate opium. He raped women. I removed him, because the people of Deh Yak came to me and asked me to. I am their servant. Your issue is with them, I can only do as they ask," the governor contested.

"Your honor, let's address that claim one issue at a time. First, if you have evidence, we'd like to see it."

"I have a video!" exclaimed the governor.

"We'd like to see it. If you have a video that proves all these things about Faiz, we'll not only drop the issue, we'll issue a formal apology for ever doubting you, and we'll even help you bring him to justice," said Aaron, the DynCorp mentor for Deh Yak.

The governor turned to one of his aides and sent him off, presumably to get the video (the aide returned about 30 minutes later, without the video). In the end, the video likely never existed.

"Okay, while your aide is getting the video, let's address your concerns about Faiz's drug use. Your honor, this simply cannot be. The ANP are all tested for drugs when they enter training, including Faiz. He passed numerous drug tests while away at training. Opium addiction isn't something that one just quits without exhibiting signs of withdrawal—as a doctor, you know this. Not once has Faiz ever exhibited signs of drug use or withdrawal during our time working with him. Moreover, if drug use is such a concern to you, we're willing to have Faiz come here tomorrow and go through a drug test in front of you to alleviate your concerns. Faiz has agreed to this," I added.

At this point Haji Fasil shot up and began rapidly exclaiming that Faiz was a known drug user, a pimp, a rapist; that just two days ago he had been in Deh Yak selling weapons and fuel to the Taliban; and that he was trying to assassinate Haji Fasil.

"Enough out of you!" I yelled at Haji Fasil. "Your honor," I said, turning back to Governor Usmani, "we know Faiz hasn't been working with the enemy, as Haji claims, because he's currently in Herat. It would be physically impossible for him to be both in Herat and here in Deh Yak. We just spoke to him on an American base in Herat before coming to dinner tonight and also two days ago. Moreover, Faiz's aggressiveness against the Taliban in Deh Yak flies in complete contrast to the idea that he's collaborating with them. Faiz has wanted to fight the Taliban in Deh Yak since the day we met him. He's the furthest thing from a collaborator and the person best positioned to bring security to Deh Yak."

"Oh no he's not! *I* am the person best positioned to bring security to Deh Yak! And I have, by firing Faiz!" the governor heatedly replied.

"Really? Then if Deh Yak is so secure, why is my truck all shot up outside? That happened after you got rid of Faiz!" exclaimed Sergeant First Class Rucker.

"Your honor, if Deh Yak is so secure, then I'm sure you wouldn't mind travel-ing to Ali Kala or Ali Kheyl villages with me right now and having a *shura* with the village elders. Perhaps we could stop and say hi to the Taliban shadow subgovernor of the district, Haji Mohammad, who lives nearby. Shall we leave now?" I asked, knowing he'd outright dismiss the mission, as it was clearly suicidal; Deh Yak wasn't secure, and everyone knew it.

"You only got shot at because you went there. You bring problems. I could go and be fine, but if I went with you, the Taliban would attack. You are the problem, not I!" the governor shot back.

"So there is nothing we can say or do that will change your mind about Faiz?" I asked.

"No, Faiz Mohammad is a bad man. He is Taliban. And if you want to challenge me, then I will go out among the Afghan people and I will lead them, and together we will fight you!" the governor replied resolutely.

The topic was clearly over for the time being, so I decided to change directions and see if his resolve held after I laid out all our evidence against him.

"Okay, your honor, then perhaps we could address a few other issues . . . ," I began to say, when he interrupted me with another wave of his hand and said, "I am here to lead the Afghan people, I will do whatever I must. Please tell me, what troubles you, my friend?"

"Well, your honor, we've heard—and again, these are accusations we have heard repeatedly from the people we meet on our patrols, your people, your constitu-ents—we've heard that you have your own private security force you use to collect illegal tolls, smuggle chromite and other illicit goods [I shot a fleeting glance at Haji Fasil, an allusion to his marijuana fields in Baley village that I'd repeatedly threatened to burn down], and most seriously, your personal enforcement squad." From this point on, our relationship with the governor was irrevocably changed, a fact made more profound by the governor's deafening silence. I turned to Janis and gave him a look that said, "Please tell me you translated that correctly."

"These are very serious charges! What is this force you speak of? There is no such force!" the governor yelled.

"Your honor, they're called the Pai looch," I calmly replied, "and the people are terrified of them."

"*What? This is shit!* Who are these *Pai looch*?" he seethed, prolonging and dwell-ing on the "looch" sound of their name. "They do not exist! How dare you use such a word in front of me? To think, the day has come when an Afghan governor is exposed to such things. Such blasphemy!"

"Well then, Agha, if they don't exist, who is guarding your office and your home at this very moment?" I yelled, exasperated at his incredulousness.

He once again began fidgeting furiously with his prayer beads.

I seized the moment. "Your honor, when we arrived, the men at your gate called themselves Pai looch. They aren't wearing uniforms. They don't claim to be ANP,

ANA, or NDS. They call themselves Pai looch. They're the same men who detained our interpreters in the bazaar the other night. You should know this, because our interpreters called *you* to get *you* to make *your* men, *your Pai looch*, let them go before *we* came to rescue them. When we stopped at the ANP checkpoint by the bus station and caught the ANP stationed there taking money from truckers, these same men, these Pai looch, stopped our investigation, as if they were in charge. After they walked away, we asked the ANP who they were. The ANP replied that they were the Pai looch, the 'governor's men,' and that they had ordered the ANP to collect money from every truck going through the checkpoint. The ANP claimed they were supposed to give these tolls to the Pai looch at the end of each shift. And if that's not enough, they're the same men we watched through our camera on the blimp above FOB Ghazni escort the illegal chromite trucks the other night. The same men who, when the NDS stopped those trucks, drove immediately to your compound, picked up Haji Fasil and Bashi Habib, and drove right back and got into a firefight with the NDS. You talked earlier about having a tape of evidence against Faiz—well, I've got *all* that on tape, and I'd be glad to show it to you!" I exclaimed, my voice rising in pitch and my pace increasing with every charge.

The room sat in shocked, deafening silence. All our cards were on the table. The next move belonged to the governor, and nothing could prepare me for what he did next.

"Karzai is the father of our nation. I serve as his humble servant. If you want to be rid of me, if I am this bad man, then he will remove me. But now, we eat," he mumbled as he stood up and promptly strode into the dining room that adjoined the lavish meeting room.

Masterful. I had to give him that. In one move, he had simply dismissed all our accusations as beneath him and not worthy of his time, and yet he had not denied a single one. He merely announced it was time for dinner and headed out as if the conversation had come to its natural conclusion. He couldn't have been more outwardly calm and yet visibly shaken as he walked away, his eyes firmly focused on the feast ahead of him.

The rest of the room erupted into intense sidebars and chatter. Sergeant First Class Rucker and Aaron began a heated discussion about whether they should let me continue my exposé; Aaron was of the opinion that it was time for the "adults" to take charge, but Sergeant First Class Rucker, ever the good NCO, realized that wasn't his place or role to decide. Majors Garrison and Goodman had made everyone aware I was running this thing and that it was likely to get heated.

Meanwhile, Bashi Habib vigorously lobbied with Janis, who kept repeating Bashi's words softly in my ear: "Bashi says not to worry, that you are his son, and that he will fix this, he will make all things good between you and the governor, but that you must let him talk for you for a little bit."

I didn't answer back. Silently, I scanned the room for the one pair of eyes whose opinion at that moment I most valued: Arnold's. His grin eased my growing fear that I had truly fucked up on a scale of epic proportions. I walked over to him and deadpanned, "So that didn't go as well as I had hoped. . . ."

Craig laughed. "No man, no it didn't. But you said what needed to be said. What all of us have been dying to say. And man, was it entertaining! I cannot wait to see how dinner goes. He sees that we know what he's been up to. That's what we wanted all along, to get him to realize that we can make life very difficult for him if he continues to mess with our ANP. So in that regard, we accomplished what we set out to do."

"Right," I sighed, my confidence still shaky. "Well, dinner should be really interesting, you're right about that. Let's go see if I can make this any worse!"

Walking to dinner, I pulled Janis aside and asked him what he thought. "You know, Matt, the governor is a bad guy. Afghans need people to stand up for them. What you did is a very good thing. You said what is right. The governor knows this. That is why he says it is ultimately Karzai's responsibility to get rid of him. You should tell Karzai to get rid of him, and then things will be better. He is very worried. Bashi tells me this as well."

At that point, Eshan jumped in and joyously exclaimed, "Matt! This was great! You told him! Afghan people are *very, very* proud of you, my friend! You are *very, very* good friend to the Afghan people! We thank you a lot a lot! Believe me! I know this!"

Walking into the dining room, I momentarily forgot about all the tension as I took in the sights and smells of the feast before us. In a modest but large room sat a very long table that easily seated 30 people. While we had argued, the governor's aides had prepared each place at the table with simple china, extremely dusty soda cans (Pepsi, 7UP, Orange Slice, and a few Iranian brands I did not recognize), a bottle of water, and the standard slab of delicious na'an. A veritable smorgasbord of Afghan dishes sat in the center of the table, their smells mixing together deliciously. As I sat down at a seat near the farthest end of the table, it struck me that I had likely never eaten a majority of the dishes in front of me. Most of my Afghan meals had been with impoverished villagers and ill-paid Afghan police, all of whom couldn't afford to feed us in such fine fashion.

Janis sat to my right, and Bashi Habib to my left. Arnold sat across and several seats down back toward the meeting room. We left the head of the table at our end open for the governor, who shocked all of us by sitting directly across from me. Clearly we hadn't finished our conversation. I turned to Janis and whispered, "I thought the head of the table is reserved for the most important man in the room—why isn't the governor sitting there?"

Perhaps the governor overheard my whisper. Perhaps he sensed the social confusion caused by his choice in seat. As he sat, he softly said, "I prefer to eat amongst you all, rather than at the head of the table. I leave it open for the day my dear uncle Karzai graces us with his honored presence." He began serving those seated to his right and left, announcing the start of the meal.

I learned early on in my Afghan tour of duty: Don't consume the dairy. Ever. Arnold, sadly, learned that lesson, as he adventurously accepted an offer to fill his cup with what can only be described as rancid, chunky yogurt with large bits of cucumber floating about. As he swallowed his first excruciating gulp, he instantly regretted his decision and continued to hate life for the rest of dinner (and for several days afterward), as with every sip a very amused Afghan would quickly top off his glass, much to his dismay. The governor, meanwhile, leisurely conversed with Aaron and Sergeant First Class Rucker, who continued to apologize for me and the argument, a futile attempt at playing good cop to my bad. The governor, however, paid almost no attention to them; his eyes remained fixed on me as we silently dueled, daring the other to be the one to mention the elephant in the room.

While Aaron and the sergeant labored away with the governor, Bashi Habib periodically leaned over, placed his hand on my thigh or shoulder, looked at me with his soft, tired eyes, and whispered (through Janis) how I just needed to trust him, that I was his favorite American nephew, and that he would make this all better after dinner. Confident that my calm demeanor all but enraged the governor, I politely enjoyed my delicious portions of a lentil paste (that I still dream about), Afghan rice, na'an, and the always gamey and oily Afghan mystery meat "meatball."

After about 20 minutes, the governor cracked. "So, tell me more about these 'Pai looch' you say I use to kill people," the governor commanded, bringing the room to an abrupt and awkward silence. Unfazed, I dipped another piece of na'an into the lentil paste, rubbed a ball of rice into the na'an, and took my time chewing. I liked that the longer I sat there in silence, the more uncomfortable he became. He had blinked first, restoring my confidence and placing me firmly in control. I was going to have fun with this.

"Well, Agha, why don't you tell me?" I replied too cockily.

"You accused me of using these Pai looch, which is a very bad and disrespectful word; tell me again why you would say such things? These lies!" he seethed, once again taking his time to enunciate the "loooooooooch."

"Your honor, if you aren't using Pai looch, then tell me who is guarding your office and this home at this very moment? They aren't ANP. They aren't ANA. And they aren't NDS. And, as I said before, they identified *themselves* as Pai looch when we arrived. So either we and they and everybody else in this town are mistaken, or you are confused or unaware of who is guarding you . . . ," I said, as he cut me off.

"Lies! You make all these lies, but you do not know. You do not know the Afghan people. You are not Afghan, you cannot know. All these lies, Karzai, my dear uncle, he has heard them. He is not happy with me. He says if they are true, he will remove me. But you know they are lies! Your lies have caused me to lose face with my dear uncle," he said, wildly pointing to the portrait of Karzai that adorned the meeting room.

He had just told me all I needed to know: His weakness was losing face with Karzai. The guy was mine.

"Your honor, you and I both know these are not lies. Faiz Mohammad is not a bad man, nor is he Taliban, nor is he trying to kill Haji Fasil. Your men, whatever you want to call them, detained my interpreters for not paying the illegal toll to enter the bazaar. Your Pai looch got into a firefight with the NDS when they tried to enforce the antismuggling laws. Your Pai looch are using ANP to run illegal checkpoints. And *your* Pai looch are currently guarding this house."

And then I just sat there. Aaron visibly cringed. Craig could barely contain a smile. Eshan and Fareed turned away to hide their grins. Janis joined me in a stone-cold, emotionless stare, while Bashi Habib rested his head in his hands, exasperated at the further deterioration of the dinner. The governor looked at me for what felt like an eternity, studying my face, my uniform, my posture, my soul. And then he spoke: "I am a doctor. You know this?"

I nodded.

"Good. I have been a doctor a long time. A surgeon in my home, Kandahar. You know this?"

I nodded again.

"Good. Then as a doctor, you know I have much training. I have studied many things, including psychology. I have studied psychology, and I can tell you this: These lies, they only exist in your head!" he confidently exclaimed as he pointed his pudgy fingers directly at my face.

I sat there, incredulous and incapable of conceiving a coherent or logical retort. What could anyone honestly say to that? And before I could muster a "Bullshit!" he slammed a mouthful of the rancid yogurt directly from the ladle, stood up, and strode out of the room.

Chaos. Aaron glared at me as if I had just lost us the war. Sergeant First Class Rucker sheepishly smiled, amused at me for standing my ground against a clearly delusional opponent. Bashi Habib continued to whisper sweet nothings about fixing everything. Eshan and Fareed looked on with awe and wonder. Haji Fasil ran after the governor like an ever-obedient dog.

And at that moment, I honestly had no idea what to do next. Faiz wasn't coming back to Deh Yak. The governor was either insane or unwilling to consider our perspective. And I probably had done some serious damage to our relationship with him, not to mention the relationships of other American units located in Ghazni. And then it hit me: If I had already done all this damage, at the least I would get a major ass chewing, if not outright be fired. So why not go for broke? I strode after the governor.

Bashi Habib was the first to sense what I was doing. "No, no, my dear nephew, don't. Let your Uncle Bashi talk with him. We can fix this," he pleaded, pulling on my arm.

"Agha, we might be in Afghanistan, but in any culture, including my own, walking away like that in the midst of a conversation once, let alone twice, is a major insult. I will not have it. He doesn't just get to have his word and walk away," I shouted, loud enough to ensure the governor heard me. Arnold shot me an odd look, confused as to my sudden loss of cool.

I realized we needed a team huddle. "All right, Agha, I ask you please, go talk to the governor and make this all better. I trust you, my dear Afghan uncle," I said to Bashi, the sincerest lie I've ever told. Bashi smiled, hugged me, reassured me all would be well, and went hobbling after the governor.

I rounded up our team and walked outside to enjoy the late-summer air and an after-dinner cigarette, leaving Aaron and the sergeant to continue to lobby the governor. Polling the group, I found the HUMINT intelligence guys thought I had played it perfectly but, like everyone else, wondered what I had planned next.

"Okay, gentlemen, here's how I see it. He's shown us that his greatest fear and thus primary motivation is Karzai. Let's use that. He's clearly too prideful to initiate any further dialogue with me, having, in his eyes, effectively ended the argument and refuted our claims. Hence the reason why I just 'lost my cool.' If I've guessed him right, he thinks I'm hurt and angry. He won't deal with me as long as I come off as cool and collected—it makes him too nervous. He needs to feel in control. So if I show some rage, some raw emotion, he can appear commanding, calming, and magnanimous if I go to him and ask him to consider our talk. And that's exactly what I'm going to do. Bashi is currently 'fixing' things for me. I'll go back pretending to have my tail between my legs. I'll profusely and sincerely apologize. And then I'll hit him with an ultimatum, one that hits directly at his fear of losing face with Karzai. What's the one thing that would cause Karzai to remove him?" I asked rhetorically.

"If we claimed Ghazni fell apart. That security had collapsed, and it was all his fault. Now, we clearly cannot do that. Karzai isn't going to listen to anything we say, let alone our superiors who could communicate that to Karzai. But, if we can make the governor think that we have that kind of power, we can use it to our advantage. So here's what I plan to offer him: I'll tell him that if he continues to interfere with the Ghazni security forces, then security is only going to collapse. I'll tell him that with every report we file, we'll blame him for the collapse in security. And we'll see where this goes."

Everyone in the group agreed to the ruse, and we returned to the meeting room. Bashi Habib ran toward me, took me by the hand, and whispered that he had fixed everything. All I had to do was offer a sincere apology to the governor, and everything would be okay. I agreed, and Bashi led me before the governor, lounging on his throne.

"Your honor, forgive me. If I have said anything tonight that has offended you, I profusely apologize. I did not mean to insult you in any way. I had no idea that the word 'Pai looch' was so offensive. Had I, I would never have used it. I know you are a good man and that you only want what is best for your country. We are friends, allies, and only together can we make Afghanistan a better place. I also recognize that we are guests in your country, and tonight I have not acted as a good guest should. Again, I apologize and ask for your forgiveness. I hope we can put this past us and move on with our friendship."

The governor sat silently, looking me up and down. Finally, he smiled. "My dear nephew, please do not think I am mad at you. We are dear friends. There is no need to apologize. All is fine between us. I am happy to have you in my home and will welcome you back anytime you wish to come," he said as he hugged me over and over again.

"Agha, many thanks, this warms my heart," I said, placing my right hand over my heart in the customary gesture of thanks.

"Agha, there must be a way we can fix this situation in Deh Yak. If Faiz cannot return, the man you've chosen to replace him cannot remain. Deh Yak is falling apart, and the last thing I want, any of us wants, is to have Deh Yak fail. The last thing I want is for Karzai to think that you let it fail. But my reports must be honest, and if you continue to make leadership changes without consulting us, things will continue to deteriorate, facts I must report to my superiors. Do you understand?"

He nodded, still smiling.

"Good, then here's what I propose. Let us come back tomorrow and agree on a new police chief for Deh Yak. Sergeant First Class Rucker and Captain Norris, the Deh Yak mentors, will come and speak with you. Agreed?"

"Yes, this is a most welcome idea!" he said, continuing to smile.

"But your honor, again, you must know that if things continue to fail security-wise in Deh Yak and Ghazni as a whole, that will get reported. The last thing I want is Karzai thinking you are to blame, but that is how the reports will be read if security fails because you keep removing effective police chiefs like Faiz Mohammad. This must stop," I commanded as sheepishly as I could (I still needed to appear contrite).

"Of course, of course, speak no more of it. All will be fixed tomorrow," he said, turning to Haji Fasil, as if to end the conversation while still in control.

I froze. We had planned everything out except the final nail in the coffin. At that moment, someone placed a baseball in the governor's hands and made a speech about how it was a gift from America to him and a sign of our deep friendship. Bashi Habib suggested we take a group photo, which afforded me much-needed time to think. I needed to leave completely in control and to have him utterly afraid.

And then it hit me: I had my nail.

Standing next to the governor, posing for the typical political photo, I flashed a fake smile, turned to him, and said, "I'm glad we're clear on this, because if Deh Yak doesn't get a new police chief tomorrow, I'm going to declare Deh Yak's ANP to be a failure, and that means we bring back the ANCOP. Indefinitely."

The governor's smile evaporated.

ANP in Ghazni province ultimately answer to his authority. But the ANCOP answer to the Minister of the Interior and thus are completely out of the governor's control. During the ANCOP's tenure in Deh Yak (May–June 2008), the governor and Haji Fasil had lobbied hard, but unsuccessfully, to have the ANCOP placed under their control. They abhorred their presence, as the ANCOP effectively patrolled Deh Yak, forcing them to temporarily halt their illegal chromite mining in Deh Yak. The ANCOP's indefinite return would mean an indefinite halt to this extremely lucrative operation. Moreover, it'd be a clear and undeniable example of how the governor's meddling with the ANP degraded security. Not even Karzai could let such a development go unpunished. No FDD-trained ANP had (at that moment) been officially declared a "failure." If they failed, Doctor Usmani would have the additional "honor" of being the first Afghan governor to have an entire American-trained police force fail while on his watch. He'd do anything to prevent the ANCOP's return.

Before he could say anything, I announced it was late, we had troubled him long enough, and restrictions on night movement meant we had to leave immediately. Thankfully, everyone in our large entourage sensed my desire to leave quickly and not afford the governor a chance to reply, as they all nearly ran for the exit. The last image I saw of the governor was of him standing with Haji Fasil, looking as if he had just watched his house collapse, holding the baseball as if unsure whether to slam it to the ground or to throw it at my head.

As we mounted up, Arnold smiled and exclaimed, "Nice move at the end there with the ANCOP. Didn't see that coming. Do you really think that could happen?"

"I haven't a clue. I made it up on the spot. But hey, he bought it!" I exclaimed.

I later learned the U.S. doesn't have a process or method for dealing with a failed FDD-trained police force; failure is, literally and procedurally, not an option.

Saturday, September 27, 2008

The governor strikes back: Major Garrison called me into his office and asked me to take a seat. Sighing, he turned to me and said, "Matt, I just got off the phone with Colonel Hall. You're never allowed to meet with the governor again."

The words were like a punch to the gut.

Days earlier, after returning from our dinner, I had immediately gone to Major Garrison and recounted the dinner's events. I wanted to give him a heads-up and to offer both my apology for potentially going too far and my analysis for what I thought would happen next: that the governor would finally play ball, as we'd sufficiently scared him at the end. I point-blank asked him, "Sir, did I fuck this up?"

"No, I don't think so. You said what needed to be said. You did good."

Much to Major Garrison's credit, he defended me. He told Colonel Hall that although I was probably overzealous in my delivery, he agreed with everything I had said. Major Garrison listed the evidence we had collected against the governor and informed Colonel Hall that the 101st simply ignored it. His defense restored any loss in pride I suffered by being sidelined by Lieutenant Colonel Batista. The irony of all of this was twofold.

First, in addition to personally being banned from meeting with the governor, Lieutenant Colonel Batista got Colonel Longfellow to order us to seek his (Batista's) permission before any future meetings with the governor (regardless of my involvement). At this point, however, Lieutenant Colonel Batista technically didn't run things in Ghazni anymore, having relinquished control of the province to the Polish days before. He would move to Paktika province by the end of the month. His days in Ghazni were effectively over, yet somehow, he still thought he ran the show. Second, no one informed the governor of the ban; after the dinner, his reps called me almost daily requesting additional meetings with me.

I remain immensely proud of what I did. Lieutenant Colonel Batista's actions, however, are just another shining example of what results from a lack of proper coordination of effort. He and his staff since our first day together dismissed us as just a bunch of worthless National Guard/Reservists who should shut up and let the mighty active-duty army handle everything. Regardless of that viewpoint, we had a mission we intended to accomplish. Had Batista and his staff bothered to hear us out, share with us their game plan, or truly consider our evidence against the governor, things would likely have gone very differently. Instead, the whole province continued to collapse closer to hell as the right hand (us) didn't know what the left hand (them) was doing, simply because the left hand continued to act as if the right didn't exist.

As for Major Garrison, I cannot adequately express my appreciation for his decision to defend me. At the same time, he willingly accepted Longfellow's directive to back off on the governor, when what we needed to do was further rock the boat. I'm skeptical we'll actually do anything with all this evidence we've collected.

Saturday, October 4, 2008

Majors Garrison and Goodman, First Sergeant Rock, the Ghazni ODA (U.S. Special Forces), the ANA, ANP, NDS, and the Ghazni governor had a security meeting today at the governor's mansion. At the end of the meeting, the Ghazni governor allegedly pulled Major Garrison, Major Goodman, and First Sergeant Rock aside and again asked for me to come to his meetings.

"He said you were his favorite American nephew, and he misses you," said an amused Major Goodman.

After the meeting, the ODA commander turned to Major Goodman, Major Garrison, and First Sergeant Rock and said, "Whatever Zeller said to him seems to have him really spooked. This is the best meeting we've ever had with him. Give him our thanks."

Major Goodman told me that they all agreed that my confronting him during our infamous dinner produced dramatic results. Most importantly, the governor announced at the meeting that he will play a reduced role in security decisions in Ghazni province, leaving it up to the ANA, ANP, and NDS, as it should have been all along. Everyone agreed that, as a result of the governor's change in attitude, I had done the right thing. I feel tremendously vindicated knowing my colleagues value my efforts.

Major Garrison also informed me that Colonel Longfellow had called him after today's meeting to see if our infamous dinner had truly irreparably damaged our relationship with the governor. Major Garrison reported the exact opposite—that I seem to have spooked him straight for the time being and that all were appreciative of the change. Longfellow asked him again if he wanted to get rid of me. Major Garrison, once again, said he wanted me to remain in Ghazni. I couldn't have been more proud.

38

Why We're Losing, Part 3

Thursday, September 25, 2008

Today serves as another shining example of why I continue to believe we're doing everything we can to lose this war. After months and months of detailed, strenuous, and at times exhausting planning, we were supposed to travel to Rabat village, in Deh Yak district, and conduct a large humanitarian assistance mission. The PRT had selected Rabat as a means of thanking the village for its active support of the Afghan government, our efforts (we recruited a lot of ANP from the village), and resistance against the Taliban.

We had spent days loading up the supply trucks with aid and getting enough medics assigned to the mission to make sure the MEDCAP (Medical Assistance Program, a day of free and effective health care for any Afghan lucky enough to be in line) went off without a hitch. We even had female medics borrowed from another unit assigned to the mission (a rarity, as almost every single embedded training team/police mentor team is staffed by men).

The PRT had first promised Rabat this HA mission prior to our arrival in country in April. About three weeks after they promised Rabat the mission, our Deh Yak ANP team visited Rabat for the first time. The villagers of Rabat assumed our Deh Yak team was the HA mission and were disappointed to find out they were not. To the average Afghan, one American is like every other American, and it's assumed we know everything every other American has done. You could imagine Major

---

A typical Afghan Qalat (mud-brick home). The walls are usually several meters thick and nearly two meters high, nearly impenetrable for our bullets.

Goodman's initial surprise when confronted by a village of thousands turning out for nonexistent aid and doctors. The PRT hadn't communicated their promise to Rabat or anyone else, let alone to us.

To compound the matter, the PRT's staff rotated midsummer, and the outgoing staff didn't inform their replacements of the promise to Rabat. When we first broached the topic with the new PRT staff (they live over at FOB Ghazni, further reducing our unity of effort), they weren't the least bit interested, as they had written off Deh Yak as a success and not in need of our assistance. Subsequent "initial" assessment missions to Rabat by the Ghazni PRT only further hurt our relationship with the village's inhabitants, who began to believe we would never make good on our promise. Taliban attacks against the village only hammered home the point that cooperating with the Americans brought nothing of value but lots of pain.

During Team One's last visit to Rabat, the villagers had announced enough was enough: The team wasn't welcome in the village (the visits provoked almost immediate Taliban attacks), the villagers doubted they'd ever see any aid, but if we were really serious about an aid mission, they'd be willing to travel to the Deh Yak District Center, pick it up there, and haul it back to Rabat on their own.

One American unit (the PRT) made a very pro-Afghan government, pro-U.S. village a promise for aid in March 2008. We arrived. The PRT knew we arrived. The PRT knew we would be going to Deh Yak almost daily. The PRT knew we were going to Rabat. The PRT did not tell us about their promise to Rabat. We visit Rabat, the villagers think we're the HA mission and are disappointed but understanding when they realize we are another unit. We approach the PRT to plan the mission, and they agree. The PRT cycles through new personnel. The outgoing personnel don't inform the incoming personnel about the Rabat promise. The incoming personnel do not think Rabat or the HA mission in Rabat is as important as other areas and blow us off for months. Meanwhile, we're visiting Rabat every two weeks or so as part of regular patrols. The Taliban attack Rabat almost after every visit (we even tried pretending to leave to set a trap for them, but they were tipped off, so the attack never came). The Rabat villagers begin to grow weary of Taliban reprisals and our inability to fulfill promises. In August, the Rabat village elders ask us to leave their village alone. In the course of five months, our inability to coordinate efforts, to share information, and to make good on one simple promise lost us the unwavering support of a village of thousands. It's as if we're trying our damnedest to fail.

We're all ready to go on this mission, our presumably last shot to repair relations with Rabat. The trucks are loaded with tons of aid. The medics are assigned. The village is on their way to the district center (we had previously set an arrival time, because the village is beyond cell-phone reception). What do you think happened? The PRT backed out, effectively canceling the mission, as they control the aid trucks, most of the security, and medics. Yet another shining example of why we're not winning.

39

Allies

Sunday, September 28, 2008

The first contingent of Polish soldiers arrived on the FOB today. The Polish have decided to do something the 101st had long since abandoned: move the Ghazni Provincial Coordination Center (PCC) from an obscure compound three miles south of us to an abandoned warehouse compound immediately outside our FOB's southeastern corner. The move makes perfect sense, as the PCC is supposed to be jointly manned by us, the Polish, the ANA, the ANP, and the NDS. Each of these services receives intelligence from a multitude of sources. Yet, sadly, most of this intelligence isn't "actioned" quickly enough to be of any use (it takes too long to bring together all the elements of the ANSF and us before the information becomes too old to be relevant).

Enter the PCC. Each of the various security forces operating in Ghazni sends a few intelligence representatives and a contingent of "trigger pullers" (infantry soldiers/regular police) who all live together on the PCC. All real-time intelligence and information (in theory) comes in to the PCC. Because every security force has someone sitting at the PCC, in theory, everyone knows what is going on, vastly improving information sharing. Moreover, since the PCC has a permanent detachment of infantry personnel from each service, getting them all together to "action" any time-sensitive intelligence becomes (in theory) relatively easy. The problem thus far has been the fact that the "old PCC" sat about three miles south of our

Arnold with two Polish officers before the infamous governor's dinner, with Bashi Habib and Haji Fasil lingering in the background.

FOB. For months, various leaders in Ghazni had talked about moving the PCC to the abandoned warehouse compounds immediately outside our FOB.

The move made all sorts of logical sense. First, our FOB could essentially absorb the compound and provide its security, freeing up the forces stationed at it to conduct patrols rather than only provide compound security. Second, the ANA felt infinitely more comfortable staging their personnel in a compound attached or "on" their FOB, as opposed to miles away. Finally, given the increasingly strict rules on where U.S. soldiers could move or live at any time, it was the only realistic way we could have a semipermanent presence on the PCC. Unfortunately, the 101st had taken to using the "old PCC" as their private prison; detainees allegedly "worked" off their "sentences" by improving the compound's security infrastructure, and thus they had opposed moving the PCC to the abandoned warehouse site. With their departure and the Polish arrival, we reenacted the plan to move the PCC to its new site.

The first thing we noticed was that the "new PCC" site sat directly (one meter) outside our FOB's hesco walls but that no passageway existed between the two. Hesco walls are constructed of sand and stone piled into a fabric shell that's held together by wire mesh. It doesn't sound strong, but it can take bullets, grenades, and most other types of Taliban ordinance. The 21st-century version of castle walls, they're cheap, easy to erect and take down, modular, available in various sizes, and extremely effective. In order to travel from the new PCC to our FOB, one had to drive out our front gate and travel half a kilometer south on the main road, highly inefficient. We needed to connect the two compounds.

Two Polish intelligence soldiers and I walked to the southeast corner of our FOB to explore the feasibility of connecting the two compounds. The hot afternoon sun beat down on our backs, while moderate wind blew the dry dusty sand of the FOB into mini–dust devils.

We decided we'd have to climb up on top of the hesco wall and tread carefully over the barbed wire in order to better survey the situation. As we hauled ourselves up onto the six-foot-high barriers, I realized we weren't well armed (pistols only) or wearing any body armor, not the best position to be in on top of the hesco wall, completely exposed to the Afghan city outside (with any eager Taliban sniper waiting to take a lucky shot). I found the whole affair quite thrilling. Atop the wall, we noticed that a door had been built into the PCC's stone walls. A similar door did *not* exist on our FOB's walls. The PCC's "back door" seemingly led nowhere.

"So what do you guys think?" I asked the Polish soldiers.

"I think this is the perfect place to put a similar entryway in your wall," replied the senior soldier.

"Agreed, so now what?"

"Do you have wire cutters and a few shovels?" the Polish soldier asked mischievously.

"I think we'd need to get this cleared with Colonel Naser [the ANA commander of the FOB] before we go and cut a hole in his perimeter."

"Agreed, we will go and ask the colonel while you get the tools, okay?" he replied.

"Sure, why not," I said, convinced he would deny their request without first consulting Major Garrison and First Sergeant Rock.

Twenty minutes later, I returned to the wall to find the Polish ready to start construction.

"He has agreed. We can begin immediately," the senior soldier confidently stated.

"Really? Well, if he said yes, then okay, go for it," I said, surprised that Colonel Naser had given his permission so quickly.

Within minutes, the Polish had clipped away the wire mesh holding the section together, cut away the inner fabric, and had piles of sand and stone streaming forth, engulfing us in dry, choking dust. With each backbreaking shovelful of dirt, the hesco came down, until an hour later we had excavated enough to cut through to the other side. Proud of what three men with two shovels could accomplish in an hour, we took a moment to admire our work.

"Okay, well, let's open that door up and make this official," I said as we confidently strode between the walls, toward the new PCC's back door.

It was locked. From the other side.

"Well, one of us will have to climb up back on the wall, use a board to traverse the meter between the FOB's hesco wall and the PCC's stone wall, drop down into the PCC, and open the door from the other side," I said, chuckling at the fact we forgot to check to see if the door was locked before we began construction on our makeshift passageway.

"I'll go," replied the junior Polish soldier.

Minutes later, he dropped into the PCC, unlocked the door, and welcomed us in with a wide grin. We had connected our FOB to the PCC.

I'd later get chewed out by Lieutenant Commander Seabolt (the U.S. Navy engineer in charge of our FOB's construction and infrastructure) for taking it upon ourselves to cut a hole in the wall. "Lieutenant Zeller, do you realize that your little stunt has left the FOB completely vulnerable to Taliban infiltration? No one is actively guarding your breach. Perhaps you weren't aware before you decided to cut a hole in the wall, but there aren't any barriers or walls between the hole and the common street. So, you've got two options. You can personally go and guard it until we build those barriers, or you can go build them yourself! What in the hell were you thinking?" he screamed.

"Well, Sir, the Polish said they had Colonel Naser's permission. It is *his FOB* after all. I trusted their word. Did they lie to me?" I asked, with a hint of insubordinate sarcasm.

"I don't know, Lieutenant! And you should have had them ask me first, as *I am responsible* for all construction!" he arrogantly seethed.

"Fine, Sir, I clearly don't want to guard the hole indefinitely. What do you suggest I do?" I sighed, resigned to the fact I'd royally screwed up.

"I suggest you find a way to make sure no one can simply walk off the street, around the PCC, and into our FOB. In short, you better learn really quickly how to put up barbed wire!" he yelled, storming off.

Captain Walter, First Sergeant Rock, and Captain Fraser, thankfully, having overheard the exchange, came to my rescue.

Smiling, First Sergeant Rock said, "Well, Lieutenant, you've learned never to do that again! Don't worry, we'll help you out. After all, if someone used that hole to breach the FOB, it wouldn't just be your problem, it'd be all of ours. Come on, we'll help you make sure no one can get through that hole."

Hours later, Captain Walter, Captain Fraser, and Master Sergeant Paton had constructed impenetrable barriers of barbed wire, effectively "resecuring" our perimeter. To this day, I cannot thank them enough for helping me clean up my own mess.

Exhausted from the day's physical labor, I returned to our compound to shower and to immerse myself in catching up on some paperwork. As I walked back on our compound, Rocko and TK trotting along happily at my side, a convoy pulled in behind me. Out jumped Captain Morriarty, Master Sergeant Postman, Private First Class Wilford, Specialist Guzman, Senior Chief Tinney, and Captain Norris, all back from leave. I could barely express my joy as I ran up to Captain Morriarty and Master Sergeant Postman and nearly tackled them with bear hugs.

"It is *so* good to see you guys! I hope you enjoyed your time away! Things just haven't been the same without you around!" I exclaimed. I hadn't seen the two of them since they left back in July to take their ANP to training.

The moment of reunion and relaxation was short lived. "Look who it is!" exclaimed a surprised but delighted Doctor Usmani. So much for that precious moment alone. I stood up and went to hug the governor in the traditional Afghan greeting.

"It's my favorite American nephew! How are you! Are you well? Is your family well? I was hoping I'd see you. You must come and eat with me again. Do not worry about last time. All is forgiven! You are my brother! My favorite American nephew!" exclaimed the governor.

"Agha, I am honored. I will check with my bosses and see what I can do," I said, trying my best not to commit to anything, my heart and mind racing at the prospect that just by talking to the man, I'd be reprimanded.

"I look forward to it! Please let my staff know when you can make it. As for now, I must return to my home. A governor's work never ends! Good-bye, my favorite American nephew!" the governor said, as he embraced me in a deep and lingering hug.

Breathing in his stench, the smell of his seldom-showered body, I couldn't help but hold my breath and think, "Favorite American nephew, my ass! You'd easily stab me right here if you had the chance." Instead I replied, "Agha, it would be my honor. Be well until we meet again." Little did we know that the next time we saw one another, I'd be making him burn $6.3 million of his own drugs in front of the Afghan press.

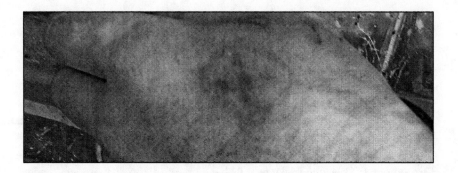

40

Up Close with Dead Taliban

Tuesday, October 7, 2008

The ANP in Andar got into a firefight while they were on their way to meet with Team Two on our FOB. I managed to get the A-10s and a QRF to respond to the ANP in a timely fashion. For once, I feel like we've actually helped. First Lieutenant Palmer told me that he and Team Two would meet the Andar ANP at the Ghazni hospital when they drop off the dead (one ANP KIA and one Taliban KIA). As he walked away, his face betrayed his emotions; he blamed himself for the death of the ANP.

The new movement restrictions essentially prevent us from getting out to our ANP; they have to travel to us for any meeting. One of our greatest fears is that the Taliban will attack the ANP in transit and exactly what happened today will occur: The ANP will take casualties. If we had been able to travel to them, this might have never happened. Walking to his vehicle, Palmer turned back and said, "Oh yeah, I almost forgot. The Andar ANP captured one of the Taliban fighters alive."

Detained fighters are a gold mine of usable intelligence.

"Phil, mind if Arnold and I come along for your trip to the hospital? I promise, we'll stay only as long as you're comfortable, but this could be a valuable opportunity," I said, clearly giddy at the prospect of gaining whatever we could out of the detainee.

My enthusiasm seemed to briefly cheer First Lieutenant Palmer up, as he flashed a smile and said, "Sure, why not? Something good should come out of this."

The five-side die tattoo sported by many Taliban fighters in Ghazni province. Not coincidentally, the governor's personal guard proudly wore these tattoos.

I rounded up Arnold and an interpreter, readied our truck within minutes, and off we went.

We arrived at Ghazni hospital moments before the Andar ANP came flying in. They secured the compound and unloaded their dead and wounded. They were professional but clearly enraged by the loss of one of their most beloved officers. At one point, several ANP had to hold an extremely distraught officer back as he attempted to rush at the detainee, clearly wanting to kill him in revenge.

Arnold and I went to work. First: Find out what happened.

The Andar ANP had been traveling from their district center to meet with Team Two on our FOB. Around a known Taliban-controlled village, they came under heavy machine gun and RPG fire, concentrated on Nabi Patang, the Andar ANP commander's, vehicle—a Taliban assassination attempt. Thankfully, Nabi survived unscathed. During the firefight, the ANP aggressively assaulted the Taliban firing positions. The Taliban fled. Most Taliban ambushes involve fighters operating in teams of two, traveling by motorcycle. The fighters decide ahead of time where they will place their dismounted soldiers. The teams of two travel separately to the ambush site, so as not to draw attention. One fighter gets off the motorcycle and walks to his firing position, while the other waits at the still-running motorcycle (the getaway driver). He initiates the ambush with an IED, RPG, or machine-gun salvo; causes as much death and destruction as possible before he runs out of ammo (or is killed/captured); and then flees back to the waiting motorcycle driver.

As the ANP assaulted the Taliban fighting positions, they sent another group to look for getaway drivers. They killed one fighter and captured his alleged getaway driver. The dead fighter lay sprawled out in the back of one of the ANP pickup trucks. His detained comrade sat handcuffed and under guard in the back of another ANP pickup truck.

"Okay, Arnold, here's what we're going to do. You go see if you can't find out the details of how they killed this guy and how they captured him," I said, pointing to the dead fighter and detainee, respectively. "In the meantime, I'll take pictures as evidence, as I suspect we'll find a familiar tattoo on the dead fighter's right hand," I said with a wink, alluding to the known tattoo of the Pai looch. "Then we'll meet back here, discuss what you find, and conduct a quick tactical questioning of the detainee before the ANP take him to jail."

Walking over to the dead Taliban fighter, I felt nothing. I couldn't care less. Before me laid a dead man, someone who only hours earlier had been alive, breathing, eating, moving, thinking, feeling, and yet, I felt nothing. His death didn't resonate with me. I could have been looking at a pile of dirt for all it mattered. As I moved closer toward his corpse, I felt glad he was dead. His loss was almost certainly meaningless for the overall state of the Taliban, but I was still glad he had died and saddened at the ANP's loss. I turned back and looked at the grieving ANP as they cried over their fallen comrade and couldn't help take in the moment. Across the courtyard, friends and relatives screamed and cried over the loss of the

ANP. In front of me, a lifeless Taliban corpse sat alone, not a mourner in sight to grieve. The whole affair was so meaningless. The Taliban killed a guy for driving up the road. In turn, the ANP killed that person in self-defense.

Looking over his body, I made sure not to touch him; it's *haram* (sinful) for an infidel like me to touch the body of a dead Muslim. Even though he was a Talib, I would have deeply offended the assembled Afghans had I touched him. But I needed him moved, as his body lay over his left hand. I called over Fareed and asked him to have the ANP turn his body over. They readily complied and rolled the corpse onto its back. It struck me that I hadn't seen his face up until that moment, and now, looking at his final expression—sheer terror—I felt nothing. His head had a massive hole where the lethal bullet had rocketed through, ending his existence. Still, I felt nothing. Examining the bullet wound, I noticed the burn marks at the entry point. The shot came at very close range. At first, I had thought the ANP had killed him while chasing him or at a distance, but his injuries told me the real story. The bullet wound to his left leg indicated the ANP had injured him at a distance as he either continued to fight or attempted to flee. Inevitably, the ANP captured him and at some point summarily executed him.

As I mulled this over, Arnold walked up and told me essentially what I already knew. "So I guess they shot this guy at a distance, captured him, and then the best friend of the dead ANP executed him with his AK-47," said an emotionless Arnold.

"Right, I came to the same conclusion. Take a look at his head wound and the entry point. The burn marks indicate a close range shot. No doubt in my mind they executed him," I replied.

"So, what do we do about it?" Arnold asked, in a tone that suggested concern over this abuse of power by the ANP, a concern I shared.

"Well, it's not our call, nor is it Team Two's, really. We weren't there, we can't prove a thing. As much as we both hate to do this, we need to drop it," I said, hating the inevitable truth of my words.

"Anyways, take a look at what else I found," I said, grinning as I gestured toward the corpse's left hand.

Arnold leaned in to examine what he already knew was there: a tattoo of the number-five side of a die, the mark of the Pai looch. He shot back a wide smile, his eyes twinkling with further evidence for our cause.

"Well look at that! Surprise, surprise!" he exclaimed sarcastically.

"Yep, I got a few choice photos. I'd like to see the governor deny this one. What did you find out about the detainee?"

"Well, as we suspected, the ANP caught him trying to flee on a motorcycle. He claims he had nothing to do with the fighting, that he was trying to run away from it and get back to his village. But his answers keep changing as to where he's from or what he was doing out. Oh, and you're going to love this, the ANP caught him with a Taliban ICOM radio," said Arnold.

"Where's the radio?" I asked excitedly, as a Taliban ICOM radio would yield loads of useful information (like what radio frequencies they currently used to communicate).

"The ANP have it in the truck with the detainee. They said we could have it for a few days, but that they'll ultimately need it back for 'evidence,'" Arnold said, as he made air quotes. We both knew that the ANP wanted the radio for their own use or to monitor Taliban radio communications.

"All right, here's how we play this. Let's give him the benefit of the doubt. I'll talk to him first and get his basic info and his reason for why he was out during the ambush. I'll tell him we believe him and walk away. Give it five minutes, and then you walk up on your own with a different terp and ask the same questions, but in a different order. We'll compare answers. If there're any discrepancies, we'll both return and confront him on it. Sound good?" I asked. Arnold nodded his approval, and I went to work.

Seated in the back of the ANP truck, stuffed in between two large, angry ANP officers, a visibly terrified man sat with a hood on his head and his hands cuffed behind his back. "Fareed, ask the ANP to take his hood off so I can see his face." The ANP complied with his request, and I got my first look at the detainee. His eyes darted, readjusting to light, the fear growing more visible as he realized an American soldier stood staring down at him. "Ask him if he wants some water or a cigarette," I told Fareed. The man relaxed a bit and said he'd really like a drink of water. I grabbed a bottle from our truck, opened it up, and held it to his lips.

He hesitated, not sure of what to make of me or my kindness; clearly I wasn't living up to his expectations, as he likely expected some sort of menacing torturer depicted in Taliban propaganda. His thirst overcoming his confusion, he leaned forward, and I gently poured the water into his mouth.

"Okay, Fareed. Ask if he wouldn't mind answering a few questions for me."

The man nodded in approval. For the next five minutes, the man nervously answered each of my questions in brief, halting replies. He was in his mid-twenties, lived in a village near the ambush, and had been on his way to the bazaar when he heard the ambush and tried to flee the carnage. He claimed he wasn't Taliban and that he didn't know the dead man, a claim that brought a hard punch from the ANP seated to his left. "Fareed, tell them not to hit him. They know better." The ANP smiled back at my request and nonchalantly promised to comply.

"Tell him I believe him and that if he's really innocent, he should calm down, as he's got nothing to fear." The man nodded and flashed a fleeting smile in thanks. As I walked away, he leaned forward, pleading something about my remaining to help him and to have the ANP let him go. I pretended not to hear it. Only the guilty are so desperate.

"All right, Arnold, you're up. I was really kind to him. Be stern," I said, effectively designating him the "bad cop."

While Arnold conducted his own brief questioning, the Andar subgovernor arrived at the hospital. A palpable tension engulfed the courtyard, as Patang and Subgovernor Disiwal do not get along. Disiwal had tried to have Patang fired since Patang's first day months prior; only our efforts had saved Patang's position. As Disiwal walked toward the ANP in a political display of concern, Patang's men protectively surrounded their commander. And that's when it hit me: Disiwal had driven the exact same route only minutes before the Taliban ambush on Colonel Patang; he had an afternoon meeting with Doctor Usmani and originally was supposed to travel with Patang's convoy. He traveled with his own, light security detail. The colonel's convoy, however, had many vehicles and nearly 50 heavily armed and trained ANP. Killing Disiwal would have been very easy for the Taliban who ambushed Patang. And yet, he drove all the way to Ghazni unharmed. Either Disiwal had a deal with the Taliban to leave him be, or, worse, he hired the "Taliban" fighters to try to assassinate Patang. The behavior of Patang's men (surrounding him as if to protect him) supported the latter theory; the Andar ANP at least suspected Subgovernor Disiwal had something to do with that afternoon's ambush.

As I mulled this revelation over, Arnold walked up and shared what the man told him. His story changed. He gave Arnold a different name. He claimed to be traveling to his home in another province and that he had been in the area because his uncle said he could find work. He maintained his innocence.

"Funny, he told me something very different," I chuckled as I repeated the answers he gave me.

"Shall we go ask him why the need for two stories?" Arnold said, laughing.

"Yeah, let's. This should be very interesting. Fareed, ask him why he's told me a different story than he told my friend."

The man said nothing. His eyes darted back and forth between my face and Arnold's. He looked down and back up. He said nothing.

"Fareed, tell him if he wants my help, he has to come clean. Either one story is a lie and the other is true, or they're both lies."

The man said nothing. He stared at me, clearly trying his hardest to remain emotionless.

"Fine, if he wants to just sit there, there's nothing I can do to help him. Hey buddy, right now, I think you're lying to me, and I think you're full of shit. I would have gladly done all I could to help you, but if you're going to lie to me or to my friend and not cooperate, then there's nothing I can do. Have fun in jail," I said and turned to Arnold, motioning it was time to walk away.

"We'll let that sink in with him for a minute," I whispered to Arnold.

The man cried out, "Wait!"

I turned back, looked at him, and half-cocked my eyebrow. The man looked at me, the ANP guarding him, the compound, down at his feet, and then back at me. He said nothing. I shrugged my shoulders and turned to walk away.

"Wait! Please! I'm not Taliban!" the man exclaimed.

"I don't believe you. Have fun in jail. Oh, and thanks for the radio," I said, holding up the radio the ANP confiscated from the man upon his capture.

The man slouched into his seat, resigned to his fate.

"I think it's time to leave. Nabi seems really uncomfortable here, and the ANP want to take the detainee over to the Ghazni jail and then get back to Andar," Palmer said as I met him in the middle of the hospital courtyard.

"No worries. We got everything we need," I replied.

"So what's the deal?" Phil asked, excited to get my insight.

"Well, I'm pretty sure the detainee was the dead guy's getaway driver. He told us two different stories and now he doesn't want to talk, but I think our talking to him will inevitably lead him to be more cooperative with the ANP's interrogators. As for the dead guy, Pai looch tattoo on his left hand, and I'm afraid your ANP probably executed him as opposed to killing him in battle."

"Yeah, they all but admitted one of the ANP guarding him shot him in the head while they went after the guy on the motorcycle," Phil replied.

"Well we got a lot out of this. More evidence against the governor, a Taliban radio, and when we get back to the FOB, you, Arnold, and I need to have a talk about your subgovernor. There's more to this than meets the eye," I said, motioning my head toward the commotion that continued between Disiwal and Patang.

"I sensed something was up based on how the ANP reacted to his arrival," said Phil, gesturing at the crowd of ANP surrounding Colonel Patang.

"Any idea, what they'll do with the dead Taliban?" I asked.

"Nabi says the fighter is apparently a resident of Andar. The hospital says they'll take the body and hold it for anyone who comes to claim him. If no one does, they'll give him a Muslim burial on their own," Phil sighed. He was clearly still blaming himself for the ANP's death.

"Hey man, not your fault. We don't make the movement rules. We've told ARSIC-E how much we don't like this. There's nothing you could have done. When we get back to the FOB and you hear our theory, I think you'll stop blaming yourself. This wasn't just some random Taliban ambush. Okay?" I said, placing my hand on Palmer's shoulder in an attempt to reassure him.

"Yeah, I guess. Okay, let's get out of here," Phil said, a bit more relaxed.

Back on the FOB, I told Phil our theory: "I think your subgovernor set that ambush up to try to kill Nabi. The subgovernor at the last moment decided to travel alone and ahead of Nabi's convoy. Everyone knows Disiwal has tried to get Nabi fired or transferred since his first day on the job back in the spring. The way that they almost went at it when he arrived at the hospital, something is up. I think Disiwal is desperate, and I don't think this will be the last attempt he makes on Nabi's life. Keep an eye out for anything that confirms or denies our theory. If you ask the Andar ANP, make sure you do it quietly. The last thing I want is Disiwal realizing we're on to him or Nabi thinking something that isn't true and taking matters into his own hands."

Phil nodded and breathed an audible sigh of relief.

"Don't worry. We're going to get to the bottom of this. We got a lot of really useful info today, and that radio is invaluable. You should be proud, your ANP kicked ass."

He nodded again, though we both knew in reality today's ambush marked the opening salvo in a lethal power struggle between Colonel Patang and Disiwal, a struggle that would not end until one or both of them died.

41

War Is Stupid

Wednesday, October 8, 2008

Arnold and I have just about had it with U.S. Navy Lieutenant Commander Seabolt. While at lunch, Seabolt cornered Arnold and proceeded to tell him that we contribute nothing, that he and I do nothing, and that we're utterly useless. In the past few weeks, Seabolt has been nothing short of highly unprofessional in his interactions with Arnold and me.

As Arnold regaled me with the details of his encounter, I felt a rage stir inside me. At that moment, nothing would have satisfied me more than to march up to Seabolt and beat the shit out of him. Thankfully, I swallowed my pride and asked Major Goodman to join us in the TOC. Arnold recounted to Major Goodman the details of our most recent encounter with Seabolt. Major Goodman thanked us for coming to him rather than just blowing up (he clearly knows me well) and said that he'd take care of it. Walking off to find Seabolt, he turned back and said, "And don't let anything that useless piece of shit said get to you. You both do fantastic work and provide infinitely more to the mission than his worthless ass."

Later that afternoon, Major Goodman pulled Seabolt aside and instructed him never to talk to Arnold or me again, as we don't work for him and he clearly cannot maintain his professionalism. Seabolt begrudgingly complied.

Ghazni hospital.

Thursday, October 9, 2008

A resupply convoy arrived today months overdue and completely unannounced. When we asked the convoy commander what route he used to travel from Gardez to us, he replied, "Tangi Valley, Lieutenant. It's the fastest."

"Sir, avoid Tangi Valley at all costs. Unless you're going in with a company of soldiers, it isn't worth the risk."

He shrugged off my concerns as meaningless. As I walked away, I turned to Arnold and just shook my head: "Some people really are out to earn medals. They are really pushing their luck."

42

Why We're Losing, Part 4, and How We Could Win

Tuesday, October 14, 2008

A quiet few days gave me the opportunity to reflect on this war, leadership, our efforts, successes, failures, and overall state of the U.S. military. I've come to a few stark conclusions. The real innovations and great, outside-the-box ideas are coming not from lieutenant colonels and colonels, but rather from company commanders (captains, lieutenants, and their respective NCO counterparts).

The U.S. Army seems to be split into two camps: those who buy into COIN (counterinsurgency), and those who ignore it at all costs. More simply, post-9/11 soldiers and pre-9/11 soldiers, trained to fight the Soviets or some other grand nation-vs.-nation war. Everything about COIN flies in the face of what pre-9/11 soldiers learned in their army careers. To them, COIN tastes too much like nation building. Our military needs to be able to, if nothing else, deter another state from going to war with us. That being said, I'm currently sitting in Afghanistan, and the tactics and strategies necessary to win that state-vs.-state battle will only result in failure should we continue to use them here. Body counts and enemy damage won't win this war; if anything, it'll hasten our defeat, as the population will rapidly turn against us (civilian deaths are inevitable, no matter how smart we make our bombs). No, to win here in Afghanistan, we must practice COIN; we have to effectively build this nation. We win when the population determines

An allegedly 22-year-old Afghan "police" officer at a remote outpost in Andar.

it's in their best interest to reject the Taliban and its ideology in favor of something that benefits our interests (a developed Afghan state that does not pose a threat to its neighbors nor can be used to harbor terrorists seeking to attack the United States).

Can we have both? Can we have a military that is ready at a moment's notice to fight and to win a major state-vs.-state battle while simultaneously being capable of winning a counterinsurgency fight? Yes, but not if we continue under our current structure.

The army needs to be split, permanently, into two separate partner forces: a conventional state-vs.-state fighting force, and a counterinsurgency/stabilization force. Each force could be used individually or in concert, depending on the conflict. Each force would undergo different training focused on their specialty (conventional continues the fast-pace, overwhelming application of force and mass advocated by General Colin Powell, while the stabilization force focuses on cultural development, societal progression, language training, community relations, civil affairs, etc., currently advocated by Colonel Nagl). I cannot fathom why this hasn't been discussed seriously.

As trainers of Afghan security forces, our entire predeployment training focused on counterinsurgency, but once we got into a conventional firefight, I felt as if we weren't adequately prepared. Contrast our experience with the 101st unit currently here with us. They are conventional war fighters, infantry door kickers. The senior lieutenants and captains get the mission, but the regular soldiers have only been trained to kill, kill, kill. They are beyond proficient in a firefight but lack the cultural awareness and counterinsurgency nuances this environment demands. Our partnership is essential. We do the counterinsurgency; they provide the big guns and bad-ass dudes when we get into trouble. I have no doubt that they could instantly put together a phenomenal attack or defense plan against a state-based army in battle, just as I have no doubt we make a great counterinsurgency team capable of training the Afghans and developing their civil society in a manner required for success.

When you have superiors who don't buy into counterinsurgency and all the cultural nuances that come with it, it's *very* hard to be productive, as you're fighting both your enemies and your command.

Counterinsurgency is a thinking man's fight, and sadly, not everyone in our military is cut out for it. I make no secret of the fact that I am, at best, an average conventional soldier. I can fire my weapon proficiently and know how to do basic soldiering skills, but if push came to shove, I'm not anywhere near the top half of the list when it comes to choosing whom you want with you in combat. That being said, I feel I'm a very proficient counterinsurgent; I read *a lot*, I pick up languages very easily, I find myself enthralled and easily able to adopt new cultures and customs, and I am proud of the fact that I only see people (I view the world without prejudice and ethnocentric bias). And I'm not alone, there are thousands of others like me; some are better suited for counterinsurgency, while others are better suited for conventional war fighting.

We can have it both ways. We can fight the state-vs.-state fight and the counterinsurgency, and we can win them both, but only if we permanently split the military into two components. We can have our door kickers and our nation builders. Should we choose to continue to require our soldiers to do both, I fear we'll end up with a military incapable of winning either, as the requirements for success in each war conflict and compete against one another.

43

Telling Off the Governor—
A Win for Captain Morriarty

Thursday, October 16, 2008

The nights have grown longer, the days shorter, and the temperature continues to drop with winter's approach. Team Four continued to prepare for their air-assault into Waghez (delayed for unknown reasons yesterday), while Team Two headed out to Andar for the first time since Nabi Patang's ambush almost a week prior.

Arriving in Andar, Colonel Patang approached Captain Morriarty and informed him that eight days prior, Disiwal, the Andar subgovernor, arrested the brother of an alleged Taliban commander. Apparently, a year earlier, the brother had signed a pledge to Disiwal promising that he would prevent his brother from returning to the Taliban or else Disiwal could hold him responsible. Under Afghan law, the pledge and the brother's subsequent arrest are both illegal. Captain Morriarty confronted Disiwal about the matter and asked him to explain himself. Disiwal admitted to detaining the man under direct orders from the Ghazni governor. As Disiwal saw it, the governor planned to use the brother in a prisoner exchange for six hostages the Taliban commander allegedly held.

Neither the Ghazni governor nor the Andar subgovernor have arrest or detaining powers; only the ANA, ANP, or NDS have these. Moreover, under Afghan law,

---

Governor Usmani looking very angry after our first contentious meeting during the infamous governor's dinner. Clockwise from left: Rucker, Dyncorps Aaron, the deputy Ghazni governor, and Governor Usmani.

no person can be held for more than 72 hours without a judge's order. The accused must go before a court within three days of arrest or be set free.

Captain Morriarty informed Disiwal that he had broken the law in making the man sign an illegal contract and illegally detaining him without due process for eight days. Disiwal, realizing that he wasn't going to back down, changed tactics. He pulled Captain Morriarty aside and claimed that in truth, President Karzai had personally sent him on a secret mission that necessitated the man's detention. Captain Morriarty asked Disiwal for proof; he replied he couldn't produce any.

Captain Morriarty is not one to be lied to, especially repeatedly, as it only fuels his anger.

Growing visibly frustrated, Captain Morriarty repeated the fact that Disiwal had illegally detained a man for eight days and that only the ANP had the power to arrest. Disiwal, sealing his fate with Captain Morriarty, protested that he hadn't detained the man but rather had the Andar ANP detain him. Thankfully, the Andar ANP, under Colonel Patang's leadership, had outgrown their fear of Disiwal and immediately disputed his claim that they had helped arrest and detain the man.

Furthermore, they insisted that they only learned of the man's detention that morning prior to Captain Morriarty's arrival. Colonel Patang informed Captain Morriarty that he had asked around and found out that Disiwal's bodyguards arrested the guy and watched over him during his illegal detention.

At this point, Disiwal insisted Captain Morriarty call the Ghazni Governor, as he had only been following orders. So, Captain Morriarty did just that. He later recounted to me their conversation:

Morriarty: Hello Governor, Captain Morriarty, United States Army here. I'm the Andar ANP mentor. Listen, I arrived at the district center this morning, and my ANP chief is telling me the subgovernor here illegally arrested and detained a man for eight days without the ANP's knowledge. After talking to the subgovernor about it, he first said you told him to do it, and then he said President Karzai sent him on a secret mission, and now he's back to saying you authorized the whole thing. So what is it?

Governor Usmani: Yes, yes. I authorized this. Disiwal is my responsibility. He works for me. I told him to arrest this man, as his brother is a very bad man who is holding many hostages. I had him use the ANP to arrest this man.

Morriarty: Well, Mr. Governor, that's not what the ANP are saying. They're saying he used his own bodyguards and that they weren't involved. I'm inclined to believe them over you or the Andar subgovernor. Moreover, as I'm sure you're aware, neither you nor the Andar subgovernor has the power to arrest anyone. Only the ANP, ANA, or NDS can do that. So, I'm going to arrest Disiwal for breaking the law and violating this man's rights.

Governor Usmani: You would arrest him as if he were some criminal?

Morriarty: Anyone who detains a man illegally for eight days is a criminal!

The governor hangs up the phone. Captain Morriarty immediately calls him back.

Governor Usmani: What is your name so that I can have it for my report?

Morriarty: Captain Morriarty. M-O-R-R-I-A-R-T-Y. Morriarty. And if you like, I'd be glad to come by your place so you can meet me in person!

Governor Usmani: Do you think I'd support the Taliban?

Morriarty: I have no doubt.

Click. Captain Morriarty hangs up the phone.

I couldn't contain my laughter or pride in Captain Morriarty as he recounted these details. "Sir, you're my hero!"

"Thanks, Zeller. You're not so bad yourself. But listen, I need to know, do I have the major's support on this one? The ANP here want to arrest the subgovernor, but only if they know we'll back them up. I don't want to tell them yes and then not be able to come through."

"Let me check with Major Goodman, as he's sitting right next to me," I replied. I quickly brought Major Goodman up to speed and passed along Captain Morriarty's request.

"Let me see the phone," Major Goodman said, his hand extended.

"Hey Morriarty, Goodman here. You do whatever the ANP want. If they want to arrest him, great, even if that means they need you to back them up. Just make sure it's their doing and their idea," Major Goodman deftly replied, walking the fine line between mentor and occupier. Captain Morriarty briefly consulted with Colonel Patang and called back.

"Zeller, tell Goodman that Nabi wants to arrest the subgovernor, but only if we back him up, so here's what we'll do . . . ," Morriarty was saying, when Major Garrison walked in the room.

"Is that Captain Morriarty on the phone?" he demanded.

"Yes, Sir," I reluctantly replied, knowing already things had changed for the worse.

"Give me the phone, Matt," Major Garrison said as he extended his hand.

"Major Garrison wants to talk to you," I said and passed the phone.

A heated conversation took place between the two, as Captain Morriarty pleaded with Major Garrison to support his decision to help the Andar ANP arrest Disiwal. Major Garrison, ever eager to not rock the boat, refused to give permission.

"Jason, we aren't here to do their jobs or fix their problems. They have to take ownership. I promise I'll take these charges up with the Ghazni governor. Just get me the proof, and I'll take it to the governor," Major Garrison calmly stated.

"What more proof do you need? I've got the guy admitting he did it!" Captain Morriarty protested.

"Just bring me the proof. Get the detained man and the ANP to sign statements attesting to what happened, and I'll take it to the governor—that's the best we can do," Major Garrison said and hung up the phone.

On the other end, Captain Morriarty seethed with anger. The Andar ANP wanted to do the right thing and arrest the subgovernor. They just needed to know we'd back them up when they went to do it. That's significant progress from how we first found them: a police force heavily infiltrated by the Taliban and incapable of enforcing Afghan law. Had we backed them up, a shit storm would have rained down on us. The Ghazni governor would have called Colonel Johnson, President Karzai, or whomever he needed to in order to try to get Disiwal released. Inevitably, an overly cautious and too-eager-to-please-their-Afghan-ally U.S. officer would get involved and determine that the only way to make nice with the Afghans would be to publically punish Major Garrison and Captain Morriarty and get Disiwal released—or at least, I think that's what Major Garrison feared. He didn't want to sacrifice his army career in order to temporarily make an example of a corrupt Afghan official.

Ultimately, Captain Morriarty took the written statements and returned to the FOB extremely irate. As he and Major Garrison had it out, I shared my thoughts with Arnold. "My prediction: The Andar subgovernor will never face justice for this crime or for the previous time he threatened our contractor, who refused to pay him a bribe. The corruption will continue and thus further undermine the Afghan people's faith in their government, laws, and civil society, which in turn fuels their support for the Taliban," I glumly said.

Arnold nodded silently in shared despair.

A terp ran in and shattered the dark silence. "The ANP just called. One of their convoys traveling to Rashidan hit an IED. They have one KIA and need help!" he exclaimed.

Sadly, the usual happened. Despite the ANP's drastic need for an air medevac, ISAF would not authorize the flight due to the lack of coalition forces on the ground with the ANP.

As the day closed, ISAF and ARSIC-E postponed Team Four's Air Assault into Waghez for a second day, leaving us to wonder aloud: Does *anyone* care about our ability to actually accomplish our mission (mentor and train the ANP)? Thus far, the Waghez ANP have been without direct coalition mentorship for more than a month since returning from their initial training. It's a credit to First Lieutenant Creger's efforts that they've continued to patrol and to attempt to do the right thing—or at least that's what they report to him during their daily phone calls.

PART III

Leave

44

Bagram

Friday, October 17, 2008

The day my leave "began." We arrived at FOB Ghazni at around 0600 to be sure we'd be among the first in line for standby seats (also known as "Space Available" or "Space-A"). Priority of seating goes as follows: those with booked seats and those seeking Space-A on a first-come, first-served basis. We had booked seats, but there was no guarantee the helicopter would have space for us once it landed at Ghazni. Depending on the helicopter's direction of travel, it's either toward the end of the "ring" or at the beginning. Pilots and aircrews also don't have passenger manifests. They simply know the rough load weight they're currently carrying in cargo and approximately how much more space they have open for people and gear. Everyone (passengers, flight crew, and landing zone coordinators) trusts that each landing zone will strictly enforce the rules of the game; people with booked seats ("Space Blocked") will get on before people seeking Space-A get on. In essence, the system is a total craps shoot. Having a booked seat means virtually nothing, as chaos ensues when a helicopter lands. The more aggressive and assertive you are about your right/need to get on a flight, the more likely you are to actually get a seat.

Despite the fact that I had diligently requested seats for every soldier going on leave, experience had taught me that Space-Blocked confirmation numbers were meaningless. What mattered was that Palmer and I arrive as early as possible and

All smiles as we ride in the helicopter from FOB Ghazni to Bagram—the first leg of my journey home for leave.

ensure our names were at the top of the Space-Blocked list, as it vastly increased our chances of getting a seat. We found a line had already formed for people waiting to get on the flight list for the day. Thankfully, we were among the only ones waiting who had Space-Blocked seats, so we instantly jumped to the head of the line. An hour later, the landing zone administrator arrived and took down everyone's info and assigned us into flight groups. We were in Group 1, meaning we had first dibs on every available seat as helicopters going north arrived. Once our group all had seats, Group 2 was up and so forth. By 0800, more than 50 people had arrived to wait for flights. The 101st was in the midst of a final and massive air-assault mission in Wardak, and the Polish were in the midst of rotating their replacement personnel into the Province. Combat operations, medevacs, and large troop rotations take priority among flights over leave flights and individual travel flights (trying to go from FOB Ghazni to Gardez, for example). For the past week, anyone seeking to travel for leave or individual movement had been out of luck: hence the 50-person line.

In the flight line, I snapped photos of helicopters performing an air-assault ballet. Four birds at a time, attack helicopters, cargo helicopters, and medevac birds would fly in, land one after the other, drop off their cargo, pick up their patient, refuel, and fly away. I'll never forget one ANA soldier as he walked off a CH-47 transport that only an hour prior had plucked him and his cohorts from a raging battle against the Taliban in Wardak. Covered in a fine, dusty film, wearing no body armor or helmet, his beret halfcocked and weapon slung aimlessly over his back, he smiled and just shook his head as if to say in the universal language of soldiers, "Well, that was stupid!"

The 101st had spent days sending helicopters full of soldiers to clear one valley of Taliban fighters. The battle raged for four days. I asked one of the soldiers who had just returned how it was. Dazed, he looked right through me as he replied, "They just kept coming, like ants. They just kept flowing down over the hills. . . . I didn't think we were. . . ." His thought trailed off as he refused to reconsider the unthinkable.

The rapidity with which the attack helicopters continued to arrive, to refuel, and to fly off to rejoin the battle confirmed the intensity of the ongoing fight.

Finally, zero hour approached, the landing-zone administrator announced our flight was inbound and ordered our group forward. I was seventh in line. If there were six seats available, I'd have to try my luck with Space-A tomorrow. Eight seats and I was golden. The CH-47 and her escort made a pass around the landing zone (LZ) and came in for their landing. The roar of the double rotors and twin turbine engines rendered talking pointless. Even the loudest of shouts could barely be heard. The aircraft dropped, pitched, with their tails angled to touch down first. A blast of intense, dusty, hot, pressurized air nearly blew me off my feet, as in my excitement I'd forgotten to brace myself for the rotor wash.

The landing-zone administrator strode out and met the lead aircraft's crew chief, turned, pointed at our group, gave us the thumbs up, and motioned for us to run to the back of the bird. This was it. I was finally leaving! As I ran toward the helicopter's tail like a kid running toward presents on Christmas, it dawned on me: I haven't left Ghazni since June and the Tangi Valley attack. It felt good to take my first steps toward leave.

Walking up to the landing-zone administrator, he struggled to yell the following over the roar of the aircraft, "We can take 12 on each bird!" I had a seat, Palmer had a seat, and the complement of "new" soldiers we'd brought from our FOB going to Bagram for a week's worth of MRAP training had seats.

I stumbled into the aircraft and took stock of its cramped quarters. Our "seats" (nylon mesh) lined the aircraft's inner frame. A floor-to-ceiling-high pile of duffel bags, rucksacks, backpacks, and other boxes of gear took up the middle of the aircraft's interior and left us little to no legroom. To the credit of our soldiers and the air crew, we got everyone and all the gear on board with room to spare. I sat down next to an FBI agent who had been in the province on a secret mission, gave him a thumbs up and a massive smile, and exclaimed "Okay! Let's go!" He smiled and flashed an approving thumbs up!

I didn't realize we had lifted off until I saw the LZ far below us out the open tail door (weather permitting, most CH-47s fly with their tails open so as to give the aircraft another gunner's platform, and because the aircraft doesn't have air-conditioning and it's really hot in the back without the tail down. I reached for my camera and snapped photo after photo of a sight I had dreamt about for months: Ghazni from the air. I took extra care to snap a quality photo of our FOB, as we lacked anything more current than an aerial photo from 2006. Flying north, I marveled at how large Ghazni appeared when seen from the air and realized I'd only traveled to a small fraction of the communities surrounding the city.

As Ghazni disappeared from sight, we climbed ever higher in order to clear the mountains that separate Ghazni from Wardak. Periodically, I would turn around and look out the window behind me to see if I could determine our location from the scenery below. Maybe if I just look out the window and try and guess where we are, I'll feel better—big mistake. We're over Salar.

Salar had turned in to a personal marker for me. I felt that in any convoy or air movement, if we made it past Salar unscathed, we'd be okay. I held my breath as the shadow of our birds raced over the village's rooftops and fields. Nothing happened.

Eventually, we changed direction and moved on a course that no longer had us parallel to Highway One. I sat in awe at the stark, alien landscape hundreds of feet below. With the rolling brown hills, subtle mountain folds, and lack of green, we might as well have been on Mars.

I must have dozed off. Looking out the porthole window, I saw fields of green, clusters of villages, and mountains towering over us. Up ahead the mountains gave way to a broad plain engulfed in a massive polluted cloud of smog: Kabul. The number, quality, and modernity of the buildings increased the closer we got to the city, as if our entire flight north was a progression through time and development. The rugged, ancient mud-walled villages of the plains and mountains gradually bled into run-down concrete carcasses from a bygone Soviet era, which were quickly being replaced with modern Westernized high-rises.

Kabul from the air appears as an endless expanse of poverty that stretches far beyond the horizon; massive, dirty, raw, it's a city of millions clinging to life one day at a time.

The helicopter flew too fast for my brain to take it all in, and before I knew it, jagged, rugged, powerful mountains towered around us in every direction. I hadn't expected the mountains; I'd never been this far north.

As we rounded a mountain's rocky edge, its jagged walls seemingly close enough for me to touch, a large bowled valley came into view, and then, finally, Bagram!

From the air, the base is truly an odd sight, standing out in stark contrast to the Afghan world in which it awkwardly coexists. Countless abandoned villages surround the base's periphery, while inside, row after row of aircraft hangers, warehouses, modular housing trailers, b-huts, and barracks ring a sea of concrete that serves as the base's runway. A double hesco high wall topped with bands of barbed wire separates the modern era from antiquity.

As the wheels of our helicopter touched down on the base's tarmac, I let out a massive sigh of relief. We'd made it unscathed. I'd only have to make that flight at least twice more before we went home for good in December. One down, two to go.

The aircraft taxied to a hanger and stopped just short of its doors. The engines died down. The rotors twirled slowly to a halt. I took my earplugs out and enjoyed a brief, calm moment of silence.

"All right folks, let's get this bird unloaded!" screamed a sergeant who entered the rear of the aircraft, shattering my moment of tranquility.

Standing up, I waited my turn as one by one we got off the plane and stretched our legs to get the feeling back after two hours of a very cramped ride. As instructed, we formed a human chain and passed bag after bag out of the helicopter. The gear unloaded, Phil and I rounded up our FOB's soldiers and set out for the transient housing tent where we were scheduled to live until our flight to Kuwait.

I started to walk after Phil and the rest of our gaggle. I hadn't been at such low altitude in quite a long time. The air felt thick and polluted. I struggled to keep up under the weight of my body armor and travel luggage. A sergeant stopped me in my tracks.

"Sir, you're going to need to remove the ammunition from your weapons, holster your clips, and put your weapons on safe," he firmly stated.

"Come again?" I replied, unsure if I had heard him correctly.

"Sir, I repeat, you'll need to remove the ammunition from your weapons, holster your ammo clips, and put your weapons on safe," he said, a little less confidently.

I couldn't believe it. I didn't believe it.

"Sergeant, this is still a combat zone, correct?" I replied, now annoyed as I watched Phil and our group walk on without me, unaware I'd been stopped. "Explain to me why I need to downgrade my combat readiness," I demanded.

"Sir, Bagram Air Force Base rules state personnel cannot walk around in an amber state. You and your weapons must be green at all times unless authorized by the base commander or his designee," the sergeant replied, mindlessly quoting regulation.

Amber: the state I'd lived in since April. Ammo clip in the weapon, no rounds chambered. In case of emergency, charge the weapon, disengage the safety, aim, squeeze trigger, kill bad guy.

Green: a state I had forgotten about. The state of large FOBs, FOBBITs, garrison life, and life outside a warzone. Ammo clips holstered or stored, weapon on safe. In case of emergency, find ammunition clip, load into weapon, charge the weapon, disengage the safety, aim, squeeze trigger, and hope you had time to do all this before the bad guy killed you.

As I begrudgingly complied with his request, I couldn't help but feel nervous. Each step further from Amber made me feel that much more in danger.

Satisfied, the sergeant let me pass, and I ran after Phil and our motley crew. I found them waiting at a bus stop on a paved street. Puffing to catch my breath after my combat shuffle, I took in my surroundings. Western women, cars, no body armor, commuter buses, people saluting every three steps. A Pizza Hut delivery guy rode by on a moped. I'd landed on some alien world. My brain couldn't piece it all together: "This is familiar, this is *your* world, this is where you belong; you just haven't seen it in a while, that's all. . . ." Something kept me from accepting it all. I was going home on leave, but I was also coming back for another two months of combat, of living life on the edge. I couldn't let go of that edge. I needed it. It kept me alive.

I refused to believe the world around me existed. I knew it should be familiar and welcoming, but it wasn't. It was foreign, nerve-wracking, unsettling, and scary. And yet I knew that in the end, this was where I belonged.

I didn't have time for this. I flagged down an SUV driven by an attractive middle-age American woman. "Ma'am, my soldiers and I have been waiting quite a while for this shuttle bus, but it has yet to arrive. Would you mind giving us a ride?"

"I mean . . . the bus should be along shortly. You just gotta be patient. I would but, I, uh, well . . . [looking back at her back seat] how many of you are there?" she hesitantly asked.

"Just us six," I said, pointing to Phil and our group.

"I would, but, uh . . . I've got a meeting, and my vehicle is awfully full. Uh . . . the bus should be here any minute . . . ," she said, trying to find an excuse to deny my request.

I started to get angry. I wasn't used to civilians saying no to me. Since April, the only people who could say no to me were senior officers.

At that moment, a bus pulled up. "Oh well, looks like you're in luck boys!" she said as she rapidly drove away.

We struggled to board the bus, as its doors weren't designed for soldiers wearing bulky body armor, ammunition, and gear. On board I took the first available seat and squeezed in, praying that the ride down the road went by fast, my comfort and patience waning. The bus didn't move. "I need everyone to take their seats before I can move. You all need to do what ya' got to do to take a seat! We ain't movin' 'til everyone is seated!" screamed a power-crazed American woman driver. There were no seats available between everyone already on the bus and all the gear.

She stood her ground. "Base rules say I can't move 'til everyone is seated. So either y'all sit, or, if there ain't no seats, some of you will have to get off. Next bus will be around in about 20 minutes." Defying the laws of physics, we found a way to make enough space for everyone to "sit." The driver rolled her eyes and drove forward. Ten minutes and several bus stops later, we arrived at the other end of the base and our transient housing tent. The struggle to get off the bus was equally frustrating as getting on, the weight and bulk of our gear and armor barely fitting through the bus's doors.

We walked toward the transient tent as the sun set over the mountains to the west of the airbase—their massive size blocked out most of the late daylight. The hum of the base's countless generators and massive streetlights announced the arrival of night.

Master Sergeant Bates, a Vietnam veteran from our unit, met us outside the transient housing tent and explained the rules. While living in his tent, we had to check in with his accountability roster twice a day, once at 0800 and once at 1800. He'd arrange for our travel to the air terminal on the day our flight left for Kuwait. Before we could enter the tent and choose a bunk, we had to relinquish our weapons and ammunition to him in exchange for a supply receipt that we'd trade in for our weapons and ammo after we returned from leave.

"Excuse me, Sergeant, I must have not heard you correctly: Did you say we needed to hand in all of our weapons and ammo right now?"

"Yes, Sir! Bagram doesn't allow you soldiers to be armed while here on a temporary or transient status," he forcefully replied. A group of soldiers sitting lounging around the smoking area laughed; this must have been a common exchange.

"Sergeant, pardon my stupidity, but what are we supposed to do if the base gets attacked?" I asked in all seriousness.

He let out a loud hoot as if that was the funniest thing he'd heard in ages. "Sir, you crack me up! They got a whole force here that does nothing but guard those walls over there! You ain't gonna need your weapon!" he exclaimed.

The place was too surreal, too strange to comprehend or to make sense of it all. I understood what he was saying, but it didn't make sense, because my way of thinking didn't make sense. I'd spent months with danger and death lurking unannounced at every corner. Here in FOBBIT-ton, life went on not much differently from a large base back in the U.S. I lived "down South, where the war is." They lived on Disney. (The main road in Bagram is called Disney after a service member killed in action . . . ironic).

I ate dinner in silence with Phil and the rest of our group in the closest chow hall, our eyes darting around from odd site to odd site: endless food, endless portions, endless rations. When we had left Ghazni, we'd run out of everything to drink but water. They had a soda fountain, with ice. I left the chow hall, returned to the transient tent, and then I did the unthinkable: I walked a mile down the road and had a Whopper from Burger King.

Bagram has a Burger King, several Dairy Queens, a Pizza Hut (that delivers), multiple massage parlors and hair boutiques staffed by what has to be a significant portion of the female population of central Asia, an Internet store, several jewelry stores, a rug store, a Subway, a movie theater, a state-of-the-art hospital, a sizeable PX (Walmart for the military), numerous Green Beans (Starbucks for the military), and countless other creature comforts from home.

Walking back to my tent, I listened to the thunderous roar of a fighter jet screaming into the sky, its afterburner a bright gaseous blue streak, the only visible evidence of its existence. A soldier stopped me. "Lieutenant, where's your PT [Physical Training] belt?" he demanded. (The military issues reflective belts to be worn while conducting PT outside in the dark).

"My what?" I exclaimed, convinced I hadn't just heard what I thought he said.

"Sir, I said, '*Where is your P.T. belt?!?*'" he repeated, enunciating each syllable.

"I haven't a fucking clue. Probably back in Ghazni," I replied, bemused yet annoyed.

"Sir, word of advice: This here's Bagram, not Ghazni. They've got a rule. After dark, you've gotta wear your PT belt, or else the MPs could give you a ticket."

I had to be imagining all this. First they made me go green, then they took my weapons. Now they wanted me to wear a reflective belt so I could be seen better. And if I didn't, they'd issue me a ticket? Where was I?

"You've got to be kidding me! Why on Earth would they want you to wear a reflective belt at night in the middle of a combat zone, to make it easier for the Taliban to shoot you?" I screamed in an increasingly frustrated tirade.

"Don't know, Sir, but them's just the rules. Anyways, have a good night, and try to remember your PT belt. The MPs can be real dicks when it comes to that shit," replied the soldier, as he walked away.

This here's Bagram, not Ghazni. Couldn't have said it better myself. I vowed from that moment on never to wear a PT belt; some rules were too stupid to abide. So what if I got a ticket? I'd never pay it, and I doubted they'd ever find me. The whole place was a realm of insanity, a desperate attempt to transplant a slice of normal America onto the moon.

Arriving back at the tent, I pulled out my phone and called my girlfriend. Hearing her voice for the first time in days brought the first real calm I had had the whole day. As she patiently listened, I rambled on and on about how weird I found Bagram and how I couldn't wait to get home to her. We talked for an hour, and then I headed to bed. That night I moved to three different bunks before I found one where the noise of the fan drowned out the roar of 40 snoring males.

The next morning, I set off to find Major Hunt and anyone else I knew on Bagram (as he'd told me to stop by if I was ever on the base). After about 30 minutes of searching, I found his office and shocked the hell out of First Lieutenant Montecillo as I popped in and said hello.

"Hey, Mike, long time no see! How have you been?" I asked with a wide smile.

"Matt Zeller, wow! How in the hell are you, man? What are you doing here in Bagram?" he replied enthusiastically.

"Going home on leave, man. Thank God. This place sucks!" I said.

"This place is a joke. Where are you staying?" he replied.

"Down at the other end of the base in the transient tent."

"Dude, that place is a nightmare. How long you going to be here?"

"Um, about a week I think. I figure with everything I have to get done, plus the time it takes to book the flight, I'll be here 'til end of the week or so."

"Dude, then you gotta stay with us. We've got plenty of extra space. You'll have your own room in an air-conditioned b-hut," he said.

"Awesome! That would be perfect, as I don't think I could take another night in there. Could you help me move my gear from the tent up here?" I asked.

"Dude, no problem. We've got our own SUVs and everything. Man, you should have called us. We could have met you on the flight line and spared you the hassle of taking the bus." I learned then and there: Always have a friend with a car and a spare bunk at Bagram. Your quality of life improves dramatically.

Bagram literally felt like a vacation; I got a filling fixed and received a real medical evaluation from an actual doctor (the first since the RPG blast and mortar rounds knocked me out back in April). The doctor pronounced me healthy but encouraged me to get a proper evaluation done upon returning to Fort Riley or with the VA once off active duty. I even went shopping at the weekly Friday bazaar (picking up several presents for my family and friends) and played piano for the first time in months at the base chapel. Friday evening, I walked over to the PAX Terminal (the place where one catches a fixed-wing aircraft flight) and got myself on the waiting list for a flight to Kuwait the next morning. I went to bed that night as excited as I've ever been in my life, barely sleeping a wink for fear I'd sleep through my "showtime."

Hours later, I rolled out of bed, packed my things, and walked into the cold Bagram night. Three blocks later, I reached the PAX terminal, handed my ID card to the attending air force airmen, and took my seat, awaiting further instructions. As the early-morning light appeared across Bagram's mountains, an airman grouped our "chalk" (the group of us traveling on the flight) together and handed back our ID cards one by one. We were officially "manifested" on the flight, which would leave in about two hours.

An hour later, the air force "locked us down" in a waiting area, where most of us passed the time sitting around, doing nothing, and getting paid for it. Thirty minutes later, we lined up and moved toward a waiting C-17 cargo plane, escorted by a stern U.S. Army sergeant who ordered us to "file in one at a time, fill up the middle seats first, and once the middle seats are filled, begin filling the seats along the wall [the way more comfortable seats that everyone wants]." True to form, the "rules" and "orders" went out the window as soon as the first person stepped on the plane and was invited by the flight's crew chief to "Take any seat you want! Glad to have you aboard! We'll be leaving shortly!" So much for my masterful plan to purposely linger and be at the back of the line; my effort failed to secure a comfy seat.

Thankfully, the flight wasn't close to full, and thus I managed to easily secure an "aisle" seat that afforded me marginal leg room. Minutes after boarding, the crew loaded the gear pallets, closed the rear cargo doors, asked us to take our seats, and gave a quick safety brief as we taxied to the runway. A monstrous roar of the C-17's four powerful jet engines slammed me back in my seat as we raced down the runway. Minutes after takeoff, the crew chief announced we had reached a comfortable cruising altitude of "way the fuck out of range of any Taliban weapon," and I took my first real, genuine, breath of relief and relaxation in almost a year. Over the next four hours, we flew over most of Afghanistan (and maybe part of Waziristan, Pakistan), skirted the coast of Iran, and arrived safely in Kuwait, which might as well be America's 52nd state (behind Puerto Rico).

45

Kuwait

Saturday, October 25–Sunday, October 26, 2008

Kuwait couldn't have been any more different from Afghanistan. The whole country, baked in a sweltering 140 degrees, seemed to be suburban sprawl with enormous mansions (some had seven stories) that gave way to empty flat desert. And, we own it all. The Kuwaitis seem to shut down the highway anytime we had to move from one airport to the other. We even have our own baselike section at their capital's international airport. We had official police escorts whenever we went off base, and those escorts were led by U.S.-manned Up-Armored Hummers.

I was dumbfounded by the number of Iraq soldiers who would pepper us Afghan guys with such questions as, "What's it like to actually be in a shooting war?" and such statements as, "God, I wish I could go there and get some. Iraq is so boring. You're so lucky!" They made no attempt to hide their envy at the fact that our war still had violence. If only they knew. These conversations made me wonder whether some combat vets end up more duck than turtle—I think so.

Kuwait was one long "hurry up and wait" prison. The base is set up in row after endless row of tents. It has a McDonald's, a KFC, a Pizza Hut, a gym, a chow hall, and a contingent of Australian soldiers who have some role on the base and quite possibly one of the *worst* desert uniforms I've ever seen (blue dots on a sea of yellow; you really call that camouflage?).

The McDonald's sign at Ali Asalim Air Base in Kuwait.

The highlight of my time in Kuwait came when I unexpectedly ran into a childhood friend, USMC Sergeant Andrea Skivington, who was randomly stationed on another base in Kuwait. She made the trip over to my base to surprise me for a half-way-across-the-world reunion.

The next morning, we got word that our flight home would leave later that evening. After lunch, the army rounded us up into a lockdown area and thoroughly searched all our gear. In a sight that would make any TSA agent envious, one by one we painstakingly dumped out the entire contents of every bag and every pocket. The army customs inspectors gave every container, canister, and parcel the most thorough search I've ever seen. The list of "contraband" included the expected (drugs and ammo) and the ludicrous (rocks and dirt). Thankfully, I only carried an extra set of clothing, my laptop, iPod, and lucky charms (pocket prayer book and my always-with-me copy of *On the Road*), so my search went rather quickly. Once "cleared" to leave for Kuwait, I hurriedly repacked my gear and followed the maze to yet another holding area, where we were once again "locked down."

For the next hours, I sat among a group of fellow army soldiers, Marines, airmen, and the odd sailor and Department of Defense civilian (instantly recognizable in their trademark "uniform" made up from the latest REI clothing catalog, cargo pants, tactical belt, and all) and just waited. Eventually word came that the buses had arrived to take us to the Kuwait International Airport for our first leg back to the U.S.

Again, I cannot overstate how much we own Kuwait. Just as in Afghanistan, civilian cars parted like the Red Sea as our convoy moved down the highway. At the airport, U.S. Airmen approved our entry into another "secure" area where we waited to board the flight. As we taxied down the runway, the lead flight attendant announced that we'd be flying into a typhoon currently over Yemen and that we should expect a bumpy takeoff. I popped an Ambien.

I've never been the best flier, but I learned something on this flight: It's serious if the flight attendant panics. And panic she did. Seated a few rows ahead of me, facing toward us, two flight attendants casually chatted as our multi-tonned flying aluminum coffin rumbled into the sky. A few bumps, nothing out of the ordinary, Ambien starting to kick in, sleep coming, nodding off. . . .

Bam!

My stomach is in my mouth. Everyone is yelling. The soldier next to me turns ghost white and asks me if God is going to punish us for the sins he committed in Iraq. His eyes beg me to forgive him for some unknown horror. I look up. The flight attendant is screaming. Someone is crying. We're falling. Fast.

And as quickly as it happened it ended.

I pop another Ambien. If I'm going to do die on this damned flight, I want to be knocked out.

When I wake up, we're landing in Germany.

So what happened? Apparently airplane + typhoon = near-disaster. We dropped several thousand feet in just a few seconds, saved only by the awesome flying and calm of our pilot.

46

The United States of I Don't Feel Like I Belong Here

Sunday, October 26–Monday, October 27, 2008

As we pulled into the terminal at Leipzig, Germany, our flight "leader" (the highest-ranking officer on the plane) gives us our "Germany briefing": Don't Drink. If anyone gets caught drinking, the whole plane has to go back to Kuwait and redo the whole lockdown. Suck it up, wait a few more hours, and drink yourself silly in the U.S.

Walking into the terminal, the colonel turns to me and says, "God I hope they listen—it's two hours, and then my responsibility as flight leader ends. God knows, I want a beer as well."

The colonel pleads with us not to drink. We begrudgingly obeyed and shuffled, forlorn, into the terminal to wait the two hours it takes to refuel the plane so we can fly on to Atlanta. And then we saw it: A plane full of Marines that landed before us is already inside the terminal, and they are rip-roaringly drunk, three beers to a man. I took a seat next to the colonel and glared.

"You've got to be fucking kidding me," the colonel said under his breath. "Just what I needed, a plane of Marines under a different set of orders. So help me God, if one person on our plane even takes one swig. . . ." His thought trailed off to some unimaginable punishment we'd all bestow upon the imaginary rogue individual.

Precila and I celebrating her birthday and my leave at the Willard Room in Washington, D.C.

Two hours later, our plane refueled, we reboarded, I popped another Ambien, and off we went toward Atlanta. I woke up somewhere over northeast Canada. Eyes glued to the night skylines below, we reveled as we flew over U.S. soil: "home."

Forty-five minutes later, we flew over Manhattan, all eyes glued to the night skyline. All sat in reverent silence. The black spot at the south end of the island came into view, reminding all aboard as to why we currently sat cruising 36,000 feet above America's great city.

Soon the sun's first morning rays illuminated the cabin and the ground below.

I couldn't believe how green it all looked. After spending nearly a year in a very brown country, the greenness of America was all the more striking and beautiful.

"Home. We're finally home," I sighed as an unknown burden lifted for the first time since April.

Upon landing in Atlanta, some sergeant boarded the plane, welcomed us home as "heroes," and gave us some "Hooah!" briefing about what we could and could not do in the Atlanta terminal. She repeated the reminder that we couldn't drink at least three times. Thinking back on the fact that I didn't have NODs until early June, I had to wonder how much more efficient we would be if the army diverted the energy it uses to prevent us from drinking into getting us proper supplies. All I wanted was to get off this fucking flight and onto my final flight back to D.C.

Eventually I found myself on an underground train taking a fellow Afghan vet and me to the next terminal. And then it happened: Civilians got on board, and it hit me that these were the first Americans I'd seen on American soil since we left Maine back in April. And I didn't recognize them. In fact, they scared the bejesus out of me.

I turned to my travel buddy and asked, "Are these people freaking you out as much as me?"

"Yep. They need to back the fuck off," he said under his breath, careful so that they couldn't hear us.

We sat like scared caged animals in the very front of the train, keeping a great distance between us and the regular everyday citizens going about their business. As the train car filled up between stops, the crowd got closer and closer, causing our nerves to rise in tandem.

Why are they all looking at us? It felt as if everyone was staring and yet not trying to stare at the same time. Finally I blurted out to no one and yet to everyone in earshot, "You people are really freaking me out. Sorry, we just got home, and this is so weird."

A Vietnam vet (identifiable by his hat) leaned down and said, "Welcome home, Son, it's going to be okay."

"Thanks, Sir. It's just . . . strange," I stammered, embarrassed that something as innocuous as a train ride could frighten me.

"Well, nonetheless, welcome home, and thank you," he replied and nodded in respect.

"You're welcome," I said, standing. "And thank you for everything you did for us," I put my hand out to shake his. Among a sea of ducks, I had found a fellow turtle; the eyes tell everything.

Several stops later the train arrived at my terminal, and I bid my travel buddy good luck. I sprinted to my gate, eager to try to make an earlier flight to D.C.

I arrived at the gate and pleaded my case to the gate agent to let me fly standby. The crowd of passengers waiting to board took notice and one by one started offering up their seats. If people ever want to see genuine American kindness to strangers in action, go down to the arrivals terminal in Atlanta on any given day and just watch. You're bound to see at least one plane full of people in uniform returning from war. As we soldiers walk into what feels like an utterly foreign land that should by all reasons be familiar, we're greeted by the warmest and loudest round of random applause from complete strangers. It's humbling, and I still don't feel as if I earned the applause, let alone having people offer up their seats so that I could get home a little faster.

Thankfully, there was a free seat. I reached into my pocket and went to dial my girlfriend [now wife] Precila to tell her that I'd made an earlier flight, but my phone wasn't working. A torrent of people rushed forward, cellphones at the ready. I made the call and for the first time since April spoke with my P on American soil.

"Sweetheart, it's me. I made it home and I'm coming in on the 11:30 flight. I'll see you in just a little over two hours!"

"Oh my God! Okay! Thanks, I'll see you soon! I love you!"

"I love you too, see you soon!"

We landed at Dulles, and the whole plane let me off first, yet another humbling experience. I sprinted into the arrival/waiting area and scanned the horizon. I couldn't see her. Where is she? And then I saw her. Leaning nervously against a metal pillar, magazine in hand, she scanned the horizon. Our eyes made contact. At first I thought she didn't recognize me or that she wasn't really that happy to see me. Later, she'd tell me my appearance shocked her. For starters, I had lost 30 pounds and looked emaciated. More importantly, she mentally struggled to believe I was actually, finally there. I ran toward her and embraced her like I've never held anyone else in my life. We walked to the car, and she remained awkwardly silent.

"Are you okay?" I asked, nervous that she would suddenly dump me (we've all heard the stories, and the thought never escapes our minds).

"Yes, I just cannot believe it. You're here! Finally! You're actually in my arms! I get to have you here with me! I'm just overwhelmed." I sat down in her passenger's seat and suddenly she came running around, jumped into my lap, gave me the longest kiss and started to cry. "I missed you so much."

As we finally drove off, you'd think I'd have just stared at her. But I didn't. While I had physically returned from the war, mentally, I was still in Afghanistan. And Precila was the first to notice.

"Are you okay?" she asked. "Yeah, why?" I replied, not recognizing the worry in her voice.

"Because you're staring out the window and your head is turning back and forth like crazy. What are you looking for?" "IEDs" I replied nonchalantly. "Matt . . . ," she said, worried, "you don't have to worry about them here, you're safe now. You're home."

I didn't stop looking. I couldn't stop. No matter what she said, every time I tried to stop, the training took over. I had to keep my eyes open and my mind focused on the lookout. We had to get to her place safely, and if I didn't look, and an IED did go off, it'd be my fault.

"Matt, calm down, it's going to be okay, there are no IEDs out there. Look at me, keep your eyes on me, tell me about your flight, talk to me, take your mind off of everything," she said, trying her best to bring me back.

Her efforts were of no use. Try as she might, I kept returning to the road and my futile scanning.

Things only got worse once we got home. Showered and in civilian clothes for the first time since April, we ventured across the street to the Cheesecake Factory in Tyson's Corner Mall. Until that moment, I hadn't been in a building that had had more than two stories in almost seven months, let alone ridden an escalator. I'd also never had a panic attack until that moment. But on the escalator ride from floor one to floor two, I nearly collapsed. I sat down on the moving stairs, pulled my knees to my chest, and started to rock back and forth. My chest tightened. I couldn't breathe.

Looking around made it worse. Unarmed, riding up a moving staircase, I watched as throngs of people milled around, shopping bags bumping along with each step. Didn't these people realize how vulnerable they all were? How could they just walk around without a care in the world, totally oblivious to the potential danger, the attack that could happen at any moment?

Precila knelt down, looked into my eyes, and said, "It's okay, it's going to be okay, we can go back home if this is too much. . . ." I snapped back into reality. "No, it's okay, I really want this burger and bourbon. I'll be fine, this is all just freaking me out. I'll be okay once we're inside the restaurant."

Events like this would repeat on and off for the rest of my leave, my condition only worsening over time. Some days were good, others really bad. I learned quickly that I didn't do well with crowds or enclosed spaces. And I can also tell you that I've never had a tastier burger than that meal at Cheesecake or a more refreshing beer than the first one I had at my favorite D.C.-area pub in Arlington later that evening surrounded by dear friends.

As the days passed, my college best friends, Patrick and Charley, visited along with my cousin Jessica and my mom, dad, and brother, Andy. By the end of leave, however, I had started to fall apart. My brother and I got into a heated argument. My dad decided to go for a walk outside their hotel while Andy and I worked it out.

Sitting in their hotel room, I tried to explain to Andy why I was acting so differently. I noticed the harder I tried to verbalize my thoughts, the harder it was for me to actually say the words. I could think the sentence, but I couldn't get my mouth to speak what I was thinking. Andy looked on increasingly concerned.

Bang! Bang! Bang!

Three shots rang out in rapid precision.

Instinctively I dropped to the floor, rolled toward the wall nearest to the hotel room door, and reached for my nonexistent pistol. Upon realizing that the pistol was locked up in a makeshift arms room in Afghanistan, I dropped to the ground, pulled my knees to my chest, and began to rock back and forth in a trance.

Andy stared in disbelief. He later told me he tried to talk to me for several minutes but that I just sat rocking back and forth, catatonic, staring into nothingness.

Unknown to me, the hotel room sat nearly across the street from Fort Myer, the home of the U.S. Army Honor Guard. Also unknown to me was that they were doing funeral detail practice right at that moment, and the shots I heard were practice shots.

Before leaving, Dad made me promise him that after I got home for good, I'd go see someone to take care of what would later become very serious issues. I'll never forget the helpless look of concern in his eyes as I hugged him good-bye before he and Andy drove back to New York.

I spent the rest of leave with Precila trying our best to savor every single moment of our time together, not wanting to admit our lingering fear that, despite our momentary joy, this could still be the end. I'd inevitably return to Afghanistan, and there was still a very real chance I'd never come home again.

As I put on my uniform in Precila's apartment on my last day of leave, I felt unexpectedly calm. It surprised me just how soothing I found the familiar sight of my army digital tan. Precila started to cry. To this day, she tears up anytime I have to go on weekend drill or regular reserve duty; she says the sight of me in uniform reminds her of this last day, and the emotions are too much. She gets overwhelmed with what we both thought at the time: This could be it, these could be our last moments together, this could be good-bye forever. I truly believe deployments are harder on those we leave behind than those of us who go. Sure, we physically suffer more, but I believe the emotional and psychological impact is just as detrimental to those we leave behind. They have to live with the emptiness; we get to go back to our adrenaline-fueled chaos. Adrenaline, our drug of choice, masks the void that those left behind must face alone.

47

Going Back to War
Feels Like Going Home

The trip from D.C. back to Afghanistan was uneventful. Precila and I had our tear-ful good-bye at the airport, filled with every movie-script cliché imaginable. Ambien ensured I spent the flights medically unconscious, awake only long enough to change planes when necessary. Three days after I left D.C., I landed back in Bagram, a return to familiarity. As I walked off to find Major Hunt and First Lieutenant Montecillo to borrow another bunk while I waited for a helicopter flight back to Ghazni, I struggled with a nagging concern: Had America softened me? Had I lost my edge? And if so, could I regain it in time before my lack of it got someone hurt or killed? Only time would tell. . . .

I spent the next several days in a Groundhog's Day–esque routine. Each afternoon around 3:00, I'd run down to the helicopter terminal to wait in line to get myself on the waitlist for any open seats on the next day's flights. They started taking names at 5:00, so I'd arrive two hours early to ensure I was at the front of the line and most likely to get a spot on an available flight. The next morning, I'd get up at 4:00, lug all my gear down to the helicopter terminal manifest area and wait patiently, hoping to get picked up for a flight "home." And every day, they'd announce that all the flights were full. I'd lug my crap back to my bunk, sleep for a few hours, mill around smoking cigarettes,

---

Beauty even in a war zone. Sunset over the Waghez mountains as seen from one of our fighting positions on FOB Vulcan. I never tired of this beautiful sight and miss it to this day.

wander over to the Internet cafe to kill a few more hours, and eventually work my way back to the helicopter terminal to wait in line and try again for the next day. On and on this went. And day after day I sat useless in Bagram, feeling useless and desperate to get back into the fight.

Monday, November 17, 2008

Four days of waiting around Bagram for a flight out, and I'd had enough. That morning as I struggled down to the helicopter terminal under the weight of my gear and body armor (I didn't remember it being this heavy when I left for leave), I vowed that no matter what, I was leaving Bagram that morning, even if it meant going to another base where I might have more luck getting back to Ghazni.

As I sat in the terminal waiting for the inevitable morning rejection announcement, I formulated my plan. If I could get out to the flight line, I'd get on the first bird going to Ghazni and just hope that no one would notice. If they did, I'd chalk it up to being a confused first lieutenant and plead ignorance, as in the old army adage, "Tis better to ask forgiveness than to ask for permission." And that's when I heard the flight managers announce that all the flights past FOB Airborne were full; if you wanted to fly, you could fly to Airborne, but after that you'd have to get off. FOB Airborne was the FOB right before FOB Ghazni and close enough for me to possibly catch a convoy later on.

I jumped up, ran to the flight managers, and stated I'd gladly fly there. Moments later I walked out to the tarmac and boarded the Chinook. The first 45 minutes of the flight went smoothly, and then something went very wrong. We banked hard, turned around, and with a thunderous thrust, sped back toward Bagram. The door gunner leaned out of the window nervously.

The problem with being a passenger in a Chinook is that you haven't a clue as to what is going on except in the immediate area inside the aircraft. Inside everything seemed fine, but the panicked actions of the flight crew indicated something was very wrong. The moment we landed at Bagram, the flight crew told us to "run the fuck off the aircraft now!"

We sprinted.

And then we just sat at one end of the airfield and waited. Eventually someone started smoking, and soon we all joined in, the nicotine soothing our nerve-racked psyches. Twenty minutes later, our flight crew walked up and informed us that one of the engines on their sister aircraft (Chinooks usually fly in pairs of two) had caught on fire and that we'd have to wait until they got another aircraft ready to fly with us, which would take about an hour. We had come back to Bagram because they feared the other helicopter was about to crash.

An hour later, we took off and made our second attempt to FOB Airborne, about an hour's flight away from Bagram. As we landed at FOB Airborne, I expected to see a mass of people waiting to kick us off the aircraft; after all, the flight managers at Bagram had informed us that all the seats were taken from FOB Airborne on. And yet, the flight line sat empty.

We spent 10 minutes at Airborne unloading gear, dropping a few soldiers and civilians off, and then we took off toward FOB Ghazni with an almost empty aircraft. I cursed the flight managers back at Bagram for their inability to properly move people and felt genuine sympathy for all the soldiers we had left back at Bagram who could have been on their way to FOB Ghazni or any other points beyond. Regardless, my plan had worked, and I didn't even need to plead ignorance. I had simply gotten on the flight, sat there, did my best to look like I knew I was supposed to be there (which clearly didn't matter to anyone actually flying the helicopter), and waited to get off at FOB Ghazni.

On the approach to Ghazni, I felt an overwhelming sense of joy, a sort of homecoming, if you can call it that, as we descended toward the landing zone and in the distance all the familiar sights (the citadel in the center of the city, FOB Vulcan, etc.) came into view.

I ran off the back of the helicopter and sprinted toward the "wall," our unit's hangout spot during resupply missions to FOB Ghazni. If lucky, we'd have a crew already there on another mission, and I could hitch a ride back. If not, then when a mission did arrive, that's where I'd be most likely to find them. Either way, I couldn't wait to get to the wall. Sadly, no one was there to greet me.

Dropping my gear, I inhaled deeply and found it surprisingly hard to breathe; I had been gone long enough to lose some altitude adjustment. As I dropped to the ground and into shadow, I realized it had got much colder in my absence. I lit a cigarette, pulled out my Afghan cell phone, called Arnold, and gleefully announced I was waiting at the wall for a ride "home." Arnold informed me he'd spin up a crew to come retrieve me at the wall and that he was looking forward to filling me in on all that had gone down since I'd left.

An hour later, Master Sergeant Postman unexpectedly drove by on a Gator (an ATV four-wheeled vehicle). I flagged him down and warmly embraced him with a hug.

"Hey you got promoted to Master Sergeant! Congrats, Al! So what in the hell are you doing over here on a gator?"

"Well, Sir, after I got promoted, they moved me over here to run the new Ghazni ANP training academy. I've been here for about a month. Arnold called and said you were here waiting. I figured I'd come get you and your gear and you could wait at our place until the crew from Vulcan arrives."

Vulcan without Master Sergeant Postman always sucked, but secretly I was overjoyed at his new assignment. As you'll recall, he had previously been attached to Team Four: Waghez. Evil, dangerous, Waghez. Now that he was running the academy, it meant he wasn't going to Waghez, which suited me just fine.

For the next hour, I hung out with Master Sergeant Postman at the academy, happily sipping chai with the Afghan trainees, sharing cigarettes, and relishing my reimmersion into Afghan culture. I was home, and it felt good.

The rumble of a Hummer rounding the bend onto the academy's grounds announced the arrival of my ride back to Vulcan. The vehicle screeched to a halt only inches from my legs, and out jumped Major Goodman.

"Welcome home, Lieutenant. I'm thrilled to see you. We actually missed the hell out of you, though we were glad as fuck when you left. You had become a royal pain in the ass before leave, and I can tell already that leave did you good. Hope you're ready to work your butt off, because things are getting really interesting."

I smiled. "Sure am, Sir, it's good to be home. I missed the fuck out of you guys. Now that I'm back, I wouldn't want to be anywhere else; it's good to be back."

Arnold jumped out of the turret, ran up to me, and bear-hugged me.

"Man it's good to see you. There's so much to tell you. Things have gotten so interesting since you left, lots of developments. How was leave?"

"Leave was great. Ate, drank, and was merry. Just what I needed. But man, I really wanted to get back to you guys—I couldn't stop worrying about you. Everyone's safe, right?"

"Yep. All good. We've done so much construction on the FOB, it's way more fortified now."

"Wow, I have been gone a long time," and then it hit me. I cockily grinned at Arnold as he jumped back into the turret. "Hey Craig, guess what?"

"What, Matt?"

"What's today's date?"

"November 17th . . . ," Arnold said, realizing why I was grinning like an ass.

"I told you I'd be back exactly one month to the day," I said as I slammed the armored door shut. "Okay, let's go home."

PART IV

My War Abroad Ends

48

Burning the Governor's Drugs

Saturday, November 22, 2008

Since I've been gone, Arnold has not only grown into his role as my replacement, he's excelled and surpassed me in some regards. He's developed a much better relationship with the ANP intel guys and has really come into his own as a leader and officer. I couldn't be prouder.

Early in the morning, our NDS contacts called Arnold to inform him that they had an urgent situation on their hands and that it required our immediate involvement. They wouldn't say more on the phone other than that it involved the governor, corruption, the Taliban, and something they recently confiscated. We immediately spun up a mission and prepared to drive to the NDS Provincial Headquarters in downtown Ghazni. As we were about to leave, our DynCorp counterparts from FOB Ghazni came roaring into the FOB.

Their leader jumped out of their truck and began to recite a tale of mythic proportions.

The night before, the NDS had stopped a jingle truck escorted by a single black car at an impromptu checkpoint on the main highway. While the truck pulled over, the car sped off to the governor's compound. Unknown to the Afghans, our aerial surveillance system had caught all the events on tape in excruciating detail. While the NDS detained the driver and investigated the jingle truck, the car arrived at the governor's compound, the passengers ran into the mansion, and within min-

---

Sitting on $6.3 million worth of drugs. Clockwise from left: Jamshid, me, Gerald, and Goodman.

utes they assembled a ragtag militia made up of the governor's personal security detail (the Pai looch), all led by Haji Fasil. Before the NDS could open the cargo container on the truck, the "militia" arrived and surrounded the NDS. A standoff ensued. Eventually someone opened fire, and all hell broke loose. The NDS held their ground and fought off the ragtag militia, which limped back to the governor's compound. The NDS drove the truck to their HQ and hunkered down for a reprisal attack that never came. As soon as the cell-phone tower started working that morning, they called both DynCorp and us and begged us to get to them ASAP. Whatever was inside that truck had them fearing for their lives.

We raced out, arriving within minutes at the NDS HQ. From the moment we arrived, one could tell two things: (1) Not everyone at the NDS compound knew we were coming, and (2) those who did know we were coming wanted *nothing* to do with the truck. While the DynCorp staff tried to calm down the NDS leadership to gain a better understanding of what had gone down the night before, I grabbed Arnold, Janis, and Major Goodman and headed off with a lone NDS officer to inspect the now-infamous jingle truck.

We found it abandoned in a rubble-filled lot, unguarded.

"So what's in it?" I asked, like a child excited to tear into his presents on Christmas morning.

"The NDS says it's drugs that belong to the governor," Janis said, interpreting what our NDS escort said.

"Really?" I said, now doubly eager to examine the cargo.

"Hold up, right now we have no authority to do anything with this truck, and we should use this as an opportunity to make the ANP do the right thing. Technically they have jurisdiction in these events, and they ought to do a proper investigation. Let's first get this truck over to ANP HQ. We'll get them to do a proper investigation and inventory of its contents while I contact our higher HQ and see what we can actually do in this situation. Remember, we're mentors; we're not here to enforce Afghan law but to advise," said Major Goodman, clearly as eager as I was to open the truck. He realized that if it was full of drugs, and if they did belong to the governor, it likely meant the corruption went way above the governor and had the potential to be an embarrassing international incident. We had to cover our asses before we could cover our Afghan counterparts.

"I'll spin up our convoy. We'll get the NDS to drive the truck to the ANP HQ, and Arnold can use his newfound positive relationship with the counternarcotics and internal-affairs officers to get a proper investigation going."

At first the NDS wanted nothing to do with our plan. They simply wanted us to take the truck and be done with it. They especially did not want it to go to the ANP, as they feared it would only be a matter of time before the governor's forces would find a way to steal it back, and all their efforts would be for naught. After a little arm twisting and repetitive promises that we'd make sure the ANP didn't run off with the drugs or let the governor do the same, the NDS reluctantly agreed to let us move the truck to Ghazni ANP HQ.

We decided to not inform the ANP we were coming. Better to arrive unannounced, as it would give us more time before the governor's informants got word, and he tried to intervene.

We arrived, and Arnold went to work corralling the narcotics officer and the internal affairs officer to do a proper investigation. The counternarcotics officer was all about it; the internal affairs officer, a man Arnold was sure had a massive hashish addiction, wanted no part of it (other than to feed his habit—he literally salivated as the police opened the cargo container). None of us was prepared for the amount of drugs inside.

The shipment contained 164 bags of hashish stored in commercial sugar and flour bags, each individually labeled with an Afghan name, number, and an Afghan city name. We hypothesized that the bags were labeled with the intended recipient or original producer, a logistics number corresponding to a yet-undiscovered manifest, and the likely destination of each bag within Afghanistan. Each bag weighed approximately 50 kilograms, and the estimated total weight of the entire shipment was 7 tons. We estimated the shipment's value was roughly US$6.3 million and contained enough hashish to meet the entire hashish demand in Poland for one year.

One bag at a time, the ANP removed the drugs, all under the observation of the NDS, the internal affairs officer (still salivating), the counternarcotics police, and us. As I watched the process, happy that the Afghans were actually doing a good job for a change, I noticed the lock that had originally secured the cargo container: a U.S./NATO-issued coalition lock. The drug runners had either stolen the locks (a serious breach of security) or illicitly manufactured them (an ingenious idea). Either way, use of a coalition lock assured them easy passage through any potential coalition or Afghan security checkpoints they may have encountered.

Near the end of the inventory, Haji Fasil sprinted into the compound. Aggressively, he lobbied to take over the inspection. He pleaded that, as the governor's representative, we could trust him, and this matter was of such grave concern that he should be given authority over the contents immediately. Arnold and I made small talk with him, avoiding answering any plea or question and effectively stalling while Major Goodman received permission from our higher HQ to take possession of the drugs.

It was now all too clear: if we didn't take control of the drugs within the next 24 hours, they'd be gone forever. Thankfully, whoever Major Goodman reached had the clout and foresight to grant us permission to confiscate the drugs under one condition: the Afghans had to be the ones to physically destroy them. We could impound the drugs on our FOB for safekeeping, but in the end, the Afghans had to destroy them (we could supply the fuel and even the lighter, but they had to do the deed) as our way of putting an "Afghan face" on the operation.

As we went to leave, Corporal Shnell jokingly picked up one of the bags and draped it over his shoulder, "All right, I got mine, let's go. I figure with this bag alone and the people I know back home, we could all retire off this shit. One bag, Lieutenant, that's all I'm asking, one bag and we all don't have to work a day in our life ever again!"

Laughing my ass off, I struggled to say no, but ultimately he put the bag down, and we mounted up. We arranged with the Polish forces (who had joined in the scene) to physically guard the drugs that night while we arranged for them to be moved to our FOB the next morning. On our way home, we decided to stop by the Ghazni Hospital to check in on the injured guys from the previous night's inter-Afghan security forces standoff (a potential foreshadowing of things to come should we leave the country in its current severely unstable format).

Arriving at the hospital, the doctors informed us that none of the injuries had been too serious, but they had just finished treating a kid who had allegedly been hurt while planting an IED in Andar. The doctors claim the kid's cousin had died in the explosion and asked us to talk to him. Arnold and I made our way to the kid's room, where he was handcuffed to his bed, an inauspicious start for a kid who swore up and down that he hadn't done anything wrong.

The boy, who couldn't have been older than 12, claimed he and his deceased cousin had found a random bullet while walking on the road. Fooling around, the cousin threw the bullet down and what allegedly happened next was unbelievable. According to the child, the bullet struck his cousin in the head, spun 180 degrees around in midair, came back, hit the child in the left arm, exiting near his torso, flew two feet, turned again in the air, hit him in right leg, and exited through his right inner thigh.

The doctors said his injuries coincided with an IED blast.

We left the kid in the good graces of the Afghan medical system with a promise to make sure the ANP came to visit him so that they could document this most miraculous account; we had to be sure no more magic bullets were out there wandering the Afghan countryside.

Tuesday, November 25, 2008

Our higher HQ, in a moment of logic and clarity, had granted us permission to seize and to impound the drugs but mandated that the Afghans would have to destroy them. In a moment of brilliance, I decided that there was only one person in the whole province with enough gravitas to do the honors at such a monumental ceremony: Doctor Usmani, governor of Ghazni Province.

I finally got my revenge on the Ghazni governor.

After a stress-filled night of guarding the drugs at ANP HQ, the Polish happily drove the load over to our FOB for impounding. While the rest of our FOB's U.S. soldiers took their obligatory cool-guy photos, I called the governor's office and informed him that we'd already called the press and announced he'd be burning the shipment in a ceremony that afternoon. Apparently TV crews were coming from as far away as Kabul to cover the event. He had to attend.

Slowly, word spread around the ANA side of the FOB that a massive amount of drugs currently sat on their grounds, and before we knew it, half the ANA battalion had gathered to help us "drive" the load to the area we'd use to burn it. They all probably wanted to steal as much as they could carry, but I think they were equally as excited to see the governor get his comeuppance.

Around midafternoon, Governor Usmani arrived with his massive entourage of personal security, high-ranking ANP officials, the counternarcotics police, a dismayed Haji Fasil, nervous NDS officials, and the internal affairs chief.

I gave the order to have the Afghans begin unloading the bags and, in a moment of pure spite, suggested to the press and the governor that he should help carry the bags from the truck to the growing pile: "It'll make for a great photo op."

The governor, doing his best not to seethe at me, smiled and said, "Anything for my favorite American nephew," and gingerly ran up to help unload a few bags.

"Thank you my Afghan uncle, we're most honored you could preside over this great accomplishment for the Afghan security forces and the Afghan people," I smugly replied.

One of the bags of hashish burst open, spilling its contents all over the ground. Before anyone could react, a random Afghan civilian who had either accompanied someone important or snuck in ran up and began stuffing his pockets full of hashish chunks. The guy stupidly thought he could steal the hashish in front of U.S. forces, the Polish, the NDS, the ANA, the ANP, the assembled civilian officials, and the press. He was shocked when a few of the guys from Team One tackled him to the ground and instantly summoned a few trusted ANA soldiers to detain him.

Within minutes the drugs sat in a heaping pile ready for burning. Joyfully, we doused the mass with an obscene amount of gasoline; we had to be sure it burned thoroughly. Sighing, resigned to the destruction and his obligation to appear on camera, the governor trudged up to the pile and attempted to light it with a cigarette lighter. I half-jokingly held out hope that, with the amount of gasoline we used, he'd burst into flames along with the drugs.

In a moment of epic letdown, nothing happened. A slow flame caught and started to climb around the massive pile. Being army guys and hoping for something more dramatic, we decided it'd be appropriate to try to use emergency flares to light the pile. The first flare didn't go off after several attempts to fire it (they're rocket-propelled, with a charge that explodes like a firework), so we tossed it onto the now sort-of-burning mass. Someone produced a second flare and fired it at the pile, smacking into it with an unimpressive thud.

Upping the stupid factor, the Polish took turns shooting at the unexploded first flare in an attempt to cause the massive fireball for which we all yearned. Eventually, enough of the pile started burning with enough heat that the whole thing really got cooking, prompting all to bust out their cameras for the obligatory cool-guy-in-front-of-burning-pile-of-drugs photos.

Satisfied he'd done his duties, the governor and his massive entourage stormed off, likely to sulk about the fact that he'd just lit millions of dollars of his own narcotics live on national TV.

While we stood around it, an explosion came from the burning pile of drugs. Instinctively we hit the deck and watched as a rocket-propelled flare streaked out of the fire and exploded into a section of the FOB's outer guard wall. Had we not hit the deck, it would have likely hit one of us, killing us instantly. Lesson learned: don't throw flares on a soon-to-be blazing mound of drugs.

The fire burned for three days straight, emitting a pleasant, calming smoke that soon overtook the entire FOB and most of the adjacent city blocks. We all took turns periodically examining the pile to make sure it was in fact still burning and that the ANA weren't stupidly trying to grab whatever they could out of the pile.

As the sun set over our half-baked (pun-intended) FOB, a contingent of our replacements-to-be randomly arrived, weeks earlier than expected. Although this would give us a proper amount of time to bring them up to speed and to prepare them for their year in Ghazni, I found the FOB immediately *way* too crowded for my liking. I had grown accustomed to our little band of brothers, stuck on our lonesome, in the middle of nowhere, simultaneously hating and loving every moment of it. Like the Illinois contingent before, I found myself surrounded by a sea of FNGs (fucking new guys), ducks, the lot of them. And then it dawned on me: we had become the old men of the FOB. Our mission would soon come to a close, and Ghazni would be their problem, their adventure. Our final duty: leave them better off than we had been when we first arrived.

49

Winning the War One Child at a Time

Sunday, November 30, 2008

For a couple of weeks, a few of the soldiers on our FOB have arranged for children from the Ghazni orphanage to come visit. During their time with us, we feed them American food (chicken nuggets and fries), teach them to color in coloring books, give them toys (soccer balls, dolls, etc.), check their health, show them pictures of America, and most importantly, use the terps to teach them literacy (in their native Dari and Pashto *and* in English). Sergeant First Class Cunningham originally organized the effort and should be commended for its success. It's something we all came to love and look forward to. This afternoon, I spent time coloring with a group of the kids and helped them write their names in Dari and English (the terps took great pleasure in using me as an assistant for a change).

One smart boy already knew how to write his name in both English and Dari and delighted in showing me. In contrast, the girls were extremely shy and soft-spoken. Every time I tried to make conversation with them, they'd sheepishly look down and away. But as soon as I pretended to glance away, I caught them all staring at me, nervously giggling. The longer we spent coloring, the more they seemed to get comfortable and open up. This effort, which we've dubbed "The Boys and Girls Club, Ghazni Chapter" is just one more way we're trying to prevent today's Afghan children from becoming tomorrow's Afghan Taliban. One girl in particular immediately stood out as special. Always giggling, the loudest of the bunch, a spitfire—if

Sitting and coloring with Afghan orphans who participated in our Ghazni Big Brothers Program.

only she had been born in a culture that cultivated her extroverted nature, who knows what she could accomplish in her life. The rest of the girls seemed resigned to accept their lower place in Afghan society, but she clearly wanted more. I'll never forget the look of awe, wonder, and joy in their eyes as Sergeant First Class Cunningham showed them pictures of Disney World while they colored in their Sleeping Beauty coloring books, letting their imaginations run wild. It's sad to think that this experience (coloring) is so normal for most American children but extremely rare for Afghans. Kids are kids, regardless of language, culture, or creed, and it's a universal truth that all kids love to color.

50

Lieutenant Colonel Clueless

Wednesday, December 3, 2008

The incoming RPAC-E commander who'll be replacing us arrived today, admonishing us immediately for our apparent "failure" throughout the past year. He landed at FOB Ghazni this morning, seething that we hadn't met him at the landing zone as soon as he arrived. The truth is, we had no idea he was coming, for he sent word of his arrival via SIPRnet (the U.S. military's secret and secure Internet). I had tried and failed to get our FOB SIPRnet connectivity working throughout our entire tour. We had resigned ourselves to using the connection at FOB Ghazni whenever we had the chance.

In his arrogance and complete lack of understanding of just how poorly our higher HQ had managed the war, Lieutenant Colonel Clueless assumed we had received his e-mail announcing his impending arrival and simply blown it off. I guess it was too logical to believe we simply didn't have SIPRnet and had no idea he was on his way and that if we had known, we'd have met him. In any case, he was there to clean house and was going to use his rank and his army-issued "Hammer of God" to show us how things would run from now on.

My introduction to Lieutenant Colonel Clueless went something like this:

Major Goodman: This is First Lieutenant Zeller: he's our intelligence, operations, air logistics, and humanitarian assistance officer. His deputy is Lieutenant Arnold. They've

---

The charred remains of an MRAP following a catastrophic IED blast. Note the turret that was blown entirely off.

compiled an impressive understanding of Ghazni and our area of operations. They will give you a thorough briefing to get you up to speed as soon as you'd like.

Clueless: He's your what? You don't need or require an intelligence officer. You should be getting all your intelligence from the ARSIC-E S2 in Gardez and the 101st S2.

Major Goodman: Sir, the ARSIC-E S2 doesn't have a clue as to what is going on here, has never been here, and uses First Lieutenant Zeller and his team's reports for their *own* situational awareness as to what is going on in Ghazni and our area of operations. As for the 101st, they left months ago and didn't give a damn about us while they were around. If you want a clear intelligence picture regarding Ghazni and our area of operations, First Lieutenant Zeller and his team are the best you'll find in the country.

Me: Sir, I can assure you I'm prepared to give you a thorough briefing on our efforts as soon as you're ready. I think you'll be pleased to learn what my team and I have accomplished given our limited resources. We have a sizeable informant network that helps feeds our intelligence efforts with our Polish allies, the U.S. Special Forces, and all the Afghan security forces operating in our AO.

Clueless: You're a mentor to the Afghan police, not the Ghazni S2. There is no Ghazni S2. You should have been mentoring the Afghan police this whole time, not doing your own collection, analysis, and coordination between allied forces.

Me: Sir, I can assure you, we've done all of our own organic work *in addition* to our immediate responsibilities to train, to mentor, and to develop the Afghan police *and* army units operating in our AO. In fact, if you ask our Afghan counterparts, they'll tell you that they think my team members are the best mentors they've ever had.

Clueless: Silence, Lieutenant! I cannot be clearer. There is no FOB Vulcan S2. No Ghazni intelligence cell. You were here to mentor, and you failed to do that. As of this moment, you and your team are dissolved. For the remainder of your tour, you'll mentor, and that's it!

Me: But Sir, if we don't do our own collection and analysis, I mean, we're keeping pretty much everyone else in our AO alive, because we're the only ones doing this kind of work. Sir, I think if you could just hear our briefing first. . . .

Clueless: You are done. End of discussion, Lieutenant!

Glaring at Major Goodman, Lieutenant Colonel Clueless immediately walked off to find his next person to "fix" or fire.

Major Goodman then turned to me and started laughing, clearly dumbfounded. "That guy is going to get so many people killed, just be thankful we don't have to serve under him for very long. As far as I'm concerned, you're not fired, you do an invaluable job here, and as soon as he leaves, which already can't come fast enough, things will be back to normal. Remember, he'll be at Gardez, he won't be able to do anything to us from there. For now, consider this a welcome reprieve.

Get some rack time, go to the gym, chill out while he's our guest. We'll make sure we don't send anyone on anything too dangerous that would normally require your team's work, and once he's gone, we'll go back to normal."

"Roger that, Sir, and thanks," I sighed, relieved at Major Goodman's sanity. And yet, deep inside, I wanted nothing more than to beat Lieutenant Colonel Clueless with my rifle. Major Goodman was right: he was going to get a lot of people killed with that attitude, and *God* help him if it was one of my guys.

Twenty minutes later, Lieutenant Colonel Clueless called a meeting of all the officers and senior NCOs on the FOB to explain the new rules. The meeting became an undeserved ass-chewing of epic proportions. He was there to tell us how things were going to be and didn't give a damn in regards to why certain things were done in a certain way. He was God. He had his hammer and to hell with logic and reality. I'd later learn that he'd never been to Afghanistan (this was his eighth day in country), that he'd done two tours in Iraq in years past, and had most recently been the battalion commander of a basic training company back in the U.S.

TRADOC (Training and Doctrine Command) is the bane of the U.S. Army. We affectionately referred to it as "Ta Da!" as in, "Ta Da! Things are going to work exactly as I say they will simply because it says so right here in this document!" There's TRADOC's Army, and then there's the real army. Lieutenant Colonel Clueless had come to bring us Afghanistan TRADOC style.

First up: we've all failed, Afghanistan is going to hell, and it's all our fault. He's here to fix it. His rules are simple and show a complete lack of understanding or desire to understand Afghanistan and counterinsurgency.

Rule #1: The terps won't be armed or wear U.S. uniforms. We hadn't armed every terp (only the ones we trusted, like Janis), but we had given them all U.S. uniforms for a simple reason: it was too easy for a Taliban sniper or informant to pick them out otherwise—just look for the one guy *not* wearing a U.S. uniform. Rule #1 meant the inevitable deaths of our invaluable terps and thus a complete inability for us to do our job. Everyone in the room, even the FNGs that had arrived last week, already knew enough to know that Lieutenant Colonel Clueless was off his rocker and that we'd all hate the remaining rules as much as Rule #1.

Rule #2: Tangi Valley Road will be used. Tangi Valley Road, where Major Garrison's team had their worst firefight, where Major Malok's team lost four guys, had been declared a black route (no one was allowed to use it) by the senior U.S. officer in our command (a major general, which last time I checked, outranked lieutenant colonel). Someone tried to speak up and point out that the CSTC-A commander had personally declared the route black, but Lieutenant Colonel Clueless paid no attention and moved on to Rule #3 as if no one in the room had said a word.

Rule #3: SECFOR (the U.S. Army security forces assigned to protect us mentors, but who in reality served as mentors in their own right) will cook for everyone after every mission. The navy cooks were going, and we'd all have to make do. As he said this, all in the room began to seethe with anger: this was a major "fuck you" to all the lower-ranking guys who already worked their asses off and honestly couldn't handle another additional duty. There's a reason we had navy cooks who only cooked; it's because the job was so demanding that it required people who did nothing else but cook. But Lieutenant Colonel Clueless had his rules and didn't care who was tired. While KBR would serve his fat ass back on FOB Lightning over in Gardez, SECFOR would be cooking for everyone, even after already doing a full day's work in combat outside the wire.

Rule #4: Our intelligence cell is disbanded, and we'll be getting all of our intel from "higher." Someone asked how that would happen, because we didn't have SIPRnet, which prompted him to stammer, "You don't have SIPRnet? But I sent you messages telling you I was coming here via SIPRnet; which by the way, why didn't anyone meet me at the LZ over on FOB Ghazni?" Yep, he completely missed the point on that one. Logic: not his thing.

Rule #5: As of that moment, all areas deemed dangerous are to be considered safe. Why? Because he had driven out to FOB Wilderness (one of the most dangerous and heavily attacked FOBs in all of Afghanistan at the time) just this past week (the start of winter and the typical end of Taliban attacks on FOB Wilderness), and nothing had happened while he had been there. As a result of his safe travels, it was clear to him that all of us who had been in country for almost a year were a giant bunch of sissies who were vastly overstating the danger and thus, everything that had been a no-go area was now green, safe as could be, and open for exploration simply because he said so, and no, he wasn't interested in the database of attacks that backed up our analysis, we had made those up too. . . .

Rule #6: "The Afghanis, . . ." They're Afghans, not Afghanis. *Afghani* is the name of their currency. The people are *Afghans.*

Rule #7: We will adopt garrison uniform standards on our FOB. I admit, in our year alone and basically forgotten, we didn't abide by the strictest of uniform standards, but that's the norm for most remote FOBs. Never once did it impact our discipline, morale, or, most importantly, job performance and effectiveness. In fact, at times, I think we had better morale than soldiers on larger FOBs simply because we didn't have FOBBITs running up to us on an hourly basis demanding to know why we weren't wearing our soft cap or PT belt when walking from our rack to the chow hall. It's the little things that can really improve morale, and for us, lax uniform standards made life a little more bearable. The irony of this particular rule was that Lieutenant Colonel Clueless's uniform was a mess. He wore his Ranger Tab at an angle, his Combat Patch was rotated backwards, and he had reversed his name tape and U.S. Army tape, wearing them both on the wrong and opposite sides, in violation of his own rule.

Three hours later, his promised "short talk" had become a tirade. At this point, we had all missed lunch, and because he had all the senior NCOs and officers on the FOB in the room, he had personally delayed Team Two's mission departure to Andar by two hours. Somewhere into hour three of his tirade, he decided he wanted to go on mission and demanded he be added to Team Two's mission to Andar. And that was it: the wrath of Lieutenant Colonel Clueless.

Or so I thought. As the meeting broke off, he pulled me aside and started accusing me of stealing other people's products and calling them my own. He claimed that all the intelligence products he had seen on Ghazni (which my staff and I created) had actually been created by the intelligence staff in Gardez and not by my team. For the first time since returning from leave, I was glad that our tour was so close to the end.

He walked off to join Team Two on their mission to Andar. I stood glaring, my anger coursing through my body, surging like a violent swell. I worried for everyone: for our replacements, for Team Two, for anyone who would ever have to encounter Lieutenant Colonel Clueless. I even worried for our dogs. It was only a matter of time before he realized three dogs lived with us, proud and important members of our team, and in complete violation of TRADOC standards. According to our higher command and TRADOC, dogs meant disease and were not allowed. I feared the moment he saw them, he'd either shoot them himself or order one of us to do it. Apparently, I wasn't the only one who worried about the dogs, because at that moment Major Goodman walked up and said, "Don't worry, if he finds the dogs we'll just tell him they belong to the ANA, and there's nothing we can do about them, because technically, we're guests on their base."

Team Two later described his presence as an unmitigated disaster. He started the "patrol" by ordering a dismount in a volatile village (one we normally went into with a lot more forces than just Team Two and their four MRAPs). He then "led" the patrol by taking the team's terp and walking off on his own, completely out of sight of the rest of the team, to "search the village." Once Team Two "recovered" (their words, not mine) Lieutenant Colonel Clueless, they took him to the Andar ANP HQ to meet the Andar chief of police, Nabi Patang. Nabi became sort of a cult hero among our FOB for his aggressiveness and sheer badassery. He didn't hide the fact that he drank heavily, loved to fight the Taliban, and, at one point, half-jokingly argued to officially rename Andar "Patang-istan."

Sergeant First Class Alderson and Nabi grew particularly close during their many months together; each man had tremendous respect for the other. As a result of this rare positive relationship, Andar's police force had actually somewhat improved since we arrived. In Nabi, the unit found a competent leader who, for the most part, patrolled his district, made sure his men got paid and had their proper equipment, and took the initiative to improve his men in our absence. Nabi and Alderson had made it clear that although Andar's force had improved, it had miles to go before it was ready to operate independently with any amount of proficiency. In fact, by CSTC-A's rules, Andar had only progressed to a CM-3 rating (CM-4 being the lowest, and CM-1 being the highest) during our deployment. Team Two gave Andar's ANP a CM-3 rating, because doctrine dictated that if a unit operated below 60 percent of its authorized personnel, then it could not be rated anything better than a CM-3, regardless of its tactical proficiency. Team Two's CM-3 rating was both fair and accurate, but not according to Lieutenant Colonel Clueless, who without any known authority other than his rank ordered SFC Alderson to rate them as CM-2. When Sergeant First Class Alderson demanded to know why, Lieutenant Colonel Clueless claimed CSTC-A had changed the rules of rating (which if true, means any measurement of progress had to be thrown completely out countrywide), and because "You've had nine months to get them to at least CM-2, and by God, nine months is long enough, they're CM-2 and that's the end of it!" Alderson refused. It didn't matter; in the end, Lieutenant Colonel Clueless made sure the ARSIC changed Andar's rating so he could claim "success" during his personal tour.

So why would he show up and declare us a total disaster without ever hearing what we had to say? Because that's how he'd get a great rating on his Officer Evaluation Report (OER). Officers in today's army get promoted almost solely based on their OERs; the better the rating, the more likely the promotion. A whole breed of officers has developed a system that almost ensures a great OER rating and thus promotion. Upon taking command, officers must write out their goals for their tours of duty. At the end of their tours, their superior officers evaluate them on how many of those goals they accomplished. The more goals accomplished, the better the rating. Thus, officers like Lieutenant Colonel Clueless arrive and declare everything that happened before their arrival to be a total disaster, and then they set out to "fix what needs fixing." If everything you find is "broken" and you change just one thing about everything and declare it "fixed," then you've done a great job and get a great OER. The result is that good policies are callously tossed out for no other reason other than they *have* to go in order to maximize the potential for an officer to claim he "fixed" as much as possible. The more one fixes, the more one accomplished, and, thus, the better the rating.

Policy efficiency and actual job performance are irrelevant under this scheme— hence a decade plus of war in Afghanistan with very few positive results. Every successive command has simply come in, declared the previous unit a disaster, and set out to reinvent the wheel. We've been fighting this war one year at a time, with almost 100 percent organizational turnover every 365 days. Combine the arrogance of rank in the army's middle management and the fact that promotions are based solely on OERs and not actual job performance, and we have a big problem; our most experienced junior officers and NCOs are voluntarily leaving the army because they do most of the fighting and are sick and tired of having FOBBITs like Lieutenant Colonel Clueless destroy all they've accomplished for the sake of increasing their promotion potential.

Lieutenant Colonel Clueless left within 24 hours of his arrival, and I never saw or heard from him again. In the end, at least for our band of brothers, his bark was way worse than his bite. God only knows what happened to the poor bastards who replaced us.

51

Old Men and Hashish

Sunday, December 7, 2008

Winter will arrive any day now. The fighting season has, for all intents and purposes, ended. The Taliban seem happy to spend their days and nights trying to keep warm while preparing for the coming spring and summer. On the FOB, we're training our replacements as best as possible. There's rumor that we may leave any day now. We've been told to ready our gear so that we could leave the FOB forever with only an hour's notice. It's night now, and I've just finished my ritual last cigarette outside my b-hut, staring up at the Milky Way above, losing myself in the clarity and beauty of the Afghan night sky.

I had just started to drift off to sleep when Sergeant First Class Turner knocked on the plywood wall outside my bunk.

"Sorry to disturb you, but the Polish just radioed us. They think they caught two guys placing an IED on the road to Andar. They're bringing them to our FOB so that we can process their biometrics into our HIIDE device."

The HIIDE device is a large digital camera that, in addition to taking pictures, scans and records a person's iris and fingerprints. It's the primary weapon in building a massive database of the biometrics of nearly every male in Afghanistan. The idea is that if a person is later caught doing something suspicious, a quick check of the biometric data record will reveal if that person had been caught doing suspicious things previously. HIIDE devices had just made their way to frontline troops like us, so the effort was still in its infancy from a national perspective.

Marijuana plants grown by our Afghan National Army soldiers in their chow-hall garden.

I sat up, rubbed my eyes, and told Turner to let the Polish know Arnold, Sergeant Bots (our newest edition to the intelligence cell), and a terp would meet the Polish on the ANA side of the FOB. As he went off to relay the message, I strapped on my thigh holster, put on my fleece jacket and hat, and went off to rouse Arnold, Bots, and Jamshid (a terp I used when Janis, Fareed, and Eshan weren't around).

I had a system for the terps. I trusted Janis and Fareed with my life, without question. I was pretty sure I could say the same about Eshan, but he and I had never been in combat together, so there was always a tiny bit of doubt. Jamshid belonged to Team Three, and they loved him. A man in his early twenties, he was by far the most Westernized of all the terps, having lived in the West for a few years in his early youth. Any time I asked him to translate for me, he happily obliged. I think he found it fun, because my translations were so abnormal in comparison to regular mentoring work.

Arnold and I smoked while we waited for Bots and Jamshid to get ready. With everyone dressed in their winter best, we walked out to meet the Polish. As I opened the gate to the ANA side of the FOB, Rocko and TK bounded up to me and brushed against my legs, excited to join us on a rare nighttime excursion outside our compound. In typical dog fashion, they raced ahead of us, happily playing and romping up the road. We arrived at the ANA S2's office and woke him up to give him a courtesy notice that the Polish would soon arrive with detainees and that he and his staff could participate in the questioning if they desired; they declined, preferring to remain indoors and warm.

Ten minutes later we heard the low rumble of the approaching Polish convoy. Their vehicles turned into the FOB and drove rapidly toward us, their intense headlights blinding us as they drew closer. Rocko and TK stopped playing and instinctively moved to our flank to protect us. God, I loved those dogs.

Grinning, the Polish soldiers jumped out of their vehicles, clearly pleased with their recent capture. The patrol leader approached me and explained what they thought had happened while his men helped the detainees out of the back of the MRAP.

The Polish HQ at FOB Ghazni had observed a group of eight men digging just off the paved road that led into Andar via their aerial surveillance equipment. The Polish command believed the men were in the process of placing IEDs in the road and immediately dispatched the patrol to disrupt the process and to capture as many of the men as possible. They had used "black out" driving (driving with night-vision goggles and without headlights) to nearly sneak up on the men, but the loud noise of their diesel engines sent the men fleeing. The Polish fired warning shots, and two men dropped to the ground. The patrol detained the two men and radioed back to their HQ for orders. HQ decided to send them to us, as we were they only unit in Ghazni with working HIIDE, and, as I'd later find out, they thought we had the facilities and authority to house detainees and intended to leave the men with us.

"What did you find on the men?" I asked, hoping to see the obvious IED components (wire, detonation cord, blasting caps, homemade explosives, etc.) so we could make this a quick questioning session and I could get back to bed.

"Well, we haven't done a thorough check yet. Their stuff is on the ground now beside them," the Polish lieutenant said, pointing to a heaping pile of assorted items wrapped up in a blanket within arm's reach of the two blindfolded detainees.

"First things first, let's separate the detainees from their stuff and from each other. We'll need to question each man individually and out of earshot of each other," I said to the lieutenant, Arnold, and Bots. "We don't want to give them any more chance to come up with a shared story, nor do we want to give them easy access to their stuff [in case there were weapons or incriminating evidence]."

The Polish lieutenant immediately barked orders to his men, who brought the first detainee over to our group while moving the second back inside their MRAP.

I instantly noticed he was at least 60 years old (ancient by Afghan standards), rail thin, and could not stop shivering from the cold. The Polish removed his blindfold, and his eyes held a look of sheer terror.

"Jamshid, here's what I want you to do. Repeat everything I say word for word. Don't yell, don't raise your voice, say this as gently as possible. Okay?"

"Okay."

"Ask him what happened."

Jamshid repeated my question, and the man began to rapidly stammer, his words hard to decipher due to his shivering. Jamshid raised his voice, repeating my question.

"Jamshid, stop. Calm down. He's clearly freezing. This will go a lot better if he isn't so cold. Ask him if that's his blanket over there," I said, pointing to the blanket that held their seized stuff.

The man said it was his.

I walked over to the blanket and told Bots to do a thorough inventory of all the items held in the bundle. I then dumped the contents on the ground and returned with the blanket, placing it around the man's shoulders.

He smiled for the first time.

"Okay, Jamshid, ask him if that's better and if he could please tell us what happened."

The man, warmer, shivering subsiding, claimed that he and the other men in his village had gone out to an irrigation canal adjacent to the road to gather water for a group of travelers and to begin irrigating their fields for their wheat crop.

"Wait, their wheat crop?" I asked Jamshid, unsure he had correctly translated the man's story.

"Yes, their wheat crop. You know, wheat, used to make the bread," Jamshid replied, his voice indicating surprise, as if I had never heard of wheat.

"Jamshid, I know what wheat is, I just didn't know it grew in winter."

"Yes. There are two kinds of wheat in Afghanistan, one for summer, one for winter. He says they farm winter wheat," replied Jamshid, relieved that I wasn't that stupid after all.

"Then I have another question: why were they irrigating their field so late at night? Doesn't he realize that makes us suspicious, because the Taliban plant bombs at night?"

What followed was an invaluable lesson in Afghan farming. The man explained that his village was part of a system of villages that shared the same irrigation canal. There wasn't enough water for all the villages to simultaneously irrigate their fields, so generations ago, their forefathers had agreed to a simple system of sharing scarce resources. Each village had a designated irrigation time. This man claimed his village's irrigation time started around 10:00 p.m. and went until about 2:00 a.m. Every night, the men would go out to the canal and break down an earthen barrier, allowing the canal to flood the field. At 2:00 a.m., they'd return and resurrect the barrier, allowing for the next village in line to begin irrigating its fields.

"Bots, what's in their shit?" I asked, wanting to know if he had found anything significant among their confiscated stuff.

"Well there are some documents that I obviously can't read, a shovel, and what looks and smells like a small block of hash," he replied, chuckling at the thought of a 60-year-old man getting high.

"Okay. Jamshid, ask the guy if he wants a cigarette, something to eat, and some water."

The guy smiled as Jamshid translated and humbly nodded his head to the offer of a cigarette and water. Arnold handed him a smoke and a bottle, to which the man replied, "*Ta Shakur* [Thanks]."

Arnold and I simultaneously turned and said, "*Kabuli Ta Shakur Naist* [to me, it's not worth your thanks; you're welcome]," hands held over our heart in Afghan custom, much to the man's shock and delight. His demeanor eased, and for the first time all night his shoulders dropped ever so slightly, relaxed.

"Jamshid, tell him to sit here and wait. We're going to talk to his friend. If their stories check out, he'll be fine. At worst, he'll spend the night in jail, we'll make sure he gets a hot meal, warm shelter, and he'll probably be released the next day. Just tell him to sit tight."

The man nodded, professed his profound thanks over and over again, saying "*Ta Shakur, Ta Shakur, Ta Shakur*," and wrapped the blanket closer to his shoulders as a strong gust of winter wind blew across the FOB, bringing with it the first snowflakes of our tour.

The Polish brought the second guy out. They removed his blindfold, revealing a man slightly younger than the first. Portly and almost jovial, our eyes met, and he smiled. I sensed confusion, but not fear.

"Okay, Jamshid, same deal, repeat exactly what I say, keep it calm and gentle. Ask him what happened."

The man, clearly more relaxed and congenial, told the same story as the first man: they had been out gathering water for travelers and irrigating their fields when the Polish surprised them.

"Why did they run?" I asked.

"Because the Polish fired shots. They thought they were being attacked. So he told the second guy to run, but the Polish caught them. He realizes that they probably should have just stayed in place and says he is sorry to have caused us trouble," Jamshid translated.

I laughed. The more I learned, the more this sounded like one of two things: either two guys who were in the wrong place at the wrong time, or two guys who had a really clever and believable cover story planned.

"Ask him what's up with the hash? Doesn't he know that's illegal?" I grinned and gave him a wink as Jamshid translated.

The man laughed and admitted, somewhat embarrassed, that the hash was his, part of a "bad habit."

"Jamshid, ask him if he's cold, does he want a cigarette, water, or food."

The man declined all, said his time in the MRAP had kept him warm enough, and nodded his head down to his portly frame indicating his fat would suffice for now.

"Tell him that as long as he cooperates, everything should be fine."

The second man nodded, never once losing his congenial nature.

"I believe them. While you get their info in the HIIDE device, I'll figure out what we'll do with them," I said, struggling to light a cigarette in the howling wind, snowflakes falling ever more rapidly. Arnold, Bots, and Jamshid walked off to enter the men's info into the device, while I found the Polish lieutenant.

Rocko and TK raced around the assembled crowd, stopping their rough play to receive the occasional pat from the Polish or me.

The lieutenant, increasingly impatient, said he wanted to get his men back to base, as their shift was nearly over. I sensed he had wanted to leave for some time. I briefed him on what I thought had happened and said that the men were probably only guilty of minor hash possession and running from the Polish at night. "So, once we're done getting them in the HIIDE system, they're all yours. Thanks for doing a great job tonight," I said turning to see how much longer Bots and Arnold needed to finish the HIIDE process.

"No, no. We leave them with you. We cannot take them with us, we don't have the proper facilities to hold them," he replied, wiping a bead of cold sweat from his forehead.

"Well, we don't have any facilities either. Nor do the ANA; I mean, what did you plan on doing with them after you came to us?" I asked, sensing a mounting minicrisis.

"We will leave them with you. This has always been the plan. Okay, we go now. We must get back for shift change," the Polish lieutenant hurriedly replied, motioning with his hands for his men to mount their vehicles. He wanted to leave before I could dump the detainees back on him.

Great. Okay, Matt, think. The ANA usually transferred their detainees to the 101st, but the 101st left months ago; it dawned on me that this was the first detainee situation we had had since they had left months ago.

"Arnold, take Jamshid and see if you can't get the ANP to come down here to pick these two guys up. The Polish are leaving, and they're basically our problem now," I sighed.

"Uh, okay . . . ," Arnold said, raising an eyebrow in curiosity. I gave him a look that made it clear I'd explain everything once the Polish left.

"Hey, Sir, just so you know, Jamshid says one of the documents indicates that the fat one is some sort of Afghan government official," Sergeant Bots called out, holding up the ID.

Wonderful, the Polish had detained an Afghan official. Silently I prayed that he wasn't some high-ranking official or cousin of Karzai. Thankfully, he was just some sort of local agricultural official.

The snow fell harder and started to accumulate beneath my feet. TK tackled Rocko and went racing off into the night. The Afghan men sat talking with Arnold and Jamshid (who had thankfully found a fast and easy way to alert the ANP to come pick up the two men). As the Polish drove away, an ANP truck pulled up, blue lights flashing in the night, illuminating swirls of billowing snow.

I turned back to the men and told them what would happen next.

"The ANP are going to take you to jail for the night. They will do an investigation. If they find you have done nothing wrong, the Polish have personally promised to drive you back to your village and give you a ton of humanitarian aid for your inconvenience. Thank you for being so cooperative. They'll take good care of you, you have my word. As for your things, I'll hang on to them for the night for safekeeping. If you're innocent, I'll make sure you'll get it all back."

The men smiled and nodded in thanks, sighing in relief. In truth, I wanted more time to examine the documents, and I didn't want the ANP to steal the shovel, hash, clothing, and other assorted items of Afghan life (pocket knife, pencil, pad of paper, etc.). As I turned to walk away, the second man spoke. "Could you get rid of the hash? He doesn't want to get in trouble," Jamshid translated.

I turned away and laughed.

"Tell him I'll think about it," I said as I walked to the ANP. I contemplated it. I wanted to dump it for the guy, as it would probably cause him trouble and force him to pay a hefty bribe to get off, but that wasn't my job. Instead, I inventoried their items, put the hash back in their bags, and hoped that when we turned the items over to the ANP that they'd ignore or miss the hash in the bag.

Through Jamshid, I informed the ANP of what had happened and that they were to do a thorough investigation and let us know in the morning what they found. I emphasized that they were to be treated with respect and given a meal and a warm place to sleep. The ANP agreed, politely helped the men into their trucks, and drove off into the cold winter night.

TK and Rocko, sensing it was time to return to our compound, raced back toward our gate as Arnold, Bots, Jamshid, and I walked through what had become a gorgeous but blinding snowstorm.

The next day we woke up to find the mountains of Waghez covered in snow. Winter had finally come. The snow-capped peaks meant our war, in terms of combat, was basically over. Almost all the fighting would stop now. Arnold headed over to FOB Ghazni and reviewed the Polish's video footage but couldn't really tell what the group of men was doing. After reviewing the footage, we called the ANP HQ to find out the status of the men. Turns out, the ANP Assistant S3 knew the guys and let them go home for Eid; they promised to return to the ANP after the holiday (that never happened). We never did find an IED hole, and I never saw the men again; last I knew their stuff, hash and all, sat in a corner of our TOC, waiting for the ANP to begin their investigation.

52

Leaving Ghazni

Tuesday, December 9, 2008

The day finally arrived. Last night, First Sergeant Rock told me to be ready to leave the FOB at 0615. Twelve soldiers would leave for FOB Ghazni to try to catch a flight to Camp Phoenix. Arnold spent the previous night working his magic and arranged an impromptu flight for us. My time at FOB Vulcan had come to an end as abruptly as it had started, with little preparation or notification.

Excited, I helped load our gear on to the convoy and took a final look around our home. It had changed so much since we first arrived; it was nearly triple the size, had massively improved defenses, and was far less intimate or desolate than we first found it. Sadly, the dogs had gone on an early-morning exploration, so I never got to say a proper good-bye; I wish I had. Within weeks the first sergeant who replaced Rock would kill TK (short for Taliban Killer), claiming he was rabid. Months later, a truck ran over Rocko, who survived but got sent to an animal hospital in Kabul, never to be seen again by any who cared for him. As for our other dog, Blondie, last I heard she's still queen dog, pumping out litter after litter of puppies. Later units would write of their fondness for her, noting she'd readily join the nightly guard patrol for their rounds, a comforting thought. I like to think she's still there, nuzzling up to a lonely American soldier as he stares off into the Afghan night, contemplating his time in Ghazni, reminding him there is still love and companionship in the world.

Snow falls over the Waghez mountains for the first time since we arrived, signaling the end of our tour and the fighting season and the coming of winter.

I also never got a chance to say good-bye to our terps; Janis, Fareed, Latif, Habib, Eshan, and a few others were still in Kabul on leave, and those left behind were still fast asleep in their bunks. In fact, other than Janis, I never saw any of them again. Last I heard, they're all still alive.

Jamshid made the front page of the New York Times a few months later in a picture snapped during a patrol in Qarabagh. Through my irregular correspondence with Janis, he tells me that most of our original terps quit after we left; they found the Illinois leadership intolerable and managed to arrange safer terp work in Kabul. I hope I'll one day get to thank them all in person for their invaluable help and friendship. I struggle to think what may happen to them should we let Afghanistan fall to the Taliban; they'll likely all flee or be executed.

We arrived at FOB Ghazni and planted ourselves on the outskirts of the LZ to wait for a flight we hoped would come with enough room for us all. The LZ, once an example of efficient air logistics operations when run by the 101st, was now the purview of a Polish lieutenant colonel with limited English.

Around 1100, Arnold's arranged flight landed in a thunderous roar, the blades kicking up dust and sending a wave of cold, bitter air all around. The Polish claimed the bird was ours and that they had 40 open seats. We ran to the open rear door. One look inside at the nearly full flight and I had my suspicions we had the right bird. Over the roar of the rotors, the flight crew confirmed my suspicions and informed me that we had the wrong bird. We were supposed to be on the other helicopter that had landed simultaneously. As hastily as one can when toting several hundred pounds of gear, we lumbered over to the second flight, not wanting to give them a chance to fly off without us.

"Hey! Great to see you! We're the ones going to Camp Phoenix!" I yelled to the flight crew.

"We'll be back for you later this afternoon! Around 1300! We've got the rest of our route to do before we pick you up!" the flight chief yelled back. We lumbered back to the sidelines. The flight never came back—lying bastards.

At this point we were at the mercy of rumor, and rumor had it another flight would land mid-afternoon that might or might not have enough seats for all of us during its flight to Bagram. We decided to chance it. North was north. At this rate, we'd take what we could get and figure out how to get from Bagram to Kabul later on. At 1530, the mythic flight landed and, to our delight, had enough room for all of us and our gear. Before the flight crew could change their minds, we quickly loaded our gear and stuffed ourselves into whatever available seats we could find.

In our haste, I never got to say a proper good-bye to Arnold. I couldn't reach his hand from where I sat in the bird, so we simply pointed our fingers at each other, as if to say, "Love ya, man, stay safe, stay alive, see you soon, it's been an honor!"

The flight was so full of gear and people that I could barely see anything other than the bags in front of me, the rear door gunner, and the Polish soldier squeezed in uncomfortably next to me.

The bird lifted off, and away we went. Good-bye, Ghazni, good-bye, Vulcan. Let's go home.

The flight to Bagram included the obligatory stop at FOB Airborne. After several boring moments waiting in the helicopter in the LZ, a loud explosion sent everything around us into panic and chaos. Without notice, our bird reared up on its tail, with the nose of the helicopter pointed vertically, the tail still on the ground. In one of the most gnarly maneuvers I've ever experienced, the bird suddenly bucked and took off back end first, flying back toward the mountains that overlook FOB Airborne to the east.

Frantically we ascended and then just as rapidly descended as we made our way up the valley toward Kabul, the bird banking sharply to the left and right as we continued to go up and down.

When we landed at Bagram an hour later, I walked up to the flight crew and asked, "What was up with the takeoff back at Airborne?"

"Oh, we were just fucking with you!" they chuckled.

The Taliban had recently taken to rocketing FOB Airborne nearly every time a bird landed on the LZ. As best as I can tell, a rocket landed, they took evasive maneuvers and didn't want to freak out a bunch of guys on their way home with the truth. The closer one gets to actually leaving, the more paranoid one gets about biting it before actually making it out alive. Short-time syndrome: you take increasingly fewer risks and become superstitious about even talking about certain things (like almost dying in a random Taliban rocket attack on the FOB Airborne LZ).

I walked off shaking my head, thankful to be alive, and headed off for the transient tent at the other end of the base, a place we'd call home until we could make our way to Camp Phoenix in Kabul.

53

The Most Difficult Good-bye

Wednesday, December 10, 2008

Everyone on that first flight out of Ghazni regarded our unexpected time at Bagram as a mini-vacation. No one was in a hurry to make it to Camp Phoenix, except me. I decided I'd give myself one day's rest at Bagram and devote each remaining day to getting to Camp Phoenix. I spent the day hanging out around the base, visiting with friends stationed there, relaxing, and reflecting on the past year. It started to dawn on me: we were going to make it home. Within a month maybe, we'd be back with our families and back to our "normal" lives, but that still felt like a lifetime away.

Thursday, December 11, 2008

Sergeant First Class Alderson and I got up *ass* early in an attempt to try to get on a flight to Kabul, only to be rejected by the two flights they had leaving that morning. Two C-130s, and they only took eight people—ridiculous.

Major Hunt saw us lugging our gear back and picked us up. I asked him if he could drive us back to our transient tent (at the other end of the base), as we'd rather not lug the 400 pounds of gear down the miles long road. He informed me

Janis and me, the best of friends.

that he couldn't drive us back to our transient tent, because the main (and only) thoroughfare on BAF is closed at the time for PT, which also happens to be the prime time to move to the PAX and Rotary Wing terminals, as most "showtimes" are between 0500 and 0700. That's right, the main thoroughfare is shut down to all traffic at the prime time for moving people and baggage so the odd runner can occupy as much asphalt as he'd like.

After a leisurely breakfast, Major Hunt drove us back to the transient tent, where we reclaimed our bunks and struck up a conversation with an incoming mentor team from Virginia. We regaled them with stories from the past year and answered all the questions they had. As we spoke, I saw the mountains surrounding Bagram for the first time, a most impressive sight, as the base sits in a bowl at 5,000 feet, surrounded by 16,000-foot peaks that seem only a few football fields away.

During our discussion, the Virginia team informed me that they were on their way to Camp Phoenix at 0930 that morning. Seeing an opportunity to use our newfound friendship to my benefit, I asked them if I could tag along, explaining how the Air Force screwed me earlier in the morning. Thankfully, they agreed to temporarily adopt me.

At 0930, I marched out on to the tarmac and joined the Virginia crew for their flight to Kabul via a Spanish Air Force C-130. The pilot, cigarette lit and hanging out of his mouth, climbed up, gave a thumbs-up, and within minutes we lumbered into the air for the 15-minute flight to Kabul International Airport (KIA). Once at KIA, the Virginia crew got their first taste of CSTC-A's massive inefficiency: Camp Phoenix (about four miles from KIA) only ran two shuttles to the airport each day, one in the early morning and one way later in the afternoon. For the next seven hours, we sat around and just waited. I showed them around KIA; they took particular interest in the fact that KIA is a NATO-run base and thus all the items for sale in the PX are priced in euros. I recalled our tour and tried to dump as much useful knowledge as I could on the FNGs from VA. Finally, as evening fell upon Kabul, the shuttle arrived and drove us the 10-minute route to Camp Phoenix.

Arriving at Camp Phoenix, I bid my VA friends good luck and good-bye and went off to see if anyone I knew still lived on base (as our brigade had already started sending people home now that most of the Illinois units had arrived). I found that, until tents opened up, the random group of PMTs, ETTs, and SECFOR that had started to trickle in were being housed in an abandoned Soviet warehouse filled with empty bunk beds.

That night, I discovered the nightly "cigar shack" hangout where officers and enlisted gathered to pass the evening smoking cigars, cigarettes, drinking near-beer, and watching the latest pirated DVDs. The shack came equipped with a surround-sound system, which eventually prompted the occasional game of Rockband. Ah, FOBBIT life. For the first time since April, though I longed for my brothers in Ghazni, I actually enjoyed being on a large FOB with no responsibilities and nothing to do other than sit around, collect pay, waste oxygen, and wait to go home. For all intents and purposes, my war in Afghanistan was over.

Friday, December 12, 2008

Major Norris and most of the crew who flew out of Ghazni with me a few days prior arrived this morning. The sight of their familiar faces sent my spirits soaring. Odd, but even a few days away and I missed those guys more than I realized, my first indication of a lifelong fraternal bond.

I spent the day relaxing, e-mailing, and reading. Janis called me and asked me type up an appreciation letter for his records and future use in his visa application. Later in the afternoon, he came to the front gate of Camp Phoenix so I could give him his letter and we could say our good-byes. Major Norris joined me.

The moment, years later, is still hauntingly heartfelt and painful to recall. I wished him and his family well, hugged him several times (I want to see my friend again), and thanked him for saving my life.

"Janis, you are my brother. I'll do whatever it takes to get you back to the United States. Be clear, just because I'm leaving doesn't mean that I'll forget about you or the other terps. I'm only an e-mail away. Please say good-bye to all the other terps for me, and please stay safe. I look forward to the day when I can welcome you to your new home in the U.S.," I said, wondering if I'd ever see him again.

Janis told me that a terp from FOB Ghazni was murdered by the Taliban a week ago while traveling home for the Eid-Al-Adha holiday. Janis had told him to go on Thursday, but he would not listen and, as a result, was dead. Major Norris and I shared a concerned look. As Janis walked away into the busy Kabul streets, his large leather and padding-stuffed coat held tightly around his body, I prayed that this was only a temporary parting and nothing permanent.

Janis rounded the corner out of the gate and physically out of our lives, and the void he left caused me at that moment to crave Ghazni for another year, a do-over even. As Major Norris and I walked back into the safe confines of FOBBIT-ton, I wondered if I'd ever return to this land of stark and immense beauty coupled with unspeakable suffering. Years later, I still yearn to return.

Janis and I keep irregular contact. We spoke via phone almost bi-weekly when I first got back to the U.S. We talk about once every two months now. Like so many other terps before him, he's suffered from his excellence. Every new unit realizes he's the best and sits on his visa paperwork, promising to forward it up the chain of command at the end of their deployment. Their end comes, the new unit arrives, his paperwork "vanishes" as they realize he's elite, and to this day he serves as a terp for U.S. forces in Kabul, desperately trying to move his wife and young son to a country he's never seen but has faithfully served for more than eight years. Janis and the others like him deserve better. We promise them five years of faithful service in return for visas, and they buy our con and keep holding out hope, because every now and then a terp or two does make it to the U.S., giving the remaining cause to keep the service going, for they could be the lucky one any day.

Janis, my brother, I haven't forgotten my vow. I will get you and your family here.

54

Endless Waiting

Saturday, December 13–Wednesday, December 24, 2008

For the next two weeks, I fell into a routine of sleeping late and browsing the Internet for hours on end, taking the occasional break. I watched movies in my rack or at the nightly cigar shack showing. At one point, I caught the Kabul crud and spent several days bedridden with the worst head cold I've ever had, made worse by the completely unsanitary living conditions of the tent I moved to after Major Malok arrived and we consolidated into our original URFs. I had come with a 16-man team from Fort Riley. Foldes died. Morrissey left weeks early to start police academy in Buffalo, and Major Mcintire volunteered for an additional 90 days. But, one by one, our original Fort Riley crew arrived and moved into our transient tent to await our any-day-now flight home. By the way, if you ever end up with the Kabul crud, overdose on Airborne and Theraflu. It'll kick your ass for the first few days, but eventually you'll beat it.

Midway through this endless waiting period, the rest of the FOB Vulcan crew arrived via helicopter. After our first crew left, the folks at Bagram canceled all flights south for a few weeks. The remaining crew eventually moved into transient tents at FOB Ghazni and spent every day hoping for a flight north, as ARSIC had banned all road travel due to the weather (Afghanistan gets a lot of snow and has no snow-removal capabilities, making the already dangerous roads that much worse).

Our bunks in the transient tent at Camp Phoenix, where we waited two weeks to begin our journey home.

In a sign of our powerful bond, every Vulcan crewmember already at Camp Phoenix made sure we were at the LZ to welcome the rest of our brothers and to help them unload their gear. Moving the bags and luggage off in organized chaos brought back memories of countless food-run trips and other bonding experiences. We were a tightly knit unit, brothers 'til the end.

Days later, we held an awards ceremony with the FOB Vulcan crew ("Team Ghazni") outside the abandoned Soviet warehouse that had come to serve as the quarters for all of the SECFOR (who would return together back to Fort Bragg, while we ETTs and PMTs would go back to Fort Riley). Standing in that awards formation, I've never felt prouder to know or to serve with any other group of people in my entire life. I doubt I'll feel that level of pride ever again.

For the remainder of our days at Camp Phoenix, Team Ghazni ate meals together and constantly visited each other, despite the fact that the brigade had divided us back into SECFOR and ETT/PMT units living in separate quarters. We were inseparable and wanted almost nothing to do with anyone else on the FOB.

The final, and perhaps, best "You-Can't-Make-This-Shit-Up" moment happened to Major Finnell and his SECFOR as they left FOB Rushmore. While waiting for their flight, their replacements basically stripped each man of all his ammo, claiming they had better use for it, because they were leaving. Major Finnell and the SECFOR begrudgingly complied.

Midway into the flight, the helicopters flew smack dab into a raging blizzard. The pilot of Major Finnell's helicopter was some lieutenant on his first combat tour and on one of his first combat flights ever. He panicked. Thankfully, his co-pilot, a chief warrant officer level-4 who had served in Vietnam, took over the flying and immediately landed the bird along with their wing flight on the first open mountain top they could see, and that's when it really got crazy.

The flight crew ordered everyone to get out of the birds and form a defensive perimeter around the helicopters until the weather cleared. Major Finnell and several SECFOR pointed out that they weren't carrying any ammo. The flight crew didn't care: they wanted the perimeter, and they wanted it now.

"What do you want us to do if we get attacked? Yell 'bang' and throw rocks?" Major Finnell sarcastically said as he walked by the very well-armed rear door gunner, who just shrugged in response.

For the next several hours, the guys lay prone in the snow, unarmed weapons pointed outward ready to scream off any would-be Taliban attack or likely die yelling.

Out of nowhere, a crowd of Afghan villagers appeared, running toward the helicopters, yelling and waving their arms frantically. One of the flight crew fired several warning shots. The villagers hit the ground and continued to yell and flail their arms.

Thankfully, a terp going home on leave had joined Major Finnell and his SECFOR. As soon as the flight crew began to fire, he jumped up and ran back to the helicopter, yelling, "*Don't shoot! They're villagers! They're trying to warn us! They say we've landed in the middle of a minefield! Don't shoot!*"

You can't make this shit up.

Thankfully, the weather cleared, the guys carefully retraced their steps to the birds, reloaded the aircraft, took off, and counted their blessings that no one had died in what could have been an all-too-tragic accident after surviving a very long, tough year.

The night before Christmas, someone passed the word that U.S. forces would begin arming Afghan tribes to fight and to defend against the Taliban, prompting all of us to wonder what the fuck we had just spent the last year doing if the ANA and ANP apparently won't cut it.

55

Leaving Afghanistan

Thursday, December 25, 2008

Christmas Day: our last day on Afghan soil.

We got word late Christmas Eve that our flight to Kyrgyzstan would leave early Christmas morning. Thankfully, we had spent the previous day having our gear thoroughly inspected so we could depart Phoenix rapidly once word came we had a flight. The army is beyond serious about preventing soldiers from bringing home war trophies and other random items like dirt, unpolished rocks, or any open bottle or container of workout supplements. The process of waiting to have every single one of my carefully packed duffel bags totally dumped out and rifled through took the better part of the morning.

I'll admit it now: I brought home a few souvenirs the army never found, like a piece of the RPG that nearly killed me in Waghez. I carried it in my backpack. The German inspectors at KIA weren't nearly as thorough in their search as the army MPs at Camp Phoenix.

We spent the rest of the day wondering if our flight would get canceled at the last moment; rumors ran wild of a massive blizzard that would ground us past New Year's.

If the flight did come, we'd have to be ready to leave by 3:00 a.m., not that any of us could sleep at this point, with the excitement of escaping Camp Phoenix and heading home. At this point, we had consolidated back into our original Fort

Boarding the C-17 cargo plane that flew us from Kabul to Manas Air Force base in Kyrgyzstan.

Riley teams, and we'd remain formally organized this way for the remainder of our deployment. Even though we had organized back into arbitrary groups, we all naturally sought out the people we had spent the past nine months with and stuck close to one another.

Captain Norris and I decided to attend midnight Christmas mass together. I'm not Catholic, but the service is close enough to Episcopalian that it suited just fine. A Puerto Rican Air Force chaplain led the service, which ended shortly after midnight. As we walked out of the plywood chapel, the chaplain greeted each of us with a warm embrace and a fond "Merry Christmas!"

I replied, "It certainly is, Father—I'm going home for good in about six hours!"

He smiled and wished us a safe journey. Thinking back on it now, I'm glad he did. We'd need all the blessings we could get.

Three hours and half a pack of cigarettes later, our motley group filed out of our transient tent for a final walk toward the Bogginsalling area near the old Soviet warehouses. A light snow started to fall, swaddling Phoenix in a gentle blanket of Christmas quiet.

We gathered at the warehouses and waited for our ride to KIA. The excitement of our group radiated throughout, joining the cold in making us shiver. Wired on caffeine and cigarettes, I've never seen so many people that happy to be up in the middle of the night to stand around for two hours waiting in the cold snow for a 10-minute ride.

At around 0515, we left Camp Phoenix forever. We drove through the deserted early-morning Kabul streets; the sun had yet to rise and call the faithful to prayer. Unlike our first ride months earlier, none of us got nervous, and no one's head darted from side to side looking out the windows expecting danger to come around the next corner. A few people power napped. I stared out the window to my left and watched the city sleep. Our original drive had been filled with such life, humanity struggling to survive on the cusp of absolute misery. This last drive, fittingly, was devoid of any living thing. The city slept, lifeless. Our tour began vibrant, raging, careless, frightened, and alive. It now closed calmly, motionlessly, tired, and passive.

We entered the grounds of KIA, and that was it, our last ride outside the wire. One flight more, and our war would be over. It felt cheap.

We spent the next several hours doing what we had come to perfect in the earlier weeks: sitting around and just waiting. The Germans made us walk through a metal detector before entering the Terminal Waiting Area, which I still find ironic, because we all carried all our weapons (sans ammo). It's the only airport screening in the world that allows you to board a plane with a machine gun, grenade launcher, and pistol.

The morning sun rose over the mountains, illuminating the airfield. Hues of pink, rose, and crimson gave way to a clear yellow. Somewhere off in the distance, the call to prayer rang, our last. Buses arrived, we boarded, and, unlike our near-panicked run when we landed, we casually drove to the waiting C-17 parked out at the end of a runway.

As I walked up the stairs into the aircraft, I turned and took one last fleeting gaze at Afghanistan. I sensed the city, the nation around me, had come to life. Somewhere south, the men of FOB Vulcan had likely risen and planned to go out on their morning patrols. Would they survive?

The snow-capped peaks that had first captured my heart had returned to surround Kabul. The sky was cloudless, bathed powder blue. A light haze from burning stove fires had settled over the city. I wondered aloud, "Will I ever return?"

God, I miss it. I miss our terps. I miss our Vulcan; not the one we gave to the Illinois unit, but *our* Vulcan, so much like the Afghans, just on the cusp of surviving, struggling, making it one day at a time. Life is more alive that way—you learn to take every moment as a gift.

Enough, let's go home. I turned my head and never looked back.

An expert at C-17 travel, I made sure to claim the first seat along the side of the fuselage I could find. Master Sergeant Postman sat in front of me in one of the uncomfortable seats with all his gear stacked on top of him, pinning him in. I offered up my seat. He declined.

I popped in my headphones, cued up my iPod, said a final "Dear God, get us the hell out of here" prayer, and leaned my head back, resigned to fate.

The engines thundered. A massive thrust threw me to my left and into the person seated beside me. We shot off like a rocket and, moments later, left Afghanistan forever.

A cheer went up inside the plane. We had made it out alive. Not all of us: those we left behind can never be forgotten. But for those of us on that plane, our war had ended. In a moment of selfish adulation, I internally expressed a profound joy at my good fortune.

A combat vet, I was on my way home from the worst year ever in Afghanistan, alive, mostly healthy, and way more mature than when I first left. I breathed easy for the first time since April and nodded off to sleep.

Hours later we landed at Manas Air Force Base in Kyrgyzstan.

We got off the C-17, boarded the same way-too-small buses we used when we first arrived back in April, and drove the very short drive to the base's gate.

At the entrance, we stopped, and two Air Force airmen jumped on board.

One, a female, wore a Santa cap. FOBBIT. A few guys on the bus cursed her under their breath.

"Merry Christmas ya'll!" she joyfully sang. "Welcome to Manas. Here are the rules. The current threat environment outside is really dangerous. Reports say Al-Qaeda and other terrorist elements could attack the base at any time . . . ," she cluelessly went on and on.

Shut up you damn duck, don't you know you're talking to a bus full of turtles?

Her speech was the first in a series none of us cared to hear. One by one, the Air Force gave us the same "Welcome to Manas, Here Are the Rules, You Can't Drink but We Can . . ." speech we had heard months prior. Back in April, we cared; most of us were strangers in a strange land. Now, we were grizzled vets, baptized in combat in Afghanistan. We realized Kyrgyzstan and everyone stationed there was a joke. They called it a combat deployment. We called it a luxury vacation in central Asia.

Briefings complete, we loaded all of our duffel bags into giant cargo pallets so that they'd be ready to go the moment we secured a flight home to the U.S. Getting anywhere at war is basically a giant game of hurry-up-and-wait and then seize the first thing that comes along. Our Air Force guards told us that the latest rumor had us leaving Manas on December 28 at the earliest, and that was if the impending blizzard didn't ground us. If the blizzard arrived, we'd be stuck there 'til at least the first week of January. The news didn't sit well with anyone. As much as we hated Camp Phoenix, we hated Manas even more.

Just like in April, the Air Force crammed us into a giant clamshell and pretended we weren't there. Unlike April, they had built a rather impressive MWR center within a short walk, which is where most of us spent our time in between eating, napping, and smoking. There was a large assortment of computers, Xboxs, pool tables, an impressive DVD library stocked with the latest pirated, still-playing-in-theaters-back-home movies, and best of all, a stadium-seating movie theater that showed movies 24-7.

Our first night in the clamshell, First Sergeant Rock and Sergeant First Class Bogginsall called me over to their bunks, brought me to attention, and read the orders awarding me a Combat Action Badge. The crowd gathered took turns punching it hard into my chest, earning me my "blood" badge. I've never felt more proud in my entire life.

Afterward I made my way over to the base's Christmas Texas Hold'em Tournament, where I quickly lost. I never went back. I couldn't stand the sight of them sitting around drinking their daily ration of two beers, believing they were "at war." The juxtaposition of their life and ours back at Vulcan made me too angry. I did enjoy, however, regaling them with combat stories any time one of them joined me for a cigarette in one of the smoke shacks (the designated areas for smoking on the base). I took some twisted pleasure in seeing the horrified looks on their faces when they realized life could get way more dangerous than they could ever imagine. By the second day, I decided to remain around our clamshell area and the MWR for the duration of our confinement.

I spent the rest of our time at Manas in moments of profound and stark self-reflection on the past year. The whole time leading up to our departure, I thought for sure I'd be thrilled to leave. But, now, with Afghanistan behind us, I felt an odd, unexplainable desire to go back. I longed to return. I felt I left my job unfinished, that I hadn't accomplished my mission, that I could still do lots more. My desire to return grew exponentially with each day we spent at Manas, sitting around uselessly, waiting for our chance flight home.

The more I tried to shake it, the more I couldn't. I didn't want to believe it. I couldn't believe it. Why on Earth would I want to go back? I still can't explain it, but not a day has gone by since that I've not at some point had the almost overpowering urge to get back any way I can.

56

The Flight Home Nearly Kills Us

Sunday, December 28, 2008

Word came as it always did, unexpected and with the usual caveats of "this could change at any time, so be ready." Our flight would leave at 0600; be ready to go to the lockdown area by 0200. I decided to volunteer for the baggage-loading detail that would help load the civilian charter flight home, because it gave me something to do (finally a purpose!) and because those who were on the detail got to pick where they sat on the plane (and I wanted a window seat up front). If the plane actually left by 0600, we'd fly to Germany and be back in the U.S. by nightfall; just like that, we'd be home.

Like our wait in Kabul before, I couldn't sleep, so I wandered down to the MWR movie theater and joined Sergeant First Class Alderson in watching a series of movies, ending with *The Terminal* (starring Tom Hanks), an ironic foreshadowing of our journey home.

At 0200 we marched over to the lockdown area. Rumors buzzed that we had to load and board the plane ASAP, because the ever-impending blizzard was due at any moment. Thirty minutes later, I joined the baggage detail for our ride out to the airfield and the start of our epic disaster.

In a stupid move, I packed my coldest winter gear into duffel bags that now sat secured in cargo pallets. Murphy's Law dictated a raging blizzard would hit the minute we started to load the bags, and that's exactly what happened. Timed

One of the engines that died during takeoff and then miraculously regained power on the flight from Kyrgyzstan to Germany.

perfectly with our arrival, a major storm raged around us, limiting our visibility, and soaking us frigidly to the bones.

First Sergeant Rock and I quickly took charge and organized a baggage-loading system. One by one, we'd unload the duffel bags from their cargo pallets and via bucket brigade hand them up to the waiting crew in the belly of the aircraft. As we did this, a civilian representative from the airline attempted to futilely figure out a way to properly balance the cargo load. A small, confused, and utterly incompetent German man, he became flustered to the point of giving up. He calculated the load once and determined there was no way we'd be able to load everything on the plane; he claimed the weight was too great. This was simply impossible. We had come to Afghanistan with more people (several had volunteered to extend their deployment, several had died) and more gear (most of us had shipped home a lot of our stuff in $20 plastic chests weeks earlier from Kabul). Clearly we had no problem getting here with more people and crap; thus, we should have no problem leaving with fewer and less. He would hear none of it. He insisted his calculations showed there was no feasible way to load the aircraft with all our stuff and safely fly.

His solution was to leave a whole pallet of duffel bags behind for some future flight home. I immediately told him this was 100 percent unacceptable, as it meant that whoever's gear got left behind would have to wait at Fort Riley for their shit to magically find its way back from Kyrgyzstan. He didn't care. If he said it didn't go on, then it didn't go on.

I dug deeper; something was amiss. It had all fit before, why wasn't it all fitting now?

A few questions later I got my answer. He had decided we couldn't use an entire cargo storage compartment in the center of the aircraft's belly.

The storm increased in intensity as we began to yell at each other with increasing anger. We yelled because we had couldn't hear each other over the wind's howl, and because it felt good to finally have someone to take all my frustrations out on.

Meanwhile, the loading process continued, First Sergeant Rock determined as ever to find a way to make everything fit, to hell with this civilian and his "solution."

The Air Force personnel who were supposed to be in charge of the baggage loading simply sat by and watched. At one point I asked them if they could intervene, but they just shrugged. They had never seen this happen before and claimed to be powerless to order the little man from Germany to allow us to use the center cargo hold.

Exasperated, cold, tired, and desperate for a cigarette, I walked off to think and to smoke (which is strictly prohibited on the airfield). I didn't have to go far, as the storm reduced visibility to about 100 feet. As the nicotine coursed through my veins, I calmed. The solution came to me through a deep puff of tobacco.

I walked back to the plane to continue my debate with the little bespectacled German.

Ding! Ding! Bang! Ding! "Come on you fucking thing! Work!"

I looked off to my right, the snow temporarily blinding me. I held up my hand to gain a clearer view. Ahead of me, the starboard (right) aircraft engine had its maintenance hatch open, with a ladder leaned against it. Atop the ladder stood a man with a hammer, a wrench, a flashlight, and rage, banging and cursing away.

"Hey buddy, is there a problem?" I asked, my nerves starting to rise.

"Dunno. The cockpit controls indicate a problem, but I can't seem to . . . if it can't be fixed we may be here for . . . certainly won't be leaving today . . . replacement parts or plane could take probably a week. . . ."

"Should we stop loading the plane?" I asked, having heard enough to sufficiently make me nervous. Nervous to fly on a broken plane, angry that we'd be stuck in Manas even longer. At this point, I'd had enough. I wanted out, we all wanted out. And we wanted it now, today, this morning, blizzard and engines be damned.

"No, no. I've seen this happen all the time," the man said, descending with a huge smile. He looked and sounded Filipino. "I used to be a pilot. This happened all the time. Shouldn't be a problem. I'll get it fixed. And if not, no worries, as I'll be on the plane with you guys!" he chuckled.

His being on the plane didn't make one bit of difference to me; I mean, what was he going to do, climb out on the wing at 30,000 feet and MacGyver a solution in mid-flight as we plummeted toward our deaths?

I trotted up to Rock and briefed him about my ongoing debate with the little German and our potential engine problems. He shrugged in his usual "oh well, that's fucking life" manner that I had grown to love and admire and said, "Roger, got it. We'll keep loading, but ain't no fucking way we're leaving people's gear behind."

"Speaking of that, I think I have a solution," I replied.

"Oh yeah, what's that?" he looked up, while handing the next bag up the bucket-brigade line.

"We came here with what, 300 people and almost every seat on the plane was filled. We're leaving with what, about 165 give or take? That means there're going to be a lot of empty seats. Enough seats that I bet you we can load with the gear the German wants to leave behind. Only the pilot could stop us from doing that, and I doubt he'll care."

"Worth a try," he replied, looking up with a proud smile.

"I'm going to going see if I can't find the pilot. I'll be back shortly," I said as I walked off to the plane in search of the one man who could solve our problem.

The storm howled. The wind gusts grew stronger with each step toward the staircase that led up into the plane.

I found the pilot and explained our issue. He looked at me, exasperated. I knew enough from his eyes and from his fleeting attention that the engine issues and the weather held more importance in his mind. The faster he dispatched of me and our baggage problem, the better.

Surprised to learn the little German had refused to let us use the center cargo hold, he readily agreed to my plan. "As long as there are enough seats on the plane for all the passengers and as long as the duffel bags and gear are tied down, I don't care how you load it. Sorry about the German, I've never worked with him before, so I don't know what to tell you."

"Not a problem. Thanks for your understanding, Sir," I said, quickly shaking his hand before I ran off to brief First Sergeant Rock.

"Okay, First Sergeant, he's good to go. We'll load up the bottom of the plane with as much as we can and whatever is left over will go in the overhead bins and in the seating area itself. I figure, what we'll do is we'll load every center seat and if there's still bags left, we'll load the seats closest to the windows. That way when the rest of the men board, they won't have to climb over gear to find a seat."

"All right, we're just about done with the cargo hold. Good job," he replied.

An hour later, we had the plane (cargo hold and seating area) loaded with all our gear, not a single bag left behind. The plan worked so well we even had extra seats once the rest of the men boarded the plane.

All the while, the mechanic kept banging away on the starboard engine, periodically emerging to converse with the pilot.

Our original departure time of 0650 came and went. At 0730, with the sun's first light warming our frozen and soaked bodies, we took our seats on the plane and watched as the remainder of our men (who had stayed back and warm in the lockdown area) boarded the plane. One by one, confused, they looked at their gear strapped down to the middle-aisle seats. And one by one, we members of the baggage detail recounted our night's activities and the impromptu solution. At one point, a major walked up to me and thanked me for my efforts. It turns out the majority of the gear in the seats belonged to his group; we had saved them from weeks of sitting at Fort Riley waiting for their gear and the unfathomable headaches that would have resulted.

By 0800 we sat ready to go . . . and waited.

Around 0845 the pilot announced that we'd be on the ground at least another 40 minutes while we waited to be deiced. Turns out Manas, which also serves as Kyrgyzstan's main airport, had one deicing machine, and we were at the end of the list in terms of priority for deicing. I looked out my window at the civilian terminal and the decades old Soviet-era passenger jets that sat, looking void of life or use. The wait defied logic, but nothing about today seemed logical.

At 0905, 20 minutes earlier than expected, the deicing machine drove up to us and began to spray our plane with the magical ice-removing elixir. Taking the pilot at his word that we'd depart as soon as they completed deicing, I popped an Ambien and fell asleep.

Four hours later, I groggily woke up. The engines hummed, but not as intensely as they should have for flight. I looked out my window and struggled to understand what I saw: the exact same view I had seen four hours prior, the civilian air terminal at Manas in the midst of a now-diminished blizzard.

Sensing my confusion, the soldier seated across the aisle from me volunteered an explanation. "We never left. They deiced the plane, but the engine is still apparently broken or something. They just announced they think they've fixed it, but there's a catch. I guess in all this time on the ground, they say we've gone from being deiced to potentially iced over again. If we don't leave in like the next five minutes, we'll have to wait to be deiced again, which could take another hour, because we're back at the end of the line again. If it starts to snow or rain, we'll definitely be grounded until they deice the plane again. So we either leave in the next few minutes or wait more . . . ," he said with his voice trailing off, resigned to the frustration of just sitting there with no control over our fate.

I've never wanted a plane to take off faster in my life. I started to go stir crazy. Manas had become suffocating. We had to leave, now. Frustration gave way to an uncontrollable angered panic.

"Come on you motherfucker, fucking go, take off!" I growled to myself under my breath.

As if the pilot heard me, the engines roared to life, and we slowly taxied down to the runway. A strong thrust slammed me back into my seat. We picked up speed. The plane skidded left to right along the icy runway. We climbed into the sky. Good-fucking-bye Manas.

I looked out the window and watched the buildings grow smaller and smaller.

And just as I sat back to revel in our victorious escape, it happened: a long wailing shriek, like a motor spinning into destruction. I looked out the window. The starboard engine sat motionless. The plane, now gliding through the apex of its arch, dipped and slowly started to drop.

Unless you've flown on a plane that loses its engines in mid-takeoff, there's no way to describe the oddity of being several thousand feet in the air and gliding in terrified silence. There is no other silence like it on the planet. It's totally unnatural and paralyzing.

It probably only lasted a mere fraction of a second, but it felt like a lifetime. I prepared for death or, at the least, a horrifying attempt to glide or to crash the plane back at Manas, as the pilot struggled to turn the plane back toward the airfield.

As suddenly as the silence came, it vanished in the thunderous roar of the port (left) engine roaring back to life. Willed into compliance, the starboard engine clicked, clunked, whined, moaned, and begrudgingly spun up. The pilot laid on the throttle and climbed.

I popped another Ambien and drifted in and out of a nervous semisleep state. Somewhere over the Caspian Sea, I woke up for good and, for the remaining five hours of the flight, stared out at the starboard engine, willing it to keep working.

Miraculously, we made it and landed without incident at the now-infamous Leipzig airport, where someone on the flight reminded us we couldn't drink.

Thankful to be alive, we ran off the plane to board the shuttle buses to the terminal, expecting the usual two-hour layover to refuel the plane. While we waited and chain-smoked away our collective nerves, German maintenance inspected the plane. The mechanics, dumbfounded that we'd actually made it, instantly grounded the plane. The aircraft, a decades-old and discontinued Boeing model, needed a whole new starboard engine that the civilian airline would have to fly in from the U.S.

Turns out, Leipzig has an entire room full of bunk beds for stranded traveling soldiers. For the next day and a half, we watched flight after flight land, ferrying soldiers, sailors, airmen, and Marines, some going to war, others going home. The system the military uses to bring us to and from war required that we remain attached to our broken plane. And so we waited, Tom Hanks–style, stranded in Leipzig, Germany. The airline handed out vouchers for free nonalcoholic beverages from the terminal shop. Three times a day, some German company came in and fed us a local fare of sausages, bread, and a variety of steamed vegetables. We glared at each new plane full of travelers who came and went around us. Some drank in front of us.

One young private boasted in front of me that he wasn't old enough to drink as he downed his illicitly purchased, delicious German beer. I told him to get the fuck out of my sight.

We lost track of time and stopped caring about the rumors that they'd fixed the plane and we'd be leaving "shortly." Eventually, word came that they really had fixed the plane, for real this time, and all they needed to do was a quick test flight and we'd be on our way.

Under our Status of Forces Agreement with Germany, we're not allowed to carry our weapons off the plane and onto German soil. During our delay at Leipzig, we'd left a few guys on the plane to watch over our weapons. The airline informed us that the weapons guards would have to get off the plane in order to do the test flight. We told them we'd have to unload all the weapons first. The Germans told us we couldn't violate the agreement and that the weapons had to remain on the plane. Another catch-22.

The solution: the weapons guards remained on the plane while the pilot took the plane out to the runway, revved up the engines to full capacity, and returned to the terminal, satisfied that they'd work sufficiently to fly us home across the Atlantic. No one liked this solution, but we were powerless.

Boarding the plane, an army doctor traveling with us handed out an assortment of pills and told us to take them before takeoff. Whatever they were, they knocked me out and kept me stoned and sedated for our flight back to Portland, Maine. At one point, somewhere over the Atlantic, I woke up and panicked, convinced the turbulence meant we were crashing. The flight attendant smiled and told me everything was okay. I fell back asleep and woke up when the soldier seated across from me shook me and said, "We're in Portland. We've gotta get off while they refuel."

I called my family and let them know we'd made it to U.S. soil. Hours later, we landed in Kansas and boarded the buses back to Fort Riley, eager to begin turning in our gear. We knew the maintenance delays had cost us a lot of time and that we'd likely get stuck at Fort Riley through the New Year's holiday, as civilians run most of the out-processing and they don't work during the holiday. Secretly, we hoped we could sprint through the process and be finished before they went off on vacation.

57

Back to the World I No Longer Know

Monday, December 29, 2008–Monday, January 5, 2009

Return to Fort Riley: Around 0500, we rolled into Fort Riley and walked into the same gymnasium we had sat in back in April waiting to board the buses for our flights to war. An army reservist chaplain stood before us and gave a "Welcome Home Heroes" speech none of us wanted to hear. People around me muttered for him to "shut the fuck up" under their breath as he explained on and on about the dangers we'd face: the urge to drink, how we wouldn't be allowed to drive for the first 24 hours back, and how we'd inevitably face civilians who'd ask us questions like, "Did you kill anyone?" and how to deal with the anger he guaranteed we'd feel as a result.

The longer he droned, the angrier we got. A personnel soldier announced that we'd be at Fort Riley for at least five days due to the holiday and the fact that the civilians necessary to run our out-processing wouldn't be working. We'd bunk in the barracks we had stayed in during our first week at Fort Riley, before we moved to Camp Funston.

Around 0630, we boarded buses and drove to another gymnasium, where we assembled in proper military formation and marched into a room full of strangers who applauded our return. An army colonel gave the shortest speech I've ever heard in my military career and dismissed us to the assembled crowd. We all looked at each other and shrugged, as we didn't know anyone clapping before us. First

Doc Caswell and me. This photo was taken approximately three hours before the April 28, 2008, Waghez ambush that nearly killed us.

Lieutenant Creger's parents walked up, having gotten word we'd arrive that morning. They had driven in from Oklahoma to greet us. He introduced the remaining Vulcan team to his family, and we walked out into the cold Kansas morning to board the buses back to the barracks.

Hours later, I walked from the barracks over to the PX and bought a bottle of Maker's Mark bourbon. That night, I ordered Domino's pizza and drank the entire bottle, sharing a few shots with Master Sergeant Postman. I got so sick I vomited and passed out fully clothed on my unmade bed.

Over the next few days, we went through the endless parade of paperwork processing, gear turn-in, and waiting for word of our return flights. Rumors drifted around that we'd get individual flights back to our individual homes. Others said we'd fly back to our respective states (NY to NY, Maine to Maine, etc.), and from there we'd be on our own to get back home. Though I had gone to war with a New York unit, I lived in D.C. and hoped for the option that flew us home individually.

At one point during the medical out-processing, we each went through a long personal interview with a medical civilian. They asked us about war injuries and then after a few clicks of a computer screen, read us the programmed response based on our specific individual conditions. Because of all the explosions I'd endured, the civilian told me I could either stay at Fort Riley for treatment (I could potentially have PTSD, hearing loss, lung problems due to the RPG blast exposure, and potential mild traumatic brain injury), or I could go home and seek out the VA for treatment. I asked him how long I'd have to stay at Fort Riley if I chose that option. He replied that I'd be there at least nine months before I could get in for the necessary tests and treatment, and that during that waiting period I'd be assigned to a Warrior Transition and Recovery Unit tasked to do odds and ends around the base. I quickly declined to stay at Fort Riley and said I'd seek out the VA as soon as I got home.

Some soldiers chose the Fort Riley option, as they had no jobs waiting at home and staying at Fort Riley meant staying on active duty and receiving a paycheck. Last I heard, most of them would change their minds after two weeks of remaining at Fort Riley. They found the process of being in the Warrior Transition Units too hellish to justify the paycheck and found unemployment far more appealing.

On the night of the fourth day at Fort Riley (January 4, 2009), our active-duty minders announced we'd leave early the next morning for individual flights home out of Kansas City, Missouri. While happy to be leaving, we sat enraged as we read our flight orders and realized that they had been prepared the day we arrived at Fort Riley. The army had known for four days we'd be leaving on our fifth day and decided not to give us more than a late-night's notice to warn our families to make airport pick-up plans. A lot of guys, like Master Sergeant Postman, got screwed with their return flights and ended up flying into airports that were upwards of a six-hour drive away from their actual homes. I got lucky and got a flight directly back to D.C.

The next morning, we boarded the bus to Kansas City, Missouri, and left Fort Riley forever. Some traveled wearing their uniforms; I chose to wear civilian clothing so I could drink in the airport bar while I waited for my flight. Two hours later, we arrived at the airport and lined up to check in with our respective airlines. I hugged First Sergeant Rock good-bye and wandered off to drink in the airport bar.

That afternoon, Major Goodman and I boarded a flight to Ronald Reagan Airport in D.C., where he'd catch a connection flight back home to Maine. As we sat in the airplane, waiting to take off, a young child turned to another soldier traveling in uniform and asked him if he had shot anyone during the war. We were shocked. The soldier replied gently that such questions were impolite, and the child turned away, disappointed.

We landed in D.C. around 1800, where my father met us in the terminal. I introduced him to Major Goodman, whom my dad heartily thanked for looking after me during our deployment. Major Goodman replied that my father should be proud, as he'd raised a good man and that it had been his mutual honor to serve alongside me. I hugged Major Goodman good-bye, wished him safe travels, and urged him to remain in touch.

A 20-minute drive later, my father and I sat down to a meal and several beers in my favorite Arlington pub and made awkward conversation that quickly gave way to the familiar and comfortable topic of sports.

Sipping my beer, I struggled to make sense of it all; my war, our deployment, had abruptly ended. I found myself struggling to answer the lingering question racing in my mind: "Now what?"

EPILOGUE

My War at Home Begins

It's taken me more than two years to write this book, and yet I haven't had a single day where I didn't think or talk about Afghanistan. I wrote everything up until leave while in Afghanistan, and then I stopped. I realize now that I couldn't deal with it emotionally or mentally until I chose to leave the war behind. As I finish this account, sitting in my kitchen, a February blizzard raging outside, I still struggle with an intense desire to go back. My New York unit is preparing to return sometime in 2012. I fear that if they go without me, I'll somehow be less of a man for not joining them. More selfishly, I fear that if I don't join them, I'll lessen if not outright lose our bond, that they'll return having gone through a second combat baptism and look at me as an outsider, as no longer one of them. I have no idea how I'd handle losing that bond.

Not that re-deployment isn't still a possibility. I'm still a member of the army reserves, so there's always the chance I'll get called again. And it's that constant possibility of unexpected deployment that has made letting go of Afghanistan that much harder. For the more I let go, the more I fear I'll lose my combat edge. I'm haunted by the fear of losing it forever. What if I need to redeploy—will I be able to get it back? It kept me alive in 2008, and as long as there's a chance I could go again, it has to remain somewhere deep within me. I feel I must keep it alive so I can make it home again. I fear that to let go of it would be to lose it forever.

I left combat behind in Afghanistan, but I brought the war and my own battles home with me. My father likes to say that the army spent years training me how to kill and react a certain way and then unfairly took only five days to dump me back out into a civilian world and way of life, a grossly foreign life I was suddenly inadequately prepared for.

Within a week of being home, Precila found herself trapped in my car as I barreled through traffic, blatantly breaking nearly every driving law in the land. I drove like a madman, freaked out by the fact that the traffic in front of me wouldn't part as it had in Afghanistan. I turned to tap my turret gunner's knee to as a signal for him to point his weapon and use it to move traffic, and found that much to my surprise, my Toyota Avalon didn't have a turret or a gunner, which freaked me out even more. I sped up. I crossed over the double yellow line and drove into oncoming traffic at 65 mph. Cars aggressively swerved to get out of my way. I took their movements as threats and aimed my car to hit them and to remove them as a threat. Precila screamed.

Blue lights and a siren roared behind me. I pulled into an empty parking lot. A Virginia State Police officer walked up to my window.

"License and registration, please. Do you have any idea why I pulled you over?" he asked as I handed him my military ID, driver's license, and registration.

"Well, let's see . . . I crossed the double yellow, drove into oncoming traffic, tried to hit a few cars that wouldn't move out of my way, I think I blew through at least two stop signs, and I know I went through that red light back there. Oh, and I was speeding. . . ."

"Uh, Son, I just had you at speeding," he said, studying my emotionless eyes.

He looked down at my military ID and looked me up and down.

"When did you get back?"

"Um, last week."

"That explains it. Please step out of the car," he commanded.

I got out and instinctively put my hands on top of my head, preparing for him to arrest me.

"Ma'am, could you please also step out of the car?" he said to Precila, who sat, thankful to be alive.

"Officer, she did nothing wrong. I did everything. She even tried to stop me. Please, leave her out of this," I said turning to confront him.

"Son, stop talking and be quiet," he ordered.

"Ma'am, please come over here," he waved to Precila. "Son, walk over to the passenger's seat," he said to me, pointing to it.

Precila and I moved as instructed.

"Son, take a seat in the passenger's seat and remain silent. Ma'am, take the driver's seat."

I got into the car and buckled my seat belt. Precila slid in next to me and looked up at the officer waiting further directions.

"Okay. Son, I want you to listen carefully. You are not to drive until she says you can, okay? You hear me? No driving. Period." he said, as I nodded.

"Ma'am, take him to the VA as soon as you can. He needs to see someone," he gently said to Precila.

"Absolutely, Officer, I agree. Thank you so much," Precila said, relieved we hadn't had an accident and that I wasn't headed to jail.

As the officer walked away, Precila turned and looked at me. I expected a verbal thrashing like no other. She started to cry. "Matt, you need help. Okay? We're going to go home and call the VA, and you're going to go, because this is not normal. You could have killed someone. You could have killed us. You need help, and we're going to get it. I'm going to be there right with you the whole time, okay?"

I nodded, in a daze. I found the world confusing. I struggled to remember what had just happened. I realized somewhere in speeding up to cross the double yellow line I couldn't recall exactly what had happened. My memory was spotty. My chest tightened. The more I couldn't remember, the more my frustration grew.

A week later, I went to the VA. Within a few hours of meeting with a counselor, she diagnosed me with PTSD and arranged for a TBI (traumatic brain injury) screening. She told me that I should start attending a bi-weekly Saturday morning discussion session that only included Iraq and Afghan War vets with PTSD. I agreed, but she never followed up to tell me where to meet the group, and I stopped calling after three failed attempts to get her on the phone. A couple of months later, another counselor performed a battery of memory and IQ tests on me, diagnosed me with mild TBI, and said that it would gradually subside. I haven't returned to the VA since spring 2009. Even though the diagnosis and treatment was supposed to be free, the VA charged me $120 for it. I called up to try and have the charges removed. The VA phone representative agreed and said he'd take care of it. In April 2010, the VA garnished $120 out of my tax return for fees owed.

I returned home on January 5, 2009, and returned to work on January 22, 2009, allowing myself two weeks to "heal." On January 20, 2009, I fought the crowds at the Obama Inauguration and witnessed it in person. The entire time, I expected a massive terrorist attack at any moment. Watching the inauguration, I felt a tremendous rush of purpose; this is why I did what I just did.

Two days later, I went back to work for the CIA. When I left the agency for war a year prior, I felt I was doing the most important job in the U.S. government. After a year on the front lines in Afghanistan, I found my work at the CIA unimportant and meaningless. I did everything I could mentally to find meaning, but nothing came close to the sense of purpose I knew I had left behind in Afghanistan, a realization that further fueled my desire to return.

For the next year-plus, I lived life on a perpetual edge, ready to snap back into combat mode. At times I found myself hoping something dramatic would happen just so I could feel the rush of craved adrenaline. I grew accustomed to walking into businesses and restaurants and letting my mind run wild with how I might react to an attack and where it might come from. To this day, I still get uncomfortable around large crowds. Whenever we go out to eat, I have to sit with as many people in front of me as possible and preferably with a clear view of the nearest exit. Any time I enter a building or a room, I make a mental plan of how best to escape or to defend myself.

Almost immediately upon returning, I started to drink nightly and heavily. Through bouts of alcohol-infused madness, I'd rant to Precila about my crazed and desperate desire to return to Afghanistan. She'd remind me that I had spent a year trying to escape with my life and that I should celebrate that, but I didn't want to listen. I missed Janis, Arnold, and the rest of my FOB Vulcan brothers to the point of painful separation. I'd call them every few weeks to get a fix, but as soon as the conversations ended, it just made missing them even worse.

The nightmares started about a week after Precila and I moved into our new house in the Fairfax, Virginia, suburbs. I'd wake up screaming, my mind still trapped in an endless and unwinnable firefight in Afghanistan. Or, the house would creak, and I'd jump up startled out of bed, convinced that someone had broken in. I'd reach for my nonexistent weapon and cower in fear. I kept a metal bat next to the bed. I started to dream vivid dreams of a bearded man breaking into our home. He'd enter through the first-floor window. I'd run out of the room, bat in hand, and we'd meet on the stairs up to our bedroom. I'd move to strike him, and, just as we came to blows, I'd find myself sitting up in bed, drenched in sweat, shaking. Precila would lean over to rub my back, but convinced the dream was true, I'd grab the bat and run downstairs, looking for the intruder who had yet to come. Eventually, I took to random nightly patrols of the house, moving from room to room in combat proficiency, with bat in hand.

Months of worthless sleep went by; exhaustion fueled my paranoia. Precila, a light sleeper, learned to realize when I was having a nightmare and, through trial and error, realized she could ease me out of them by gently rubbing my back. Some nights, she had to jump on top of me and pin me down to prevent me from hurting her as I violently thrashed about in my sleep.

I made on and off attempts to reduce and to eventually quit smoking. While I'm nowhere near my Afghan amounts, I've never fully quit.

As for the drinking, it nearly killed my relationship with Precila. For a year, I craved the sweet caress of bourbon on my tongue. I'd rush home from work just so I could sit down in the darkness of my living room, bottle in hand, and jump back and forth from the latest war movie and my computer, where I'd read endless blogs and articles on Afghanistan. I had become obsessed with everything regarding the war. A combat junkie, I chased the dragon and got my fix where I could, be it through aggressive driving, black-out drinking, online news and blogs, movies, TV shows, or 3:00 a.m. phone calls via Skype to Janis or Arnold back in Afghanistan.

And then there's the anger. My dad was right. The army taught me to react a certain way, and I slowly adapted those instinctive reactions to normal American life. Driving became one endless bout of road rage and increasingly dangerous maneuvers. Once, on my drive to work, the above-ground metro line flew by me as I sat stopped in early morning rush-hour traffic. The train sparked right next to me. My body tensed. My stomach churned. I braced for the expected blast of an IED that I believed had just exploded. A car's horn blaring at me to move forward snapped me back to reality. I shook in fear and drove on, struggling to understand how nothing had happened when I was sure an IED had just gone off next to me. I snapped at the littlest of things and at times even sought out confrontations, hoping they'd turn physical. The angrier I got, the more I wanted to return to Afghanistan, where I could do horrible things to evil people.

In April 2009, Precila and I went to Syracuse, New York, for the brigade's official welcome home ceremony, known as a "Freedom Salute." It was the first time I got to see any of my brothers since returning. Instinctively, Sergeant First Class Alderson, Master Sergeant Postman, Major Garrison, and Captain Norris stuck to one another. Major Hunt and a few other PMTs and ETTs attended as well, but for the most part, non-PMT and ETT or SECFOR soldiers (the FOBBITS) comprised the audience. I found myself treating the non-Vulcan soldiers differently. I'm ashamed now to admit that I arrogantly looked down upon their service, but at the time, that's how I was. I was angry at a lot of things in my life, and part of that anger was toward those who I felt did far less than we had in the war. I've grown out of that now, thankfully, but only because I've learned to realize that we all had our parts to play and that I must hold all service in equal honor. To do anything different would degrade the efforts of my brothers to develop me into a better man and leader.

In May 2009, I went to Rochester, New York, for Doc Caswell's wedding, which became the unofficial reunion for a lot of the FOB Vulcan crew. Captain Morriarty, Sergeant First Class Alderson, Doc Sullivan, Sergeant Blasker, and a few others came. We ended up drinking Doc Caswell's open bar dry. We've had a few impromptu and one planned reunion of the FOB Vulcan crew since we came home. Through these gatherings, I've come to realize that my brothers are the people I relate to most comfortably to in life, and I fondly look forward to anytime we're together.

In April 2010, I left my job with the CIA to run for Congress in my ancestral home in upstate NY, an effort that, although I lost the election, saved my life. Through campaigning I escaped the war and finally started the long process of coming to terms with my inner demons. The rigors of campaigning forced me to almost immediately quit drinking. I learned to manage my anger by attending countless constituent meetings, where throngs of angry people would scream their frustrations with the government at me. Though I wanted to lash out, I quickly realized I had to have patience and channel my anger into something positive; otherwise no one would vote for me. And eventually, I learned to laugh away the anger; in comparison to the struggles I endured in Afghanistan, what now ails me simply isn't worthy of such an intense response. Most importantly, I found purpose in my life. I worked my ass off and ran as a Democrat in a heavily Republican district where the previous congressman (a Democrat) resigned amid a sex scandal, leaving the seat vacant and the constituents in uproar. Though I lost, I ran believing I would win and as if I had nothing to lose and everything to gain. I gave it my all, and not because I wanted to win for the sake of winning. No. For the first time since I climbed aboard the C-17 in Kabul on Christmas Day, I wanted to be the change I wanted to see in the world. And you know what? I still believe I can be.

As for Precila and me, we got married in May 2011, and she's pregnant with our first child. What I've learned through my struggles to leave the war behind and to adjust to life in my postwar skin is that, despite all that happened, despite how much I'm forever changed, ultimately, life gets better one day at a time. Every step forward is a success.

Acronyms and Jargon

1LT: An abbreviation for *First Lieutenant*

ACOG: An abbreviation for *Advanced Combat Optical Gunsight*

Amber: A state of "readiness" in which one has a loaded magazine of ammunition in one's weapon, but has not chambered a round; also a state of post-combat readiness in which one has expended about half of one's ammunition/supplies; also a road/route that has been judged as moderately dangerous (i.e., a moderate likelihood of being attacked) prior to traveling on it.

ANA: An abbreviation for *Afghan National Army*

ANCOP: An abbreviation for *Afghan National Civil Order Police*

ANP: An abbreviation for *Afghan National Police*

AO: An abbreviation for *Area of Operations*

ARSIC-E: An abbreviation for *Afghanistan Regional Security Command-East*

ASV: An abbreviation for *Armored Security Vehicle*

ASV 1: An abbreviation for *Armored Security Vehicle #1*

ASV 2: An abbreviation for *Armored Security Vehicle #2*

b-hut: A plywood building used as barracks or offices; pronounced "bee-hut." Stands for "basic-hut," as it is of a very basic design and use, spartanlike.

BAF: An abbreviation for *Bagram Airforce Base*

Black: A road/route that has been deemed too dangerous to drive on without receiving the explicit permission of a U.S. general officer prior to traveling on it—that is, a "NO-GO" area. The road has been judged as guaranteed to be attacked while traveling on it, and the attack will be so catastrophic as to cause a significant or total loss of one's unit/resources; also a state of postcombat readiness in which one has exhausted all of one's ammunition/supplies.

BUB: An abbreviation for *Battle Update Brief*

CAA: An abbreviation for *Close Air Attack*, which refers to helicopters providing air support to troops on the ground

CAB: An abbreviation for *Combat Action Badge*

CFF: An abbreviation for *Call for Fire*

Chinook: A type of helicopter

CIB: An abbreviation for *Combat Infantryman's Badge*

CID: An abbreviation for *Criminal Investigation Division*

CLS: An abbreviation for *Combat Life Services*

CM: An abbreviation for "*Charlie Mike*" (i.e., "Capability Milestone"), or a level of proficiency assigned by CTSC-A to rate the level of readiness of an individual unit of the ANP. One determined the rating by measuring such factors as the number of personnel assigned/present, number of patrols undertaken over a period of time, state and amount of equipment, and, most importantly, the unit's ability to independently conduct operations without the presence or mentorship of coalition advisers.

COIN: An abbreviation for *Counterinsurgency*

CONEX: A shipping container, such as a TEU, which is an abbreviation for *20-foot equivalent unit*

CSTC-A: An abbreviation for *Combined Security Transition Command-Afghanistan* (now known as NMT-A, which is an abbreviation for *NATO Training Mission-Afghanistan*)

D-Fac: An abbreviation for *Dining Facility*

DC: An abbreviation for *District Center*

EMT: An abbreviation for *Emergency Medical Technician*

EOD: An abbreviation for *Explosives and Ordinance* (a unit that seeks out and dismantles, disarms, and destroys IEDs and mines)

ETT: An abbreviation for *Embedded Training Team*

ETT/PMT: An abbreviation for *Embedded Training Team/Police Mentor Team* (ETTs work with the ANA, and PMTs work with the ANP)

Exfil: To tactically leave an area (i.e., exfiltration)

Fam-fire: An abbreviation for *Familiarization Firing*

FDD: An abbreviation for *Focused District Deployment*

FNG: An abbreviation for *Fucking New Guys*

FOB: An abbreviation for *Forward Operating Base*

FOBBIT: A person who spends the entire war living in a FOB

FRAGO: An abbreviation for *Fragmentary Order*

Gator: A type of all-terrain vehicle

Green: A state of readiness in which one's magazines are *not* loaded into one's weapon and one's weapon does *not* have a round chambered; also a state of postcombat readiness in which one has not expended any ammunition/supplies; also a road/route that has been judged safe or having a low likelihood of attack prior to traveling on it.

HA: An abbreviation for *Humanitarian Assistance*

HE: An abbreviation for *High Explosive*

HE 203: A High Explosive Grenade Round used in an M203 grenade launcher mounted on an M4 assault rifle

HIIDE: An abbreviation for *Handheld Interagency Identity Detection Equipment*, which is a device used for acquiring biometric information

HMMMV: A Hummer vehicle; we used the M1151 variant

HUMINT: An abbreviation for *Human Intelligence*

ICOM: A portable, unsecured communications radio, equivalent to handheld Motorola radios available at Radio Shack

IED: An abbreviation for *Improvised Explosive Device*

ISAF: An abbreviation for *International Security Assistance Force*

IV: An abbreviation for *Intravenous* (e.g., getting an IV of fluids in a hospital)

KBR: An abbreviation for *Kellogg Brown & Root*

KIA: An abbreviation for *Kabul International Airport*; also an abbreviation for *Killed in Action*

Lightning Main: The call sign of our higher headquarters at FOB Lightning in Gardez, Afghanistan; also the HQ of ARSIC-E

LZ: An abbreviation for *Landing Zone*

MEDCAP: A medical humanitarian assistance mission in which NATO forces provide free medical screenings and services to the Afghan civilian population

MEDEVAC: A medical evacuation by a helicopter, a vehicle on the ground, or being carried out on foot by one's comrades

MOI: An abbreviation for the Afghan *Ministry of Interior*

MRAP: An abbreviation for *Mine Resistant Ambush Protected Vehicle*

MRE: An abbreviation for *Meals Ready to Eat*

MWR: An abbreviation for *Morale, Welfare, and Recreation*

NCOIC: An abbreviation for *Non-Commissioned Officer in Charge*

NDS: An abbreviation for *National Directorate of Security* (the Afghan equivalent of both the CIA and the FBI; it has both domestic and foreign intelligence responsibilities)

NODs: An abbreviation for *Night Optical Devices*, or night-vision goggles

OC: An abbreviation for *Officer in Charge*

OCS: An abbreviation for *Officer Candidate School*

ODA: An abbreviation for *Operational Detachment-Alpha*, which is a generic name for a U.S. Special Forces unit/team

OER: An abbreviation for *Officer Evaluation Report*

OP: An abbreviation for *Observation Post*

OPCON: An abbreviation for *Operational Control*, being assigned to another unit other than one's own for operational purposes

OPFOR: An abbreviation for *Opposition Forces*

Pai looch: Pashto for "Those Who Walk Without Shoes"; also used as a derogatory slang by the Afghan public to refer to members of the Taliban. In Ghazni, the governor's personal security detail openly referred to themselves as the Pai looch.

PAX terminal: A Personnel Terminal, which is the terminal where people acquired plane flights at Baghram

PCC: An abbreviation for *Provincial Coordination Center*

PCI: An abbreviation for *Pre-Combat Inspections*

PMCS: An abbreviation for *Preventative Maintenance Checks and Services* of personnel, vehicles, and gear

PMT: An abbreviation for *Police Mentor Team* (they work exclusively with the Afghan National Police)

PRT: An abbreviation for *Provincial Reconstruction Team*

PT: An abbreviation for *Physical Training*

PT Belt: A Physical Training Belt, which is normally a reflective belt worn while performing physical training on a U.S. military installation

PTSD: An abbreviation for *Post-Traumatic Stress Disorder*

QRF: An abbreviation for *Quick Reaction Force*

Red: A state of readiness in which one has a magazine loaded into one's weapon *and* a round chambered in the weapon, ready to be fired; also a state of post-combat readiness in which one has exhausted 90 percent of one's ammunition/supplies; also a road/route that has been judged as highly dangerous (i.e., there is a high likelihood of being attacked) prior to traveling on it.

RIP: An abbreviation for *Relief in Place*

RPAC-E: An abbreviation for *Regional Police Advisory Command-East*; they were the next higher unit within our command (i.e., I was on PMT Ghazni; we fell under RPAC-E, which fell under the authority of ARSIC-E, which fell under the authority of TF Phoenix VII, which fell under the authority of CSTC-A). Of course, as far as I know, none of that exists anymore, as CSTC-A has been replaced by NTM-A (NATO Training Mission-Afghanistan).

RPG: An abbreviation for *Rocket-Propelled Grenade*

RUMINT: An abbreviation for *Rumor-Based Intelligence*

S-1: An abbreviation that refers to the Personnel Section/Officer

S-2: An abbreviation that refers to the Intelligence Section/Officer

S-3: An abbreviation that refers to the Operations Section/Officer

SECFOR: An abbreviation for *Security Forces*

SF: An abbreviation for *Special Forces*

SITREP: An abbreviation for *Situation Report*

Snafu: An abbreviation for *Situation Normal: All Fucked Up*

SP: An abbreviation for *Start Point*

Space-A: An abbreviation for *Space Available*

Status Red: See "Red," above

TACSAT: An abbreviation for *Tactical Satellite Radio*

TBI: An abbreviation for *Traumatic Brain Injury*

TIC: An abbreviation for *Troops in Contact*

TMC: An abbreviation for *The Medical Center*

TOA: An abbreviation for *Transfer of Authority*

TOC: An abbreviation for *Tactical Operations Center*

TRADOC: An abbreviation for *Training and Doctrine Command*

UAH: An abbreviation for *Up-Armored Hummer*

UAV: An abbreviation for *Unmanned Aerial Vehicle*

URF: An abbreviation for *Unique Unit Requirement Form*; CENTCOM validates force requirements using a database called the Force Requirements Enhanced Database. Each mission has a URF that contains the administrative data for the requirement, the mission, the capabilities, and any additional clarifying information, such as whether a joint solution could work or specific training guidance. The URF, which is also linked to previous and future rotations, establishes the unit's initial mission requirements and is an important point of contact information for when it arrives in theater.

VBIED: An abbreviation for *Vehicle Borne Improvised Explosive Device*

WIA: An abbreviation for *Wounded in Action*

XO: An abbreviation for *Executive Officer*

Places

Ajiristan: A district of Ghazni province
Alu Kheyl: A village in Deh Yak district, Ghazni province
Andar: A district of Ghazni province
Camp Phoenix: A U.S. Army base in Kabul that was the HQ of CSTC-A
Deh Yak: A district of Ghazni province
FOB Vulcan: The FOB I lived on, which was located in Ghazni, Afghanistan
Fort Riley: A U.S. Army base located outside Manhattan, Kansas; the location of our predeployment training as ETTs/PMTs
Gardez: The capital city of Paktia province, Afghanistan, and the location of FOB Lightning
Ghazni: A province of Afghanistan; Ghazni city is the capital of Ghazni province
Jaghato: A district of Ghazni province
Kabul: The capital of Afghanistan
Kandahar: A city and province in southern Afghanistan
Khogiati: A district of Ghazni province
Kyrgyzstan: A country in central Asia
Leipzig, Germany: A city in Germany that we landed at going to and coming from war
Manas: A U.S. Air Force base on the outskirts of the capital of Kyrgyzstan
Mash village: A village in Andar; I met with one of its elders during an Andar *shura*.
Sangor village: A village in Deh Yak where Team One was attacked while on a patrol with their Afghan Police and elements of the 101st Airborne Battalion that served with us in Ghazni
Tian Sian Mountains: A mountain range running throughout central Asia, specifically in Kyrgyzstan

CPSIA information can be obtained at www.ICGtesting.com
Printed in the USA
LVOW08s1809081213

364409LV00002B/240/P